MAKING DATA

MAKING DATA

Materializing Digital Information

EDITED BY
IAN GWILT

BLOOMSBURY VISUAL ARTS
LONDON • NEW YORK • OXFORD • NEW DELHI • SYDNEY

BLOOMSBURY VISUAL ARTS
Bloomsbury Publishing Plc
50 Bedford Square, London, WC1B 3DP, UK
1385 Broadway, New York, NY 10018, USA
29 Earlsfort Terrace, Dublin 2, Ireland

BLOOMSBURY, BLOOMSBURY VISUAL ARTS and the Diana logo
are trademarks of Bloomsbury Publishing Plc

First published in Great Britain 2022

Copyright © Editorial content and introductions, Ian Gwilt, 2022
© Individual chapters, their authors, 2022

Ian Gwilt has asserted his right under the Copyright, Designs and
Patents Act, 1988, to be identified as Editor of this work.

For legal purposes the Acknowledgements on p. xxii constitute
an extension of this copyright page.

Cover design: Louise Dugdale
Cover image: *Snow Water Equivalent* sculpture by Adrien Segal

All rights reserved. No part of this publication may be reproduced or transmitted in any form or by any means, electronic or mechanical, including photocopying, recording, or any information storage or retrieval system, without prior permission in writing from the publishers.

Bloomsbury Publishing Plc does not have any control over, or responsibility for, any third-party websites referred to or in this book. All internet addresses given in this book were correct at the time of going to press. The author and publisher regret any inconvenience caused if addresses have changed or sites have ceased to exist, but can accept no responsibility for any such changes.

A catalogue record for this book is available from the British Library.

Library of Congress Cataloging-in-Publication Data
Names: Gwilt, Ian, editor.
Title: Making data : materializing digital information / edited by Ian Gwilt.
Description: London ; New York : Bloomsbury Visual Arts, 2022. |
Includes bibliographical references and index.
Identifiers: LCCN 2021052915 (print) | LCCN 2021052916 (ebook) |
ISBN 9781350133235 (hardback) | ISBN 9781350133242 (epub) |
ISBN 9781350133259 (pdf)
Subjects: LCSH: Information visualization–Social aspects. |
Data structures (Computer science) | Object (Philosophy)
Classification: LCC QA76.9.I52 M35 2022 (print) |
LCC QA76.9.I52 (ebook) | DDC 001.4/226–dc23/eng/20211130
LC record available at https://lccn.loc.gov/2021052915
LC ebook record available at https://lccn.loc.gov/2021052916

ISBN: HB: 978-1-3501-3323-5
ePDF: 978-1-3501-3325-9
eBook: 978-1-3501-3324-2

Typeset by Integra Software Services Pvt. Ltd.
Printed and bound in Great Britain

To find out more about our authors and books visit www.bloomsbury.com
and sign up for our newsletters.

CONTENTS

List of figures vii
List of contributing authors xi
Foreword xix
Acknowledgements xxii

Introduction   *Ian Gwilt* 1

SECTION ONE   MAKING DATA: THEORIES 7

1   **Data-objects: Thinking with your hands**   *Adrien Segal* 9

2   **Shifting data between the material and the virtual is not an immaterial matter**   *Dew Harrison* 25

3   **Data as environment: Physicalization strategies for communicating environmental data**   *Laura Perovich and Dietmar Offenhuber* 41

4   **Designing explanations of data-based interactions in socio-technical systems**   *Aaron Fry* 57

5   **Moving data: Visualizing human and non-human movement artistically**   *Michele Barker and Anna Munster* 73

SECTION TWO   MAKING DATA: PRACTICES 87

6   **Uncanny landscapes: Tactile and experiential encounters with ecological data**   *Zoë Sadokierski, Monica Monin and Andrew Burrell* 89

7 Exploring digital-material hybridity in the post-digital museum   *Daniela Petrelli and Nick Dulake*   107

8 Socio-material translations of data and value(s)   *Bettina Nissen*   125

9 Personal data manifestation: A tangible poetics of data   *Giles Lane and George Roussos*   141

10 Data and emotion: The climate change object   *Karin von Ompteda*   153

SECTION THREE   MAKING DATA: TECHNIQUES   167

11 Hybrid data constructs: Interacting with biomedical data in augmented spaces   *Daniel F. Keefe, Bridger Herman, Jung Who Nam, Daniel Orban and Seth Johnson*   169

12 Sonic data physicalization   *Stephen Barrass*   183

13 Making with climate data: Materiality, metaphor and engagement   *Mitchell Whitelaw and Geoff Hinchcliffe*   195

14 Waterfalls as a form of AI-based feedback for creativity support   *Georgi V. Georgiev and Yazan Barhoush*   211

15 Data as action: Constructing dynamic data physicalizations   *Jason Alexander*   223

SECTION FOUR   MAKING DATA: TRAJECTORIES   237

16 Making data: The next generation   *Ian Gwilt and Aaron Davis*   239

Index   247

FIGURES

1.1 *Tidal Datum*, San Francisco, 2007, by Adrien Segal. Wood and Steel, 26″ x 32″ x 72″. Photo courtesy of the artist. The tide data represented in three-dimensions (x, y, z) are: (x) observed water level height; (y) 24-hour daily tide chart; and (z) 29 days or the duration of a full tide cycle 13
1.2a *Arctic Sea Ice/Albedo*, 2017 Cast Glass. Artwork by Adrien Segal 15
1.2b *Trends in Water Use*, 2011. Carved Plywood and Steel. Artwork by Adrien Segal. Photograph by Fredrik Nilsen Studio 15
2.1 The *Shift-Life* installation in action (Harrison 2009) 35
4.1 Working toward an 'Affinity Map' in a design thinking session for the Visualizing Finance Lab. Parsons School of Design, NYC. February 2019. Photo by author 67
4.2 A map of first and second-order effects. Used for an innovation exercise within an American automotive company in March 2020. This is the author's version of a template derived from the collaborative whiteboard platform 'Miro'. Photo courtesy of Megan Staake 68
5.1 An example of typically formatted movement data containing x,y coordinates as longitude and latitude positions and timestamps. Fraser KC, Shave A, Savage A, Ritchie A, Bell K, Siegrist J, Ray JD, Applegate K, Pearman M (2016) Data from: Determining fine-scale migratory connectivity and habitat selection for a migratory songbird by using new GPS technology. Movebank Data Repository. doi:10.5441/001/1.5q5gn84d. Published under Creative Commons license, Universal Public Domain Declaration 76
5.2 Screenshot of two moving image channels combined in *pull*, 2017, Michele Barker and Anna Munster, multi-channel audiovisual installation. The left shows high-speed cinematography; the right movement data rendered as 3D CGI 78

5.3	Left: Cinematographer Chris Bryan filming under waves and wearing the GPS enabled watch capturing movement data. Right: Screenshot of the motion path produced by x, y coordinates of the cinematographer's geospatial location correlated with timestamp data over a 3-hour period taken from the visual interface on the GPS enabled watch	81
6.1	Film still from *Clever Country* (Zakpage 2019)	94
6.2	Semiconductor's *Cosmos* in Alice Holt Forest, UK. Photograph by Laura Hodgson, 2014	96
7.1	The elements of Fort Pozzacchio installation (from bottom left to right): the pebble; the interactive bench with the testimonies slots; the printed postcard; the animation in station 1 being played (top). Images: Daniela Petrelli/Nick Dulake	113
7.2	The interaction with *My Roman Pantheon* (from top left): collecting the lamp from Juno's shrine; in the museum offering a light; back at the shrine returning the lamp and collecting the 'oracle'; four different personalised postcards. Images: Daniela Petrelli/Nick Dulake	116
7.3	The Interaction at the Atlantic Wall exhibition (from bottom left – clockwise): the replicas representing the different perspectives; a visitor using the sugar box to listen to the stories of the Dutch civilians; the personalized website; and the postcard. Images: Daniela Petrelli/Nick Dulake	118
8.1	(a, b) *Block Exchange* workshop. Photo: Bettina Nissen; (c, d) *Weaving Crypto-Ledgers* workshop. Photo: Bob Moyler; (e, f) *Strings of Distributed Value* workshop. Photo: Bob Moyler	129
8.2	(a, b) *GeoCoin* experience. Photo: Bettina Nissen; (c, d) *Currency After Money* installation. Photo: Yuxi Liu; (e, f) *Alternative Rates of Exchange* installation. Photo: Bob Moyler	131
9.1	*Lifestreams* by Proboscis (2012) installed in the group show, *The New Observatory*. FACT, Liverpool (2017). Image: Gareth Jones	145
9.2	*Lifestreams*, Parkinson's Disease Lifecharms by Proboscis (2016). Photo: Alice Angus	147
10.1	*Climate Clock* (2019). Designer: Ka Leng Kong. Photography: Ka Leng Kong	155
10.2	*Disruption: The Materiality of Global Temperature* (2018); (a) sculpture in OCAD University's Great Hall; (b) detail of object representing the year 2016. Designer: Paz Pereira-Vega. Photography: Paz Pereira-Vega	158

FIGURES

10.3 *Burning Acres* (2018). Designer: Kathleen Stever. Photography: Nicole Torres and Karin von Ompteda — 161

11.1 *Bento Box*. Top-left: Digital visualizations of blood flow in the right atrium use animation to make it possible to see the flow develop over time and interactive techniques to select and filter the data. Bottom-left: Physical representations provide the most solid understanding of the 3D form, where it is possible to encode additional data variables 'on top of' the form using a pattern of data glyphs, but these physical printouts are inherently static. Right: Optimal understandings of the data may come from a hybrid construct that combines the best of both strategies. Image credit: Interactive Visualization Lab, University of Minnesota-Twin Cities — 173

11.2 Initial hybrid design studies focus on bringing the interactivity that works so well in digital spaces to physical data constructs. Image credit: Interactive Visualization Lab, University of Minnesota-Twin Cities — 177

12.1 (a) Parametric tuning fork programmed in OpenJSCAD (Barrass 2015); (b) Parametric Tuning Forks (Barrass 2021); (c) Tuning Fork and Variations (Barrass 2014) — 186

12.2 (a) 3D printed Bells in Steel, Brass and Bronze (Barrass 2021); (b) Binaural Data Bells (Barrass 2021) — 188

12.3 (a) Tibetan Singing Bowl cast in Bronze (Barrass 2021); (b) Blood Pressure Singing Bowl with profile mapping (Barrass 2021); (c) Hypertension Singing Bowl (Barrass 2021); (d) Chemo Singing Bowl with Bezier spokes (Barrass 2021) — 190

13.1 (a, b) Initial software sketches; (c, d) Paper prototypes with hand annotations; (e) Laser fabrication and material tests; (f) ANU Climate Change Institute Canberra Climate Update, February 2018; (g) Canberra 2017 Climate Coaster. All works and images by Mitchell Whitelaw (a–d) and Geoff Hinchcliffe (e–g) — 198

13.2 (a, b) Initial sketches testing boundaries for daily and monthly temperature peaks; (c) Finished website; (c1) Locations listed in map and text views. Map points are coloured according to annual average temperature; (c2) Timeline shows annual average temperature from 1991 to 2018. Allows selection of different years; (d, e) Exported images; colour version (d) for printing and social media, vector version (e) for laser cutting. All works and images by Geoff Hinchcliffe — 201

14.1 Design thinking conversation during the initial testing of the real-time analysis and evaluation system (a) Design thinking conversation feedback with separate; (b) and compound; (c) plots of real-time conversation data. In example (c), four semantic measures are plotted on the y axis, taking values on the axis z over time on the axis x. Images: Yazan Barhoush 215
14.2 Feedback with an anti-gravity illusion waterfall. Image: Yazan Barhoush and Georgi Georgiev 218
15.1 EMERGE, a physically dynamic bar-chart; (left) a user directly interacts with a bar by pulling it; (right) linkages connect linear actuators to bars. Image credits: Faisal Taher (Lancaster University) and Jason Alexander (University of Bath). Reproduced with permission 228
15.2 Two ShapeClip modules (left); A row of ShapeClip modules (centre); A PolySurface physicalization of a volcano (right). Image credits: (left, centre) John Hardy (H&E Inventions), Faisal Taher (Lancaster University) and Jason Alexander (University of Bath); (right) Aluna Everitt (University of Oxford) and Jason Alexander (University of Bath) 229

CONTRIBUTING AUTHORS

Jason Alexander
Jason is Professor of Human-Computer Interaction in the Department of Computer Science at the University of Bath, UK. He has a particular interest in developing novel interactive systems to bridge the physical-digital divide. His recent work focuses on the development of shape-changing interfaces – surfaces that can dynamically change their geometry based on digital content or user input – and their applications, including the design and implementation of dynamic data physicalizations. His other work has investigated novel interaction techniques using eye-gaze, haptic feedback and gestural interaction.

Yazan Barhoush
Barhoush's work is focused on digital fabrication and virtual reality, as well as software and hardware development for Human-Centred design applications. He is currently employed as a doctoral researcher in the Center for Ubiquitous Computing, at the Faculty of Information Technology and Electrical Engineering at the University of Oulu. He is a member of Associate Professor Georgi Georgiev's Design Research group. Barhoush has an international education: a diploma from United World College of the Adriatic (Italy) in 2013, a BSc in Computer Engineering from Union College (NY, USA) in 2017 and an MSc in Computer Science and Engineering from the University of Oulu (Finland) in 2019.

Michele Barker
Michele Barker is a media artist with a strong focus on experimental cinema and responsive media environments as a way of exploring the multifaceted complexities of the human and more than human via perception, embodiment, movement and duration. Her work has been shown extensively both nationally and internationally.

Developing projects that integrate a vast range of technological platforms, Barker has collaborated extensively with Anna Munster for over twenty years, with recent works including évasion, an eight-channel responsive installation working between dance, performance and the moving image; and the multi-channel interactive work, *HokusPokus* which explores the relations between perception, magic and early moving image technologies and techniques. In the moving image works *pull* and *hold*, they use water as mechanism for exploring duration and felt experience. Continuing their preoccupation with duration and felt experience, they are now using drones to delve into what they call 'geotime', an exploration of time and perception through the lenses of water and land as forces situated outside humans' short 'moment' in geological time.

Stephen Barrass

Stephen Barrass is a researcher in Sonic Information Design and Founder of SONIFICATION.COM which is dedicated to using data sonification to make the world a better place. His Doctorate on Auditory Information Design (Australian National University 1996) was one of the first on sonification worldwide, and has been very influential in this field. He initiated the development of the open source Mozzi sonification software for the Arduino microcontroller, and the MozziByte PCB board for rapid prototyping of sonic ideas and embedding sonifications in things. His recent experiments with the 3D printing of data physicalizations modelled on musical instruments provide a new method of Acoustic Sonification that produces interactive sounds from a complete dataset in real time.

Andrew Burrell

Andrew Burrell is a practice-based researcher and educator exploring virtual and digitally mediated environments as a site for the construction, experience and exploration of memory as narrative. His process is one of wording in virtual space – visualizing otherwise unseen connections and entanglements. His ongoing research investigates the relationship between imagined and remembered narrative and how the multi-layered biological and technological encoding of human subjectivity may be portrayed within, and informs the design of virtual environments. He is a Senior Lecturer in Visual Communication, faculty of Design, Architecture and Building at the University of Technology Sydney. He lives and works on Gadigal Country.

Aaron Davis

Dr Aaron Davis is an award winning educator, designer and facilitator. Dr Davis works as the Facilitation Manager of NOVELL Redesign at the Florey Institute of Neuroscience and Mental Health, and as a Lecturer and Research Fellow at the University of South Australia. He works across a range of interdisciplinary teams and at the intersection of built environment, community, health and technology. Dr Davis's background is in Architecture but his research interests include social practices, sustainability, innovation and entrepreneurship, the social shaping of technology, and the processes of knowledge formation and sharing.

Nick Dulake

Nick Dulake (MA) is Senior Research Fellow and Industrial Designer at ADMRC/ Design Futures, Sheffield Hallam University in the UK. He has more than twenty years of experiences working across diverse market sectors, applying a user-centred and co-design methodology approach to create innovative design solutions. Working in areas such as a digital heritage, wearable medical products and e-health, clients include English Heritage, Kenwood, Adidas, Trulife and Unilever. These collaborations have produced six national/international patents and numerous products to market.

Nick is a founding member of the Digital Materiality Lab, the lab explores the many ways in which the digital and the material worlds collide, fuse, converge or clash and how people interact with this in multiple domains. He has a broad experience of applying technical and creative design methods and developing interventions with a focus on digital tangible interactions.

Aaron Fry

Born in New Zealand, Aaron is an artist and design educator, he has taught studio art and design, art and design history and theory, basic design and design-business. Formerly a practising artist, Aaron's research interests are expressed through his writing at the intersection of design, business and the social sciences. Aaron is co-director of the Visualizing Finance Lab (VFL), a research initiative that explores the capacity of emotionally, culturally and metaphorically rich 'narrative visualization' in Financial Literacy Education (FLE). Aaron is author of numerous articles and speaks regularly at conferences and workshops internationally on design thinking in business strategy and design's role in supporting financial literacy.

Georgi V. Georgiev

Dr Georgi V. Georgiev is Associate Professor leading the Design Research group at the Center for Ubiquitous Computing (UBICOMP), University of Oulu, Finland. His experience and research interests encompass design creativity, digital fabrication and prototyping, idea generation, user experience and design cognition. He earned his PhD in Knowledge Science from JAIST, Japan, in 2009. Dr Georgiev is actively involved in the foundation and development of the Special Interest Group Design Creativity at the Design Society, International Conference Series on Design Creativity and International Journal of Design Creativity and Innovation.

Ian Gwilt

Ian Gwilt is Professor of Design at the University of South Australia. Current areas of research include the application of design in the context of healthcare and well-being, and the development of novel information visualization techniques to facilitate the understanding of data for non-specialist audiences. He is also interested in how we can incorporate visual communication design practices into interdisciplinary research teams using inclusive, participatory practices to facilitate knowledge translation, and to include community insight and lived experiences into the design and implementation of complex products, systems and services.

Dew Harrison

Dr Dew Harrison is Professor of Digital Media Art and Director of CADRE (Centre of Art Design Research and Experimentation) at the University of Wolverhampton, UK. She was the Principal Coordinator for the 2016–20 EU Horizon 2020 project, 'MinD', co-designing for and with people with early-stage Dementia. As a practice-led researcher her work explores a computer-mediated approach to the territory between art, technology and cognition and she considers the dialogue between the virtual and the material as a semantic space for creative exploration where she collaborates with AI programmers to create mixed-reality works.

Geoff Hinchcliffe

Geoff Hinchcliffe is a founding member of the ANU School of Art and Design's innovative new design program and Associate Dean Education in the College of Arts and Social Sciences at the Australian National University. Geoff's research focuses on enlivening data and digital collections through visualization, interface and interaction design. Novel representation, exploration and discovery are core to his web-based works, with audience contribution and participation being key areas of interest. His research results in both theoretical and applied outputs, ranging from the practical to the experimental, playful and occasionally provocative.

Daniel F. Keefe, Bridger Herman, Jung Who Nam, Daniel Orban and Seth Johnson

This research was conducted by the Interactive Visualization Lab (IV/LAB) within the Department of Computer Science and Engineering at the University of Minnesota. Dan Keefe is the director of the IV/LAB and a Distinguished University Teaching Professor and Associate Professor of Computer Science and Engineering. His current and former PhD students, Bridger Herman, Jung Who Nam, Daniel Orban and Seth Johnson, each led a design study described in the chapter as part of their doctoral research in computer science.

Giles Lane

Giles Lane is founder and director of the non-profit creative studio, Proboscis, and is currently also Specialist Researcher in Art-Science at Central Saint Martins, University of the Arts London where he has co-founded the interdisciplinary Manifest Data Lab research group. Giles's work spans artistic practices, participatory research and community engagement across multiple disciplines and sectors, involving a wide range of partners and collaborators from industry, government, academia, the arts, civil society and grassroots communities.

Monica Monin
Monica Monin is a practice-based researcher and educator investigating the effects, possibilities and role of computation, code and data within poetics (making). Through a critical coding practice, her research explores how intensive media ecologies transform the production of knowledge and meaning-making. She is a Lecturer in Visual Communication, Faculty of Design, Architecture and Building at the University of Technology Sydney.

Anna Munster
Anna Munster is Professor in Media Arts and Theory, Faculty of Arts, Architecture and Design, University of New South Wales, Sydney Australia. Her current research interests are in radical empiricist understandings of technologies with a focus on machine learning, platform cultures, arts and politics. She has led several large research projects on media, data, perception and embodiment including, 'Re-imaging the Empirical: Statistical Visualization in Art and Science' (2017–21), supported by the Australian Research Council's Discovery Project scheme. She is the author of *An Aesthesia of Networks* (MIT Press, 2013) and *Materializing New Media* (Dartmouth Press, 2006). She has also published with *Theory, Culture & Society, The Journal of Cultural Analytics and Leonardo Electronic Almanac*. She collaborates artistically with Michele Barker using audiovisual, immersive media and data to draw out their affective and errant tendencies.

Bettina Nissen
Dr Bettina Nissen is a Lecturer in Interaction Design and researcher at the Institute for Design Informatics at the University of Edinburgh. Her practice-based design research focuses on engaging audiences with complex technological concepts and data through data physicalization, tangible interactions and playful installations. Bettina completed her AHRC-funded PhD in Human Computer Interaction at Newcastle University in 2018. She has recently worked on research projects spanning topics of trust and consent in pervasive environments (EPSRC-funded PACTMAN), privacy and online harm (EPSRC-funded REPHRAIN), the future of value(s) in the digital economy (ESRC-funded After Money) and collaborative feminist economic perspectives of care and social justice (Creative Scotland funded Crypto-Knitting Circles).

Dietmar Offenhuber
Dietmar Offenhuber is Associate Professor at Northeastern University in the fields of Art + Design and Public Policy. He holds a PhD in Urban Planning from MIT, Master degrees from the MIT Media Lab and TU Vienna. His research focuses on the relationship between design, urban technologies and governance. Dietmar is the author of the award-winning monograph *Waste is Information* (MIT Press), worked as an advisor to the United Nations and published books on the subjects of Urban Data, Accountability Technologies and Urban Informatics.

Laura Perovich

Laura Perovich is Assistant Professor at Northeastern University in Art + Design. She holds a PhD and an MS in Media Arts and Sciences from the MIT Media Lab. Her research focuses on ways to create physical, contextual and interactive experiences around data and social challenges.

Daniela Petrelli

Prof Daniela Petrelli has a mixed background across fine arts and computing. Her most recent research focuses on bridging the gap existing between material culture and the digital world in the context of cultural heritage. This theme was investigated in depth in the European project meSch, let by Dr Petrelli, that explored tangible and embodied interactions in museums and heritage sites. meSch has received international awards and is the first to use the Internet of Things and Cloud Computing in museums. Dr Petrelli's other research interests include personal and family memories, data visualization, multimedia and multilingual information access. In her career, she has published over 100 international peer-reviewed contributions and received 12 awards from both academia and industry. Dr Petrelli is Professor of Interaction Design at Sheffield Hallam University in the UK and director of the Digital Materiality Lab, an interest group looking into new digital-material hybrids.

George Roussos

Prof George Roussos leads the Pervasive Computing Group at Birkbeck College, University of London, an internationally recognized research centre in mobile computing and the IoT with particular expertise in networked RFID and mobility analytics.

His work pioneered participatory cyber-physical computing as the predominant methodology for the construction of mobile and pervasive computing systems. With contributions in systems architecture, privacy protection and human dynamics, his work demonstrated how the user's activity can be exploited as the core ingredient for building such systems.

Prof Roussos is the author of four books and over 100 research papers. He was a member of the EU-China Internet of Things Expert Group in 2010/12, the 2011 Medalist for best environmental project at the British Computer Society awards and since 2004 serves on the ACM US Public Policy Committee.

Zoë Sadokierski

Dr Zoë Sadokierski is an award-winning book designer, educator and writer. She completed her PhD on the narrative function of graphic devices (photographs, illustrations, experimental typography) in 2010 at the University of Technology Sydney, where she is now Senior Lecturer in Visual Communication. Her current research investigates narrative approaches to ecological communication: how might we communicate the moral, ethical, social and cultural dimensions of climate change and biodiversity loss, to inspire critical dialogue and substantive change? Current collaborations include *Precarious Birds* with Dr Timo Rissanen, and *Uncanny Landscapes* with Dr Andrew Burrell, run through the Speculative Narratives and Networks Studio.

Adrien Segal

Adrien Segal is an artist based in Oakland, California. Drawing from science, history, landscape, emotion and perception, her sculpture synthesizes information into knowledge as an intently subjective experience. Her work has been exhibited internationally since 2007, and is published in several books and academic journals. She has been awarded numerous Artist Residencies across the United States, Canada and Europe. Adrien was the Latham Fellow at ITT Institute of Design in Chicago, and has held Visiting Artist positions at San Diego State University and California College of the Arts, where she teaches art and design. Adrien pursues her creative practice out of her studio on the former Naval Base in Alameda, California.

Karel van der Waarde

Dr Karel van der Waarde started in 1995 a design-research consultancy in Belgium specializing in the testing of pharmaceutical information design. The main activities are the readability tests for package leaflets, usability tests for packaging and prototype development. This company develops patient information leaflets, instructions, forms and protocols (www.graphicdesign-research.com).

Karel van der Waarde publishes, teaches and investigates visual information. He is a life-fellow of the Communications Research Institute (Melbourne, Australia), a board member of International Institute for Information Design (IIID, Vienna, Austria) and editorial board member of Information Design Journal, Hyphen, She Ji and Visible Language.

Karin von Ompteda

Karin von Ompteda is Assistant Professor of Graphic Design at OCAD University in Canada. Her background is in both science and design, having undertaken an MSc Biology (University of Toronto), BDes Graphic Design (OCAD University) and currently completing a PhD Visual Communication (Royal College of Art). Karin's doctoral research is focused on integrating scientific and design knowledge on typeface legibility, with a focus on low vision readers. Working with data plays a central role in her research, practice and teaching, and she has developed her data manifestation pedagogy internationally over the last decade through courses and workshops with students, professionals and the public. Her work has been presented internationally through conferences (IEEE VISAP, RGD

DesignThinkers), exhibitions (Brno Biennial, BIO Biennial), publications (Laurence King, RotoVision) and press (BBC's The Forum, China Daily). Projects have been funded through research councils in both Canada and the UK, and clients have included BBC Research and Development and the National Film Board of Canada.

Mitchell Whitelaw

Mitchell Whitelaw is an academic, writer and maker with interests in digital design and culture, data practices, more-than-human worlds and digital collections. His teaching and research uses digital design to seek out moments of insight and delight that intensify our engagement with a complex world. His work has appeared in journals including *Leonardo, Digital Creativity, Digital Humanities Quarterly, and Senses and Society*. He has worked with institutions including the State Library of NSW, the State Library of Queensland, the National Archives and the National Gallery of Australia, developing 'generous' interfaces to their digital collections. His current research investigates environmental and biodiversity visualization, and digital design for a more-than-human world. Mitchell is currently Associate Professor in the School of Art and Design at the Australian National University.

FOREWORD

Karel van der Waarde

There seem to be two distinct activities related to data-objects.

The first activity attempts to make sense of raw data, or combinations of different kinds of data. It aims to *find and show patterns and structures in raw data* in order to discover new ideas. Such a discovery needs to be recorded and included in a narrative. This becomes a story that the data appears to tell, and that needs to be made perceivable in some sort of physical form.

The second activity is *the interpretation of physical forms by people*. The idea is that these physical forms, or 'data-objects', help people to make sense of a story. The shapes and materials provide an alternative presentation that is worth looking at because it reveals additional, enhanced and more detailed interpretations.

Making data-objects
Original data can be tangible or abstract, analogue or digital, current or historical, and can be provided by a single source or by a combination of several sources. Many disciplines such as science, fine-arts, dance, heritage, economics and medicine to name but a few actively look again at these different kinds of data. This leads to discoveries and ideas that might be new and relevant. What all disciplines share is a need to develop ideas and to make ideas easier to grasp and make them applicable. Initially for the makers themselves, and later for other people.

It is always necessary to make a selection out of the available data and to provide a motivation for this selection. Raw data is rarely available as a clean set, without any outliers, absolutely representative, and without any errors. Decisions need to be made which data to include, about the boundaries and about the data that will be excluded or ignored. The influence of the provenance of the data, the sensors, the inclusion criteria and the embedded software algorithms need to be acknowledged.

Two kinds of tools are necessary to deal with data and objects. The first tools help to transform data and objects into manageable structures. Software can sift through digital data and provide structures. The second type of tools helps to transform these structures into visual and tangible data-objects. Sculpting of large amounts of data needs a digital interpreter which calculates and acts in a three-dimensional space. However, for some data, it might still be possible to sculpt manually.

Furthermore, it is essential to make conscious decisions about the most suitable media to present data within a story. This decision partly determines the combinations of materials to make a data-object.

Both steps – from data to an idea, and from an idea to a data-object – require substantial practical skills and experience. Both are in constant flux and demand continuous learning and reconsideration of the tools and materials. The only way to gain this experience is by taking the steps, simply because there are no established practices yet. It is an iterative process of trying, reflecting, improving, changing and re-sculpting.

To summarize, making data-objects requires a series of conscious decisions: Which data? Which data-selection criteria? Which analysis tools? Which sculpting tools? Which materials? What do I need to learn to answer these questions? The scope of these decisions shows that there is not a standard single process that leads to a single optimal solution. It is a sequence of decisions that leads to a very wide variety of objects.

Interpreting data-objects

For people who look, touch, smell and listen to data-objects, this variety does not make it easy.

At a first encounter, a data-object might not be immediately understandable. Data-objects more or less encourage people to take an active stance – by simply forcing people to move around, touch, consider and rethink again. The interpretation requires an engagement and motivation to invest time and energy to deal with an object.

The interpretation is separated by time and location from the original data. Questions about the data, the reasons why certain data were selected, the motivations for the choice of materials and the aims of the makers are common starting points. The role of the interpreter – that is the person who tries to make sense – is vital. Further questions focus on the accuracy of the original data, their reliability and their representativeness. Each interpreter is required to find a balance between trust and critical scepticism, and this is influenced by worldviews, existing knowledge and previous experiences. Because of their physical form, data-objects might be beneficial to explore meanings collaboratively through discussions during the encounters.

Interpretation of visuals, diagrams or objects is rarely formally taught. It is assumed that these 'speak for themselves', and that the ability to successfully deal with objects only needs to be acquired through repeated encounters. However, it is very likely that it takes training and practice to interpret data-objects, similar to the time required to reach some fluency in reading texts. 'Tactile literacy' is probably an oxymoron, but suitable words for 'objectacy' or 'dataracy' seem to be missing.

And probably the most important point of the interpretation is the reactions. What are people going to do, what are they enabled to do with this newly acquired interpretation? What is the impact on knowledge, opinions or behaviour?

All these actions of interpreters require conscious decisions too. Should I deal with this? Do I know how to deal with this? Is this really correct? What can I do with this? What is the maker suggesting that I should do?

Does all this matter?

Does this division in 'making data tangible' and 'interpreting tangible objects' matter? It's clear that both processes consist of a series of decisions. Some of these decisions can be motivated, while others are probably less relevant for a particular data-object.

In some situations, the aim of the provision of data-objects is clear. Inform people about climate change or inform about a pandemic to make sure that people are aware and are enabled to take the most appropriate decisions. The interpretation and the resulting actions are vital and paramount.

Other aims are possible too, and even 'aimless' objects can be made. Data-objects can give pleasure and they might provoke emotional experiences. They might create memories or can be used to remember. They might be convincing, and they might stimulate reactions.

The opportunities for people to get involved in the exploration of data and the making of data-objects are very substantial. And so are the opportunities for people to interpret data-objects. Whether people really want to do this depends on individual motivations and curiosity.

This book

This book contains a collection of provocative articles. It shows a rough and unexplored area for practice, research and education. I found it a delight to read that authors expressed their questions, insecurities and personal reflections. It shows that it is an area where the borders and limits are not defined yet, and where it is not possible to offer solutions, guidelines and standards.

And that is probably the core of this anthology. It provides an overview of opportunities that are likely to stimulate others to try alternative ways of making and interpreting data-objects.

However, a book of a few hundred paper pages, or even an e-book, is probably not the most obvious medium to describe the making of data-objects, to describe data-objects or to involve people in experiencing data-objects. It only increases the longing to be in the same space as the objects but it can't yet make the same impression.

I'm sure this book will inspire readers to explore data in order to make things. But more importantly, it will inspire to critically feel, experience, interpret and discuss the physical forms of data.

ACKNOWLEDGEMENTS

I would like to thank all the wonderful authors and contributors to this book, and also recognize the pioneering makers, artist, designers, computer-scientists, engineers, thinkers and theorists mentioned and not mentioned, who have been collectively exploring and contributing to the world of data physicalization. With a special mention to the organizers and participants of the Schloss Dagstuhl Seminar on Data Physicalization which took place near Saarbrücken, Germany in 2018 and was a catalyst for this publication.

Also to Dr Jack Wilde who stepped in to lend laser-like editorial precision and a carefully considered perspective on this assemblage of words, ideas and references in this book.

To my family Alison and Dylan for their patience, understanding, coffees and toast on this long journey, and to the people at Bloomsbury Publishing for their support and for entertaining this unusual subject matter.

Ian Gwilt

INTRODUCTION

Ian Gwilt

For many outside of the scientific community, data and the forms it takes – such as statistical lists, spreadsheets and graphs – can appear abstract and unintelligible. This book investigates how digital fabrication and physical making approaches are increasingly being used to translate and represent data in new ways that can communicate and generate interest to a wide range of people and communities. The chapters in *Making Data: Materializing Digital Information* investigate a range of emergent practices and approaches that move data beyond the computer screen and into the physical world in ways that exploit potentials of both physical and digital paradigms. From personally collected biometric information to large-scale multidimensional data, this publication explores ethical, political, philosophical, creative and cultural implications fashioned when we translate and design digital data into physical forms.

The disciplines related to Computer Science still embody a specialist set of knowledge. Still today, only a small percentage of people in the word are able to programme, understand computer code or read and analyse digital data. Fortunately, we continue to develop techniques and design tools that allow none-specialist audiences to interact with these digital technologies. Since the 1990s advances in human computer interfaces, web browsers, information visualization techniques, computer modelling software, dashboard interfaces and the rise of mobile apps have taken advantage of the exponential growth in computing power to help make the access and manipulation of digital information easier. More recently, Augmented Reality (AR), Virtual Reality (VR) and Artificial Intelligence (AI) systems now operate as enabling technologies to facilitate engagement with digital content. These increasingly ubiquitous and distributed technologies are creating a range of readily accessible digital platforms and devices that have given rise to the notion of situated data – the experience and access to digital data 'in situ', when and where we want or need it. An everything, anytime culture.

Yet, however inviting, and as Mitchell Whitelaw champions, 'generous' these interfaces become, this ready access to digital content can at the same time mediate and diminish our experiences of the physical world and the embodied understanding that comes with this. The intangibility of the computer screen, the digital overlays of AR, and even the increasingly perfect modelled and rendered 3D worlds of immersive VR can still struggle with accommodating the multisensory ways in which we experience data in the physical world.

Before digital computing, people used and crafted physical objects from the natural environment to count and record things, places, persons and phenomena of interest. These pre-digital *data-objects* often held not just economic but cultural, religious, scientific and political knowledge and importance. From the mercantile clay tokens of the Mesopotamians to today's 3D printed representations of environmental data in the Anthropocene, tangible interpretations of information have played an important role in recording how we interact with the natural and man-made phenomena of our Euclidian realities.

Campbell-Stokes Sunlight Recorder is an elegant example of scientists having applied analogue technologies in the service of capturing data from the physical world. Since the mid-seventeenth century this simple device has been used around the world to measure the number of hours of sunshine in a day. Simply by burning the information directly onto a scaled sheet of paper through the use of a magnifying lens as the sun travels across the sky (Sanchez-Lorenzo et al. 2013). The Sunlight Recorder speaks to data that lives over time, connected to our physical experience of the world. Like the Mesopotamian counting tokens, data collecting and recording artefacts like the Sunlight Recorder offer examples of how different people and cultures have used the materials, technologies and tools of their time to help to tell the story of data and to share this information with other people. In today's interconnected multidimensional dataspace these narratives are increasingly becoming an important mechanism for helping people make sense of this complexity.

However, in the era of Big Data we might be forgiven for thinking that we are simply counting greater numbers of things or trying to make sense of more complex events, objects and phenomena. Since the turn of the twenty-first century 2D information visualization techniques have increasingly been used to help make complex digital data more accessible through the use of visual design, metaphor, diagrams and animations, but already this process has drawn criticism in some quarters for at times over-embellishing information to confuse or not faithfully representing the underlying data. More worrying is the accusation from some quarters that data visualization may have had its day and has lost its impact due to over-use and cultural saturation (Lima 2009). If this is indeed the case, then the offerings from the key thinkers contributing to this book, who outline the theoretical positions, making practices, methodologies and applications for the creation of data driven material/physical artefacts, are all the more important in order to demonstrate how we can continue to make big data and open data sources more communicable to public audiences.

Many of the examples described in this book also address a contemporary interest in how we can build stronger relationships between the physical world and the digital paradigms encapsulated in the term Industry 4.0 (the Internet of Things, smart environments, AI, cloud computing etc.), by using design techniques, creative practices and these same emerging technologies to build the hypothesis that data-objects will play an important part of the next generation of information visualization methods. And proposing that the making of data into physical objects and digital inflected hybrid artefacts is the next important development in the data visualization phenomenon. For instance, as digitally enabled printing and fabrication technologies become more accessible, these technologies are being employed by artists, designers, theorists and scientists to create new and novel ways of representing data, moving beyond the conventional ways in which we typically experience and interact with digital information.

Through a collection of expert practitioner chapters, this anthology uncovers the creative methods, processes, theories, cultural and technological issues surrounding the making of physical representations of digital information. It is a smorgasbord of ideas, case studies, theories and technological experiments from academics, artists, designers, engineers and computer scientists, who are all exploring this emergent practice of making data in a post-digital age.

Topics within the book range from the concept of data as transaction, with a focus on the design of economic, ethical and knowledge translations; data realities which creatively examine the ontological relationships between digital and material data cultures and hybrid combinations; ideas around data ownership, open data and community use; the individual and implications of collecting biometric data, and ideas of the quantified self. Other chapters offer a selection of exemplar forms and techniques for the generation of data-objects such as the use of smart surfaces, AR technologies, next generation technical interfaces that blend physical and digital elements, and experiments in physicalizing sound. These are documented through a range of sociocultural contexts for the application of data-objects, including healthcare, cultural and heritage interactions, education, and new forms of techno-creative practices. A recurring theme throughout the book is the use of data physicalization strategies to explore environmental data and contexts. A number of the authors have explored through their own practices or the review of international projects that employ data physicalization techniques as a way of making sense of incomprehensible phenomena using human scales, senses and affordances. These data physicalization techniques combine a concern for effects of the Anthropocene and a desire to represent and communicate environmental data and climate change statistics in understandable and impactful ways.

The book is made up of three main sections: making data theories, practices and technologies. Chapters in the first section focus on the overarching concepts related to the making of physical data artefacts and offer insights into some of the different ontological and epistemological considerations which arise when translating and transforming digital data into a physical or digital/material hybrid form. In these conversations the act of data physicalization is discussed at a meta, philosophical level, while also drawing on particular examples and applications. Section 2 foregrounds a range of practices and processes in the creation of data-objects and offers a further set of contextual circumstances in which these practices might be used. In Section 3 the focus shifts towards an exploration of the technological potentials which support the materialization of digital data, once again supported through engagingly described exemplar projects and experiments.

'Making Data: Theories', the first section in the book, opens with a series of observations on the crafting of the data-object by the artist/maker Adrien Segal. Segal explores the nature of materiality and data and sets out the ontological and epistemological precepts for physicalized data. This is followed by a chapter by Dew Harrison who reflects on the interchange between digital and material realities, virtuality, and the *interstate* of hybridity in relation to the crafted art object. In the first of a number of chapters that examine encounters with ecological data, Laura Perovich and Dietmar Offenhuber explore why it is that a significant number of physical data displays and projects choose to address climate change, pollution or the loss of biodiversity. After analysing a range of prescient examples Perovich and Offenhuber offer us a set of guiding questions to think about when designing effective and meaningful environmental physical data displays. Aaron Fry takes a look at duality through a different lens in his chapter that explores the political and economic tenets of data. How our transactions with data should be thought of in terms of a socio-technical system, wherein the infrastructures of digital systems are always physical and material, political and economic is the topic of Fry's chapter. Movement and temporality, and the way this is expressed through the practices of visualizing data – both analytical and artistic – is the subject of Michele Barker and Anna Munster chapter, a theme they explore through the theory and practice of their artwork installations rounds out this section.

In Section 2 'Making Data: Practices' we return to the communication of environmental data, as Zoë Sadokierski, Monica Monin and Andrew Burrell present a conceptual framework for strategies that attempt to make global phenomena relatable on a local and individual scale. Tackling data that is drawn from events that can occur over huge timescales or processes which might be invisible to the naked eye, this chapter showcases a number of creative exemplars wherein ecological data narratives have been interpreted in novel and engaging forms. Digital-Material information hybridity is again explored in Daniela Petrelli and Nick Dulake's chapter on the use of data-objects in the museum space. Petrelli and Dulake document the potential for using technologically enhanced objects to guide museum visitors through a personalized experience of an exhibition, and to tap into personal visitor preferences which can be used to suggest further and future engagement, and to help curators understand the effectiveness of their exhibits.

Continuing with the theme of knowledge mobilization, Bettina Nissen looks at the value of tangible data translations for education and pedagogy. Taking contemporary economic constructs and systems such as blockchain, cryptocurrency and distributed ledger technologies as a site of enquiry, Nissen employs a material-oriented ontology to help make sense of these complex concepts. Giles Lane and George Roussos invite us to consider the world in which we are 'datafied' in everything we do, and to consider how we might hold onto our sensory perceptions and affordances to help us make sense of and interpret personal biometric data using tangible means that have the potential to offer bespoke insights into the data of our well-being. We return to the creative interpretation of environmental data to conclude Section 2. The intimacy of physicalized data is the topic of Karin von Ompteda's chapter which explores through a collection of her student projects how we can exploit quotidianly occurring objects such as the humble wall clock and sensorial materials such as burnt wood, to create emotionally charged representations of climate change data.

Section 3 'Making Data: Techniques' further explores the notion of tangible data enabled through new technological forms. This includes smart surfaces, AR techniques, sonification and next generation technical interfaces that use AI to blend physical and digital visualizations. The section begins with a chapter by Daniel F. Keefe and his collaborators who highlight and explore a new application area in biomedical data as the site of their research. In this chapter a combination of digital visualization and physical data constructs showing blood flow in the heart are used by medical practitioners, engineers and scientists to help understand difficult-to-see spatial relationships. Building on this conversation around the advantage of drawing from both physical and digital paradigms Stephen Barrass reminds us that in the world of data physicalization, sound is often an overlooked medium. The chapter shows that sounds can tell us how big things are and what they are made of. Barrass expertly takes us through a series of technical experiments that use 3D-printed instruments to create sonic data physicalizations. Mitchell Whitelaw and Geoff Hinchcliffe's chapter looks at how hybrid approaches to data visualization can exploit the tangible affordances of physicalized data in conjunction with the updateability of digital interfaces, to create an enhanced and customisable experience of data. Climate Data is again used by Whitelaw and Hinchcliffe as a lens through which to explore bespoke making techniques, materiality issues, engagement and metaphoric ideas of the data-object. Georgi V. Georgiev and Yazan Barhoush affirm that data is a fundamental constituent of computer technologies and is something that is not only shaping technology and our relationship with it but also our understanding of ourselves. In a tip to a technologically enhanced near future Georgiev and Barhoush propose that an AI-based system that drives a data physicalization can be used to provide real-time feedback on human creative decision-making processes and conversations by controlling a miniature waterfall as a form of communication no less. In the final chapter from this section Jason Alexander continues the exploration of dynamic data materializations through an exploration of techniques and technologies that facilitate active data-objects that can physical change shape in response to real-time inputs.

A brief overview of the book plus some thoughts and observations on where to next with the making of data is offered in a concluding chapter by myself and research colleague Dr Aaron Davis.

I hope that you find the theories, creative practices and technological ideas outlined in this book as exciting and as engaging as I have in bringing them together. Ranging from the cultural history and techniques of making data-objects; to the concept of data as an economic, ethical form of knowledge transaction; to data realities which examine the relationships between digital and material data cultures and the hybrid combinations of both; to the implications of the quantified self and even the quantified planet, this publication touches on some of the concerns and potentials enacted through the physicalizing of digital data. However, like any activity at the forefront of its discipline the ideas presented in this book raise more questions than answers and point towards our dynamic future engagement with digital data. Currently the skills and labour required in the creation of physical data translations make this a rarefied activity, but as technologies and cultural expectations of our digital data continue to evolve we will undoubtably see the kinds of data typologies described within move into the mainstream.

References

Sanchez-Lorenzo, A, Calbó, J, Wild, M, Azorin-Molina, C and Sanchez-Romero, A 2013, 'New insights into the history of the Campbell-Stokes sunshine recorder', *Weather*, vol. 68, pp. 327–31. https://doi.org/10.1002/wea.2130

Lima, M 2009, 'Information visualization manifesto visual complexity VC blog', accessed 29 April 2021, http://www.visualcomplexity.com/vc/blog/?p=644

SECTION ONE
MAKING DATA: THEORIES

Chapters in this section introduce the general concept and application of the data-object, as well as exploring theory associated with the physical data artefact as a means of recording, reading and valuing information. It begins a conversation around the social, cultural, political, economic and philosophical significance of data-objects and draws out the relationship between digital data and data which are physically materialized through these lenses. Recognizing that digital and physicalized data are not necessarily in binary opposition and that there are many examples wherein hybrid forms of data can invoke nuanced understanding and insight through the interplay between these two paradigms.

Ontological and epistemological relationships between digital and material data cultures, and hybrid combinations of data and meaning are explored. Ideas around the politics of data ownership, data physicalization as a pathway to behaviour change and data as movement within a creative practice are also discussed.

1
DATA-OBJECTS: THINKING WITH YOUR HANDS

Adrien Segal

The path is revealed by walking along it.
— SPANISH PROVERB

Introduction

There is nothing inherently digital about data. Some of the earliest representations of data were physical objects and artefacts used to record and track quantified data (Dragicevic & Jansen 2012). These representations were forms and constructions made from raw materials. Incan civilizations used a complex system of knotted cotton or wool ropes, called quipu or khipu, that represented information through colour, knot patterns and cord twist directions as devices for data storage and communication (Salomon 2013). The Marshall Islands stick charts abstractly represented the interaction of the ocean's currents, swells and islands, and were physically constructed from sticks and seashells (National Geographic Society 2013). Mesopotamian clay tokens were created by preliterate cultures to count, store and communicate economic data dating as far back as 7500 BC, around the time that agriculture began. These tokens were made from clay shaped into geometric symbols including cones, spheres, cylinders and tetrahedrons, representing commodities such as barley, oil and units of work, and in different sizes, denoting quantity (Schmandt-Besserat 2009).

Data is an abstract representation, a reduction of the rich reality that is the world around us, divided into elemental parts, captured as quantifiable measurements. No matter how much data one can amass, without form, organization and context, data itself has no meaning. The immensity of data we find ourselves swimming in today is a direct result of the digitization of life through the expanded daily use of technology, computers and devices that are constantly tracking, measuring and quantifying. This is perhaps why data today is often perceived to exist primarily in digital form.

However, the roots of the word 'digital' stem from the analogue world. Up until the mid-twentieth century, the common conception of 'digital' (in print form) was almost exclusively found in books about human and animal anatomy, in reference to the movement of hands and feet (Quain 1828). Digital, from its Latin root *digitalis* or *digitus*, simply means finger or toe, pertaining to numbers below ten, or exactly that which can be counted on your hands. It was not until circa 1945 that the connotation to computation and digital computers, which run on data in the form of numerical digits, established the modern meaning of digital (Harper 2017a).

From a very early age, we are admonished from counting with our fingers, and encouraged to 'count in your head'. As students advance through Western educational systems, their level of intelligence is constantly evaluated through standardized testing, pop quizzes and multiple answer exams that require the retrieval of information purely committed to memory. This institutional emphasis on explicit, propositional statements, also known as 'a priori' knowledge, or knowledge that can be derived from the world without needing to experience it, does not account for all kinds of knowledge that fall outside this mental boundary. Embodied, tacit or 'a posteriori' knowledge is everything that cannot easily be expressed through language, such as learning how to ride a bike or play a musical instrument. It is acquired through first-hand experience and 'hands-on' actions, and is equally, if not more valuable to human existence.

The current accepted principles of data visualization reinforce the common convention that all thinking and reasoning happens through the eye and only in the mind. This limited view of disembodied thought leaves out the potential that lies in representing information physically, that is, communicating ideas through objects and artefacts whose form and materials are driven by data in physical space. In fact, much of the data that has been collected about the natural world is inherently physical – tree rings, ice cores, layers of sedimentation – information is embedded in the physical structure of these material formations. Even wind, clouds and the jet stream, seemingly ephemeral natural phenomena, are in effect physical processes involving masses of air and water vapour shifting due to pressure and temperature flux. From these natural formations, we decode records of changes in the environment over time as we seek to understand the world in which we live, to learn how it came to be this way and to predict how it might change in the future.

As an artist, designer and specifically a sculptor, I know through first-hand experience that representing ideas in physical forms and materials can be an effective and powerful medium for expressing and communicating ideas.

DATA-OBJECTS: THINKING WITH YOUR HANDS

There is strong scientific evidence supporting the idea that the way humans perceive physical space is an integral aspect of thinking processes. In her book *Mind in Motion* (2019), cognitive psychologist Barbara Tversky describes how spatial thinking and physical expression are developed in humans long before spoken language. Tversky proposes the theory that spatial cognition isn't just a peripheral aspect of thought, but that it is the foundation of thinking processes.

Thinking that engages the body in movement, interaction and physical space can increase understanding, reasoning and problem-solving. For instance, the abacus had been in use centuries before the adoption of the Hindu-Arabic numeral system, much like the Mesopotamian clay tokens were a tactile data processing tool – the counters were meant to be grasped, rearranged and manipulated with the fingers (Schmandt-Besserat 2009). Imagine how challenging it would be to play a word game such as Scrabble without having letter tiles that can be spatially reconfigured to find new combinations of words. In contrast to the traditional concept of cognition, which only analyses internal processes of the mind, 'distributed cognition' calls for a shift towards a manner of thinking that examines the relationship between the mind, the body and its environment (Hutchins 2001, pp. 2068–72). Using this approach, researchers at Kingston University tasked test subjects with a series of statistical reasoning problems and found increased success in solving the problems when participants were given a pack of cards with information that they could spread out and rearrange, as opposed to solving the problems with just a pen and paper (Vallée-Tourangeau, Abadie & Vallée-Tourangeau 2015). The researchers concluded that 'people are more creative and more efficient when solving problems with their hands: thinking is an embodied activity embedded in a physical environment' (Vallée-Tourangeau & Vallée-Tourangeau 2016).

Our senses are the instruments by which our body takes in information from the surrounding environment and transmits those sensations to the brain where they are interpreted – it is an interdependent system. There is no internal hierarchy that defines information read from a book through the eye as more important or useful than information which you smell, hear, touch or otherwise experience somatically.[1] Some kinds of information simply cannot be learned from a book or a visual graphic – it must be lived and experienced directly by a thinking, feeling person. To ignore the potential that lies within representing data and communicating information to people physically is a missed opportunity for the field of data representation as a whole.

This proposition raise's questions around, what, specifically, can spatial, tactile and physicalized data express and communicate that tabular or purely visual data cannot? How does one begin to translate data into physical forms and materials? And what can we learn from designers and artists about effectively representing ideas in three-dimensional space?

On representation in three dimensions

The famous pipe. How people reproached me for it! And yet, could you stuff my pipe? No, it's just a representation, is it not? So if I had written on my picture 'This is a pipe', I'd have been lying!
— RENÉ MAGRITTE (Torczyner 1977, p. 71) on the *Treachery of Images*

To lay the foundation of how to communicate data concepts visually (or physically) we should first touch on the concept of representation. In this case to represent data is to give it shape and substance. Given structure, organization and context, raw data becomes 'information' through its representation in a new form. This is the point at which we step away from pure objectivity and enter the realm of a subjective human, in terms of both who decides what shape to give the data, and also how the audience interprets, decodes or reads what the representation is communicating. The relationship between these two actions, the act of representation and the act of perception, is immensely important for artists and designers.

Although there are a number of important early examples of visualized data in the graphic forms of diagrams and maps (Friendly 2006), many of the conventional and generally recognized data visualizations we see commonly in use today were a relatively recent invention from the eighteenth century.[2] It was in the twentieth century that the first comprehensive theoretical foundation of information visualization, *Semiologie Graphique (Semiology of Graphics)* by Jacques Bertin (1918–2010), was published.[3] In his book, Bertin (1967) outlines six visual variables that can be employed by the designer to create information graphics in two planar dimensions: size, value, texture, colour, orientation and shape. When data is represented in three-dimensional space, we gain access to at least three additional variables: space, form and material. These additional design elements appeal to our spatial and tactile nature as humans living in the world, and when utilized to represent data, they make information accessible to our perceptual senses, including but not limited to the visual.

In Bertin's *Semiology of Graphics*, a Cartesian coordinate system with two axes (x, y) define the two planar dimensions on which numerical data can be visually mapped. This system positions the location of points in space in relation to an origin (0, 0). In basic terms, adding a third axis (x, y, z) creates an additional channel through which data can be mapped. For example, the three axes represented in the artwork series *Tidal Datum* has one dimension representing water level, and two additional dimensions that capture time (Figure 1.1). The additional dimension (z) allows the representation of data in *volumetric form* which a human can move around in three-dimensional space. In terms of human experience, as the body moves around a physical artefact, new perspectives and understandings are gained, which is not possible when viewing a flat, two-dimensional graphic. Additionally, physical forms are spatially enhanced with light and the shadows that are cast from their volume, allowing for a rich interactive experience and a physical, sensory and intellectual engagement with an audience.

Material as metaphor

Objects can be seen as the blank slates upon which we project our needs, desires, ideas and values. As such, material culture contains a wealth of information about who we are, who we want to be.

(Hirst 2018)

The root of the word material emerged from Latin *materia* meaning 'substance from which something is made', 'matter', and the 'hard inner wood of a tree' (Harper 2017b). In fact, the earliest known human wood worked artefact, the Clacton Spear, dates to around 400,000 years ago, long before it is believed that spoken language existed (Allington-Jones 2015). Influences of material culture and the ways we work with raw materials can be found in language used today. Describing someone as a 'chip off the old block', meaning a person whose character or personality closely resemble their parents, is a reference to stone work and its use dates back to the third century BC (Ammer 2013). Working 'against the grain' references the craft of woodworking, referring to a situation when one cuts against the direction of fibres in a piece of wood. Used figuratively, 'against the grain' means in opposition or contrary to what is commonly practised or accepted.

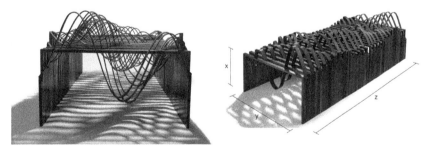

Figure 1.1 *Tidal Datum*, San Francisco, 2007, by Adrien Segal. Wood and Steel, 26" x 32" x 72". Photo courtesy of the artist. The tide data represented in three-dimensions (x, y, z) are: (x) observed water level height; (y) 24-hour daily tide chart; and (z) 29 days or the duration of a full-tide cycle.

Let's look specifically at wood as *a material* to understand the practical, aesthetic, functional and symbolic meanings materials can carry. The physical characteristics of wood vary greatly depending on which species you are working with. Easily misleading, the designation of a species as hardwood or softwood is not related to the degree of its physical hardness, but dependent upon whether the tree is coniferous (cone bearing evergreen) or a flowering tree (angiosperm). Balsa wood (*Ochroma pyramidale*), for example, has excellent sound, temperature and vibration absorbing properties. It is very light in colour, has almost no visible grain pattern, and it is remarkably buoyant (Meier 2009). Balsa is very soft and easy to cut, shape and carve, however, technically it is considered to be a hardwood. Conversely, Yew *(Taxus baccata)*, perhaps the hardest of all softwoods, is a species with a long history and deep cultural ties. The Clacton spear was made from Yew wood. Because of its strength and flexibility, it is ideally suited for use in archery bows, and was the material of choice for English longbows used in medieval warfare. Yew is a tree species that carries symbolic weight in its association with death, due to their common presence in cemeteries, and because the tree's needles and berries can be fatal if ingested (Cherrell 2019). In Shakespeare's *Macbeth*, the witches concoct a poison including 'slips of yew, sliver'd in the moon's eclipse' (Shakespeare 1623). Working directly with Yew wood can cause skin, eye, respiratory and other bodily irritations, learned first-hand while carving a piece during an artist residency in Ireland.

In my creative work (which is often described as 'data sculpture'), I strive to find a balance between the physical characteristics and unconscious associations that a material brings, while maintaining accuracy in representing the dataset that drives the form. I work across different media, allowing the data concept to determine what material will best convey the idea to an audience. For example, *Arctic Sea Ice/Albedo* (2017) (Figure 1.2a) is an artwork representing sea ice patterns as cast glass, utilizing the material properties of transparency the graduated tones of blue seen in the ocean's depth. The casting process retained tiny bubbles embedded in the glass, similar to the porous structure of sea ice. Another sculpture, *Grewingk Glacier* (2015), represents data measuring the retreat of a glacier in Alaska as cast ice. A time-lapse video captures the sculpture melting away, referencing the fluid and temporal nature of glaciers. When the physical ice sculpture has been shown in a gallery context, viewers express a desire to touch and feel the sensation of cold.

Trends in Water Use (2011) (Figure 1.2b) is a sculpture created from water consumption data in a report published by the United States Geological Survey (Hutson et al. 2004). Learning that the largest river in the American West, the Colorado River, runs dry before it reaches the Gulf of Mexico, was the catalyst for researching the consumption of water in the United States. The reports contain an analysis of all the water consumed in the United States dating back to the

DATA-OBJECTS: THINKING WITH YOUR HANDS

Figure 1.2b *Trends in Water Use*, 2011. Carved Plywood and Steel. Artwork by Adrien Segal. Photograph by Fredrik Nilsen Studio.

Figure 1.2a *Arctic Sea Ice/Albedo*, 2017 Cast Glass. Artwork by Adrien Segal.

year 1950. The data sculpture implies the absence of water through the aesthetic forms seen in the arid landscape of the American West. Constructed using finely layered plywood the piece reflects the geologic formation of a canyon and the stratified rock layers that are revealed as water carves and erodes material away. Mirroring the physical process of weathering and erosion, the plywood is carved back into a smooth, undulating surface using handheld abrasive tools and grinders. The width of the walls of the sculpted canyon directly correlate to the amount of water consumed. The vertical height of the canyon correlates to fifty years' time, from 1950 at the top to the year 2000 at its base.

From a practical standpoint, the decision to manifest data in physical materials requires the knowledge, skills, tools and techniques necessary to successfully transform the material into the desired form. Form and material must be considered in tandem – one cannot arbitrarily choose a material without understanding the form and its structure, and a form cannot be manifested without a material from which it is made. Materials can be fragile or durable, have fibrous structures, weaknesses, will expand or contract with humidity, will deform with heat, or may not hold a sharp edge depending on their physical properties. For example, wood cut very thin or cut across the grain can more easily break, and cast glass can take days or even weeks to properly cool in a kiln to avoid cracking, depending on its thickness. These physical characteristics also relate to aesthetic features, such as surface quality, texture, reflectivity, transparency, tone or colour. All of these features can influence how a form is interpreted and experienced, and they can be utilized to strengthen the communication of a data concept, or can distract from it, if not thoroughly considered.

Beyond their physical and aesthetic properties, materials offer many subtle qualities, such as familiarity, traditional use, perceived value, historic significance, symbolic meaning, site-specificity and cultural association. These nuances can be both conscious and unconscious. For example, the warmth and familiarity of a natural material such as wood may invite touch and interaction, whereas a fragile or sharp material like glass may be unnerving or can bring an awe inspiring but cautious presence. Common, inexpensive or industrial materials like concrete or polymer plastic will be perceived and treated with a different reverence than a precious material like gold, associated with value and currency, or marble, which has become a symbol of tradition and refined taste in some cultures (Gwilt 2013). The links between the significance of a material and its signified meaning are not universal or absolute. Like the alphabet, a flag or the colours of a stoplight, what is being communicated must be learned and interpreted, and is specific to a culture. Although there are no universal rules about how a material will be interpreted, cultural familiarity and sensitivity can help to avoid unintended miscommunications. Artists and designers can provide guidance in understanding how materials can be used to effectively convey an idea while being thoughtfully considerate of these qualities, both tangible and symbolic.

The degree of familiarity and symbolic significance of a material spans a wide spectrum. Traditional materials even after they are refined into an artefact tend to retain the qualities of their raw sources, such as the grain structure in wood reflecting the tree from which it grew. Furthermore, the artefacts one creates cannot truly be seen in isolation from the places from which their materials are sourced and extracted. Carrara marble is named for the city from which it is quarried in the northernmost tip of Tuscany, Italy, which is uniquely distinct from Yule marble sourced from the Rocky Mountains in Colorado. Found or repurposed materials retain evidence of their previous existence, sometimes symbolically. London based sculptor Cornelia Parker salvaged the materials for her work titled *Mass (Colder Darker Matter)* (1997) and *Anti-mass* (2005) from two incinerated churches in the American South, one struck by lightning and the other by arson. Parker's choice to repurpose wood remnants from places of worship brings a historic, geographic and cultural context to the work. These symbolic meanings are conveyed through material itself, which is interpreted by a human subject, thus impacting the way one perceives, thinks and feels about the experience of encountering the sculptural installation and the events that are being represented.

In contrast to the more recognizable natural materials we see, touch and interact with daily, in both the natural and built environment, there are many man-made, industrial, synthetic or engineered materials (polyurethane, PVC, epoxy resin, fibreglass, plastics etc.) that are *perceptually* more removed from their earthly sources. Their material disassociation from tradition and history has been employed by artists and designers such as Gaetano Pesce and Roberto Cuoghi to represent modernism, futurism, hybridity, metamorphosis, and to question perception and expectations through their material obscurity. Pesce, an industrial designer, created a line of furniture objects including an armchair titled *Senza Fine Unica* made from extruded polychrome PVC (Pesce 2011). The object is a bright, amorphous form made up of flaccid, multi-coloured, plastic tubes bundled into a seemingly functional, yet alien, seat. Cuoghi's work is similarly extrinsic with a somewhat darker aesthetic. In his exhibition '*da id. ā e pin˙ galā a id. ā e id. ā o pin˙ galā e pin˙galā.*' Cuoghi's sculptural work is realized in a variety of highly textured, unconventional and unidentified media (Aspen Art Museum 2015).

Despite their ambiguous appearance, even engineered materials are themselves not entirely removed from their natural sources or the landscapes from which they are extracted. Polylactic Acid (PLA), a common filament material used in 3D printing, is a bioplastic which is in part made from fermented plant starches such as corn (Auras et al. 2010). Polyvinyl Chloride (PVC), from which Pesce's chair is made, is derived from chlorine from sea salt and fossil fuels through an extremely complex chemical process. The metals, minerals and compounds used in digital devices like smartphones[4] (the average mobile phone contains a total of sixty-two different types of metals), which are physically extracted from sites across the globe (Graedel et al. 2013). The more processed the raw material is, the farther removed it appears to be from its source, and the less we tend to recognize or associate it with a particular site, environment or culture. Natural or synthetic, familiar or obscure, common or rare – all materials are imbued with underlying associations and meanings from which they cannot be fully disassociated.

The field of archaeology underscores the importance and longevity of the material artefacts left behind by human civilizations as evidence of their culture and values and the study of physical artefacts reveal much of what we know about human existence in past eras. Prehistoric epochs are named for the tangible artefacts left behind, more specifically for the materials from which they are made; the Stone Age, Bronze Age and Iron Age, commonly known as the Three Age System.[5] It has been proposed that the material legacy of the current epoch, the Anthropocene, in which humans are noticeably altering the surface geology of the planet with the production of long-lasting, man-made materials, will be marked by the inclusion of a layer of plastic to the geologic record (Zalasiewicz et al. 2016).

Method of production

The translation of perception and experience into different forms is one of the most important mechanisms of the creative process.
(Jenny 1981, p. 18)

The objects and artefacts we create must be considered as integral to the processes by which they are formed from raw materials. The complex nature of working with materials may deter practitioners of data visualization that would otherwise like to try their hand at representing data in physical materials. Designers and artists have also faced the challenge of creating work that requires skills, equipment or technical abilities outside of their expertise.

Some artists choose a primary medium and work with it directly and continuously throughout their career. Others rely on partnerships and collaborations to help them translate their work into materials that require specialized working processes. Many designers and artists create scale models and prototypes in an easily formed medium and then rely on master craftspeople to realize the final piece in more permanent materials (Sennett 2009). The renowned French sculptor, Auguste Rodin's (1840–1917) original works were often sculpted in clay or plaster. He employed highly trained assistants, plaster casters, carvers and founders to translate his models into larger finished works in marble and bronze.[6] The mould-making and casting process were particularly important. This approach not only allowed Rodin to translate his work into permanent materials and to reproduce them in multiples,[7] it became an integral part of his process of sculpting and spatial problem-solving.

> Rodin often had several casts made of an original, allowing him to create a number of different versions, as well as to cut casts up as a means of working out further possibilities. Over time he built up a huge repertoire of plaster moulds and models, using them to devise new figurative combinations and juxtapositions, or to find fresh solutions to compositional problems.
> (Victoria and Albert Museum 2011)

In recent times, designers have increasingly come to rely on new technology and digital fabrication equipment, such as 3D printers, robotic arms and other Computer Numeric Controlled (CNC) machines, to aid in the prototyping and production of three-dimensional objects, including for the purpose of data physicalization. These machines are appealing in that they are seemingly quick and easy to use (hence the term 'rapid prototyping') and relatively accessible,[8] although they can be limited in the variety of material and quality of output.[9]

Typically, a form is designed using Computer Aided Design (CAD) modelling programme. The geometric information that defines the shape (x, y, z coordinates) is translated into instructions (computer code) that control the movement of the machine. For example, when 3D printing with a Fused Deposition Modelling (FDM) printer, the machine is loaded with cartridges or rolls of mouldable synthetic material. The material filament is heated to an amorphous state, extruded through the printer head which is attached to a 3-axis system moving in the x, y and z dimensions. The form builds up layer by layer, and the material sets as it cools (Varotsis 2019). In other types of 3D printers, plastic or resin is squeezed through a set of nozzles and set with infrared light, or the printer heads only move in the x, y dimensions while the machine bed raises or lowers in the z dimension. Objects made in this way retain evidence of how they are made – the surface is made up of thin, layered horizontal lines of uniformly coloured plastic. The layers are less visible with a higher resolution print. Plastics and resins tend to lack durability compared to other materials in that they are relatively easy to break if not handled carefully and will deteriorate over time and with exposure to the sun – factors which inform how they are culturally perceived.

It is rare that an art object in its final form will be produced exclusively using digital fabrication tools. Often 3D printers and other digital fabrication tools are used to test ideas, to refine a form's proportions, as a prototype, or to cut parts that are processed further. More importantly, the choice to use a machine as the primary means of production of tangible artefacts removes some, if not all of the physical interaction normally required to 'make' something. In this case, the embodied knowledge involving the hands and the sensation of touch is almost but not quite eliminated from the act of making, as many of these digital process still require some 'finishing' by hand.

Conclusion

Stop thinking about artworks as objects and start thinking about them as triggers for experience.

– ROY ASCOTT (Eno 1996, p. 368)

To fully understand how physical objects can convey information through space, form and material, we need to stop thinking about them simply as inanimate, static matter, but as what American philosopher and educational reformer, John Dewey (1859–1952) called the 'expressive object'. Theories set forth in his book *Art as Experience* (1934) have deeply influenced views on how objects can expressively communicate ideas, information and meaning through human experience. Why is experience so important in the field of data representation?

If data in-and-of-itself has no meaning, and data in context becomes information, then how does information become meaningful to the person perceiving it?

Sensory perception is a direct pathway for acquiring information from objects in our surroundings, therefore form, space and materiality fundamentally shape what we experience and perceive, and how we learn, reason, understand and gain knowledge from those experiences throughout our lives.

In parallel with the process of visualizing a dataset, creating an expressive object begins with a raw material that is refined into an intensified and concentrated form through a series of actions and decisions – the act of doing or making. For the data visualizer, creative practitioner, artist or designer, tasked with representing a dataset, it may seem that the goal is simply to present objective facts. This approach, however, falls short by neglecting awareness of the second part of representation – the act of perception and the resulting experience of the subjective human observer. Dewey proposes that the expressive object effectively connects two distinct experiences – the act of making or doing, and the act of perceiving or undergoing. 'What is done and what is undergone are thus reciprocally, cumulatively, and continuously instrumental to each other' (Dewey 1934). In an expressive object, the making and the perceiving are presented in relation to each other, thus the action and its consequence become joined in an experience. If we acknowledge the expansiveness of human perception in how we choose to represent data, information presented as an expressive object will be more meaningful and engaging than purely visual representations because it will fully consider how humans learn, understand and experience the world around them.

Creating an experience is an instrumental step for information to be perceived, synthesized and transformed into knowledge. Until it is interpreted by a subjective, living, feeling person, data will forever remain meaningless. Soren Kierkegaard, the Dutch philosopher, proposes that 'subjectivity is truth', in that truth is not found simply by learning objective facts, it is how one relates oneself to those facts that matters (Kierkegaard & Hong 1976). Raw data is objective, but to serve its purpose is to become subjective through this process because ultimately, humans do not make decisions or find meaning in life through pure objectivity. By being represented with the full faculties of human perception in consideration, data thus becomes accessible simultaneously to the mind and the body as a more complete form of experience.

Acknowledgements

Much appreciation to Charlie Nordstrom, Donald Fortescue and Julia Harrison for their time, encouragement, editing suggestions and knowledgeable feedback throughout the process of writing this text.

Notes

1. Although each of the senses are indispensable to human experience, for the purposes of this writing we are primarily interested in physicalized data (or data physicalization) rather than the distinct areas of sound (data sonification), smell or taste. Also, it should be noted that there are more than five senses. Internal sensation, or interception, detects stimuli from internal organs and tissues. Many internal sensory and perceptual systems exist in humans, including proprioception (body position) and nociception (pain).
2. William Playfair (1759–1823), a Scottish engineer and political economist, is credited with inventing several types of diagrams including line, area, bar and pie charts.
3. Coincidence or not, the term 'information overload' seems to have been established and popularized around the same time as Bertin's book was published. It was first used in Bertram Gross' book, *The Managing of Organizations,* published in 1964.
4. Bastnasite, for example, which is used in magnets, camera lenses and batteries.
5. The Three Age System define the three archaeological periods spanning roughly 2.5 million years ago to 1200 BC. Controversy of Eurocentrism aside, this concept of naming ages based on metals originated with Danish archaeologist C. J. Thomsen (1788–1865), director of the Royal Museum of Nordic Antiquities in Copenhagen, as a means to classify the museum's collection of artefacts.
6. Rodin's bronzes were cast by Rudier Foundry in Paris – the mark of the maker 'ALEXIS RUDIER/Fondeur PARIS' can be found near the base of these works.
7. According to the Victoria & Albert Museum (2011), Rodin authorized more than 300 bronze casts of 'The Kiss' during his lifetime to disseminate his work to a broad audience.
8. It is important to note that most people in the world do not have access to rapid prototyping equipment.
9. The two most common and inexpensive materials available for consumer market 3D printers are Acrylonitrile Butadiene Styrene (ABS) and Polylactic Acid (PLA), both thermoplastics.

References

Allington-Jones, L 2015, 'The Clacton Spear: The last one hundred years', *Archaeological Journal*, vol. 172, no. 2, pp. 273–96.

Ammer, C 2013, *The American heritage dictionary of idioms*, Houghton Mifflin Harcourt, Boston.

Aspen Art Museum 2015, *Roberto Cuoghi: da id. ā e pin˙ galā a id. ā e id. ā o pin˙ galā e pin˙ gala*, 13 February–14 June 2015, Aspen Art Museum, Aspen, Colorado.

Auras, R, Lim, L-T, Selke, SEM, & Tsuji, H 2010, *Poly(Lactic Acid) synthesis, structures, properties, processing, and applications*, John Wiley & Sons, Inc, Hoboken.

Bertin, J 1967, *Semiology of graphics: Diagrams, networks, maps*, trans. W Berg, Esri Press, Redlands, California, 2011.

Cherrell, K 2019, *The Yew: Tree of the dead*, Burials & Beyond, accessed 17 February 2021, https://burialsandbeyond.com/2019/08/31/the-yew-tree-of-the-dead/.

Dewey, J 1934, *Art as experience*, Minton, Balch & Company, New York.
Dragicevic, P & Jansen, Y 2012, *List of physical visualizations*, accessed 15 February 2021, http://dataphys.org/list/.
Earth Observatory 2012, *Rare Earth in Bayan Obo*, accessed 17 February 2021, https://earthobservatory.nasa.gov/images/77723/rare-earth-in-bayan-obo.
Eno, B 1996, *Year with swollen appendices: Brian Eno's diary*, Faber and Faber, London.
Friendly, M 2006, 'A brief history of data visualization', in C Chen, A Unwin & W Härdle (eds), *Handbook of computational statistics: Data visualization*, Springer-Verlag, Heidelberg.
Graedel, TE, Harper, EM, Nassar, NT & Reck, BK 2013, 'On the materials basis of modern society', *Proceedings of the National Academy of Sciences*, vol. 112, no. 20, pp. 6295–300.
Gwilt, I 2013, 'Data-Objects: Sharing the attributes and properties of digital and material culture to creatively interpret complex information', in D Harrison (ed), *Digital media and technologies for virtual artistic spaces*, IGI Global, Pennsylvania.
Harper, D 2017a, *digital | Origin and meaning of digital by Online Etymology Dictionary*, accessed 18 February 2021, https://www.etymonline.com/word/digital.
Harper, D 2017b, *material | Origin and meaning of material by Online Etymology Dictionary*, accessed 18 February 2021, https://www.etymonline.com/word/material#etymonline_v_43757.
Hirst, KK 2018, *What can the material culture of a society tell scientists?* accessed 16 February 2021, http://www.thoughtco.com/material-culture-artifacts-meanings-they-carry-171783.
Hutchins, E 2001, 'Cognition, distributed', *International Encyclopedia of the Social & Behavioral Sciences*, Pergamon, pp. 2068–72, accessed 15 February 2021, https://doi.org/10.1016/B0-08-043076-7/01636-3.
Hutson, SS, Barber, NL, Kenny, JF, Linsey, KS, Lumia, DS & Maupin, MA 2004, *Estimated use of water in the United States in 2000*, U.S. Geological Survey, Reston, VA.
Jenness, JE, Ober, JA, Wilkins, AM & Gambogi, J 2016, 'A world of minerals in your mobile device', *U.S. Geological Survey*, accessed 18 February 2021, https://pubs.er.usgs.gov/publication/gip167.
Jenny, P 1981, *Sign and design*, Lehrstuhl Für Bildner, Gestalten, Architekturabt, Eidgenöss. Techn. Hochschule, Zürich.
Kierkegaard, S & Hong, EH 1976, *Søren Kierkegaard's journals and papers*, Indiana University Press, Bloomington and London.
Mabillard, A 2021, *Macbeth Glossary*, Shakespeare Online, accessed 17 February 2021, http://www.shakespeare-online.com/plays/macbeth/macbethglossary/macbeth1_1/macbethglos_yew.html.
Meier, E 2009, *Balsa | The Wood Database - Lumber Identification (Hardwood)*, Wood-database.com, accessed 16 February 2021, https://www.wood-database.com/balsa/.
National Geographic Society 2013, *Marshallese Stick Chart*, accessed 2 March 2021, https://www.nationalgeographic.org/media/icronesian-stick-chart/.
Parker, C 1997, *Mass (Colder Darker Matter)*, Phoenix Art Museum, accessed 18 February 2021, https://phxart.org/arts/mass-colder-darker-matter-monton-materia-mas-oscura-mas-fria/.
Parker, C 2005, *Anti-Mass*, Fine Arts Museums of San Francisco, accessed 18 February 2021, https://art.famsf.org/cornelia-parker/anti-mass-20062.

Pesce, G 2011, *Senza Fine Unica*, Gaetano Pesce, accessed 18 February 2021, http://gaetanopesce.com/.
Quain, J 1828, *Elements of descriptive and practical anatomy: For the use of students*, W. Simpkin and R. Marshall, London.
Salomon, F 2013, 'The twisting paths of recall: Khipu (Andean cord notation) as artifact', in KE Piquette & RD Whitehouse (eds), *Writing as material practice: Substance, surface and medium*, Ubiquity Press, London, pp. 15–44, accessed 15 February 2021, *JSTOR*, http://www.jstor.org/stable/j.ctv3t5r28.7.
Schmandt-Besserat, D 2009, *Tokens and writing: The cognitive development*, Denise Schmandt-Besserat, accessed 15 February 2021, https://sites.utexas.edu/dsb/tokens/tokens-and-writing-the-cognitive-development/.
Sennett, R 2009, *The craftsman*, Penguin, London.
Shakespeare, W 2019, *Macbeth*, The Complete Works of William Shakespeare, Act 4, Scene 1, Line 27, accessed 16 February 2021, http://shakespeare.mit.edu/macbeth/macbeth.4.1.html.
Torczyner, H 1977, *Magritte: ideas and images*, Harry N. Abrams, New York, 71.
Tversky, B 2019, *Mind in motion: how action shapes thought*, Basic Books, New York.
Vallée-Tourangeau, F & Vallée-Tourangeau, G 2016, *Why the best problem-solvers think with their hands, as well as their heads*, The Conversation, accessed 17 February 2021, https://theconversation.com/why-the-best-problem-solvers-think-with-their-hands-as-well-as-their-heads-68360.
Vallée-Tourangeau, G, Abadie, M & Vallée-Tourangeau, F 2015, 'Interactivity fosters Bayesian reasoning without instruction', *Journal of Experimental Psychology: General*, vol. 144, no. 3, pp. 581–603.
Varotsis, AB 2019, *Introduction to FDM 3D printing*, 3D Hubs, accessed 2 March 2021, https://www.3dhubs.com/knowledge-base/introduction-fdm-3d-printing/.
Victoria and Albert Museum, 2011, *Auguste Rodin: production techniques*, Victoria and Albert Museum, accessed 28 April 2021, https://www.vam.ac.uk/articles/rodin-production-techniques/.
Zalasiewicz, J, Waters, CN, Ivar do Sul, JA, Corcoran, PL, Barnosky, AD, Cearreta, A, Edgeworth, M, Gałuszka, A, Jeandel, C, Leinfelder, R, McNeill, JR, Steffen, W, Summerhayes, C, Wagreich, M, Williams, M, Wolfe, AP & Yonan, Y 2016, 'The geological cycle of plastics and their use as a stratigraphic indicator of the Anthropocene', *Anthropocene*, vol. 13, pp. 4–17.

2
SHIFTING DATA BETWEEN THE MATERIAL AND THE VIRTUAL IS NOT AN IMMATERIAL MATTER

Dew Harrison

Introduction

Within the field of Fine Art, articulating the idea of the art object had made redundant the desire for the hand-crafted artefact to the extent that by the early 1970s text, language and dialogue had become the tools of a post-Duchampian Conceptual practice. Duchamp's *Readymades* had an immense impact on art-thinking and art-making by liberating our understanding of what constituted an art object to the point where the art object no longer needed to exist materially but could exist virtually as a concept of interrelated ideas played out in different forms. In the twenty-first century artists install readymade objects in galleries as a means of visualizing the data of complex situations in an actuality. Meanwhile designers and craft makers are exploring new materials and using data in 3D print processes to create statements in new forms. Often, this is through a hybrid dialogic process of a maker's thoughts translated into code in the virtual world for production in the real world, resulting in unique crafted objects created without the 'touch' of the hand-made, while encapsulating craft-thinking in the machine-made. Artists are then, moving objects across the virtual from the real and back again into solid form, so cyberspace gains a foothold in the real through the process of materialization.

It is now timely to consider the opposite directional flow, away from the digital code of the virtual object transitioned into a materialized physical object, and from downloading to uploading. For this we need to move our thinking away from the *Readymades* and into the *Large Glass* where Duchamp's amazing visionary ideas about the technological potential for augmenting human consciousness and creative practice remain encased. Interfaces between our real/physical world and a computer sustained virtual space (the fourth-dimensional space-time termed 'cyberspace') are becoming less mechanically remote and more intuitive through the employment of haptic or gestural means of access. Although we are nearing a smooth transition between these different states, there exists a hesitation between the two, a liminal space of becoming, of being neither one nor the other, a threshold between two dimensions – hybridity, the mixing of data across media that upturns our thinking about data and form.

The interstate of hybridity will be paralleled here with the artwork known as the *Large Glass* which Duchamp intended would transcend the third dimension by acting as a signifier to the fourth. He was exploring ways of portraying his 'Bride' in the fourth dimension and began with painterly abstractions of the figure, finally rejecting paint and canvas in favour of the flatness of glass. For Duchamp, the work exists on a two-dimensional plane approaching the theoretical state of having no thickness, of being ultrathin or 'inframince'. He conceived his 'Bride' in the Large Glass as a 'two-dimensional representation of a three-dimensional bride who herself would be the projection of a four-dimensional bride in the three-dimensional world' (Duchamp 1914). The state of Duchamp's *inframince* can therefore be understood as the transitional portal existing between dimensions, between real and virtual worlds, a space to create hybridized artworks of inter-connected data.

Art forms, digitality and hybridity

There are artists who follow a conceptual path and whose interests lie in *l'inframince* and hybridity allowing for the movement between states through mixed-media installations to offer holistic understandings of a complex situation. However there are other artists who might not use computer technology but are none-the-less concerned with presenting complex concepts through various forms including material representations of data information. The more common forms of practice here can be described in three groups:

- artists who print art objects from code in hybridized new materials;
- those that collate or create real-world items to evidence and critique the statistical scale of an event;
- those who visualize digital data in a material form.

All these forms of practice sit within a lineage of art arising from Duchamp's *Readymades* in the last century. As we are now twenty years in to the new century, I propose that we need to look beyond the *Readymades* and into his *Large Glass* if we are to create work in the new dimensions of space, virtuality, reality and the space in-between where an audience can encounter new experiences and new art forms.

Accessing and experiencing virtual platforms means a stepping from one world to the other, a conceptual moving from one state of being to another. Contra to the avatar-to-human experience, virtual objects can be transformed into a solid materiality by crossing this threshold. The threshold is then a magic alchemical space, an interstice between the real and the virtual, a moment of change, of becoming other. These considerations and terms such as 'alchemical' 'change' 'threshold' 'transformer' 'conceptual' etc., when used as part of our art vocabulary are the direct descendants of the work and ideas of Marcel Duchamp for instance 'interstice' = *inframince*. The digital computer enables interactivity as a fundamental paradigm of dynamic relations to occur between the artist, spectator and artwork, itself a Duchampian positioning related to his seminal paper *The Creative Act* (Duchamp 1956) where the viewer completes the artwork. The computer screen acts as the interface to the machine constructed virtual world, a looking-glass into the other world beyond the real physical site of the viewer, a direct parallel with the *Large Glass* itself allowing the viewer a glimpse into another dimension and in so doing acting as a continuum between old and new technologies. To better find a key into the *Large Glass* we need to consider how the ideas encased within it were developed in a culture of new scientific and technological discoveries, and how the Artist's idea of the *Readymades* generated at the same time brought radical change within art theory and the subsequent disappearance of the art object, now returning through the technological affordances of data visualization and materialization, the virtual and the real.

The disappearance and re-materialization of the art object

In her seminal text *Six Years: The Dematerialization of the Art Object from 1966 to 1972 …* (Lippard 1973) Lucy Lippard considered that as work was designed in the studio for professionally crafted execution elsewhere, the art object had become merely the end product. She saw that a number of artists were losing interest in the physical evolution of the work of art and that the studio was again becoming a study. To Lippard, this 'trend' appeared to be provoking a profound dematerialization of art (Chandler & Lippard 1968, p. 31). Central to her texts is the understanding that Conceptual Art means 'work in which the idea is paramount and the material form is secondary, lightweight, ephemeral, cheap, unpretentious and/or "dematerialized"' (Chandler & Lippard 1968, p. 31). To support her understanding of Conceptual Art, Lippard identifies the historical source for this form of dematerialized practice as Marcel Duchamp and the re-reading of Duchamp's work undertaken by practitioners in the 1960s ensured that Duchamp was a major catalyst in the turning of the Modern to the Postmodern.

Duchamp's *Readymades*, industrial objects reclassified as artworks, challenged the traditional concepts of beauty, creativity, originality and autonomy in 1917, when Duchamp declared as a work of art an object designed for reproduction – a urinal, which he entitled *Fountain* (1917) and signed with the pseudonym R. Mutt. This object only became a work of art by virtue of the fact that an artist had submitted it for exhibition. With the introduction of the Readymade Duchamp challenged the conventional concepts of artistic skill and aesthetic value leading to a redefinition of the art object. By taking an everyday manufactured object and exhibiting it in an art gallery, the object became an art object because the artist said it was. This led to the practice of not making objects for critical assessment but applying critical assessment to a chosen object. Duchamp had proposed 'a new thought for that object' (Duchamp 1917). Following the Duchampian appropriation and claiming of the Readymades, the Conceptualists invested concern with the idea-structure in art, and non-object art emerged as information, systems and actions. A prime example of non-object art was the huge column of air hovering over Oxfordshire in 1968 taken as a hypothetical object for critical discussion by the Art & Language collective (Atkinson & Baldwin 1968, pp. 868–73). Text and language became prominent forms for displaying idea, text being inserted into the field of the art object and also, text presented as art, as exampled in the *Indexes* of the Art & Language group (see https://www.lissongallery.com/artists/art-language).

In his paper *Words and Objects after Conceptualism* (Beech 2009), David Beech suggests that art objects are 'inert without their texts', inertia in this case, being a social characteristic of art and not a physical one. He refers here to the various forms of dissemination which are part of the art piece reaching out as multiples, invites, publications, websites, blogs etc. 'To rearticulate the relationship between art objects and their texts is, therefore, to reinsert art into its social context' (Beech 2009). Beech argues that Lippard's 'dematerialization' wrongly characterizes Conceptualism in that it never fully escaped materiality, and that this could now be remedied if we consider the Conceptualists as re-contextualizing the inert traditional art object. He aligns this position with Walter Benjamin's concept of aura as the supernatural activity which rescues art objects from deathliness, and asserts that without that aura, 'the life of objects is given back to them through the social processes in which they participate' (Beech 2009). Postconceptualism therefore redeploys art's social relations. Although this redeployment is affective within current social art practice, this is also evident in the new craft-thinking currently emerging (Adamson 2010; Buszek 2011; Veiteberg 2011) and exampled by artists such as Michael Eden who is creating machine-produced digitally enabled designed objects in direct response to classical craftware but with RFID codes patterned into them, which connect to websites of information. Eden, a highly successful potter for over twenty years, still considers himself a 'maker'.

Lippard (1973) had documented Conceptual Art from 1966 to 72 as being highly politicized in that artists were indeed sharing 'distinctively modern concerns' and were in the process of facing the 'forces' in order to change their world. Lippard declared Conceptual Art as a product of the political ferment of the times, and states that her own version of Conceptual Art practice is 'inevitably tempered by my feminist and left politics' (Lippard 1973, p. 7). This politicized understanding of a Conceptual Art practice pertained to her own and to that of others, for example in 1971, Hans Haacke set out to expose two decades of unscrupulous activities by one of New York City's biggest landlords. *Shapolsky et al. Manhattan Real Estate Holdings, a Real Time Social System, as of 1 May 1971* (1971) employed cross-referenced texts (visually similar to the *Indexes* of Art & Language) to display the corrupt associations between stakeholders demonstrating a blatant disregard for the welfare of the tenants. The exhibition of this new work at New York's Solomon R. Guggenheim Museum was cancelled six weeks before the opening due to its contentious content (not unlike *Fountain*). Such work revealing actual documents and linked texts have prevailed into the new century as new technologies and social communication channels have allowed contemporary artists to consider both a return to the studio and to the method of crafting objects outside it. A revision of the situation where the idea is still paramount, but now exists within an art object with extended reach contextualizing it into the larger socio/political world. Thus, the material form can now be placed on equal footing with the idea. From dissecting and distilling language to science to art itself, Conceptual artists have expertly evaporated all in the high realm of ideas, creating works that challenge ideological authority, questioning the limits of what is true, and to do this they use information in material form, including texts and the visualization of digital data.

Ai Weiwei's highly politicized installations of masses of sunflower seeds, steel rods etc. are a fine example of a contemporary conceptual art practice using materials/readymades to offer a true and critical position of an actual event, and in so doing is visualizing information/data to a public audience in a succinct holistic gestalt. *Straight* (2008–12), steel reinforcing bars, 600 x 1,200 cm, Royal Academy, London 20 January 2016–12 January 2017, concerns the poorly constructed school buildings in the Sichuan Province located on seismic fault lines which were destroyed in the earthquake of 2008 killing over 9,000 children. The work consists of 150 steel reinforcing bars, 90 tons in weight, recovered from the ruins of the schools and hand-straightened by labourers, the floor-based installation was laid out in broken ripples designed to resemble the fault lines that caused the earthquake. A work both provocative and poignant, as for *Sunflower Seeds* (2010), 12 October 2010–2 May 2011, at the Tate Modern, where 100 million life-size sunflower seeds were poured into the Turbine hall. Each seed having been hand-crafted in porcelain, individually sculpted and painted by specialists in small-scale workshops in Jingdezhen. The work represents traditionally hand-crafted porcelain as one of China's prominent exports and questions the 'Made in China' aspect of cultural and economic exchanges today. As an artist and activist Ai Weiwei is well aware of the power of social media and has an internet blog, website, Twitter account, Instagram and Facebook page to support his activities, artworks and ideas.

The numbers or data apparent in the above works are significant in visually representing the situation accurately, in a similar way the *Blood Swept Lands and Seas of Red* (2014) installation at the Tower of London July–11 November 2014 by Paul Cummins and Tom Piper marked the centenary of the First World War with 888,246 ceramic poppies, one for each military fatality during the war. Wafaa Bilal's 2010 work ... *and Counting* is more physical performance than installation where for 24 hours his body becomes a borderless map of Iraq with 5,000 red dots representing actual American deaths and 100,000 green UV dots for the Iraqi deaths near the cities where they fell and invisible unless viewed under a black-light. The British group of artists Stan's Café have been creating data landscapes the world over by mapping a single grain of rice to one person in order to convey various statistics such as city populations or deaths in the holocaust. The size and theme of the show change in accordance with the location and its personality. The largest installation involved 104 tons of rice with the rice being weighed and poured manually to form a huge pile. Other artists visualize large amounts of data more directly from computer code to offer a direct understanding of an issue, Doug McCune calls himself a 'data artist' and builds physical thematic maps from online statistics turning 'horrible data' such as murders and natural disasters into beautiful objects, his *Stalagmite Crime* 2013 shows elevation maps of crime rates in San Francisco: narcotics-related crimes (green), prostitution (blue) and vehicle theft (orange) (www.dougmccune.com). Artist duo Ruth Jarman and Joe Gerhardt created a semiconductor sculpture *Cosmos* in 2014 as a model of carbon exchange in a wooden ball, this two-meter spherical wooden sculpture located in Alice Holt Forest, England, represented the take up and loss of carbon dioxide from the forest trees across one year (www.semiconductorfilms.com).

The above pieces are examples of artists representing data information frequently gleaned from the internet as real-world installations, often using readymades in their actual number, or objects materialized from/influenced by code, for greater impact. Either way this is big data in material form showing the complexity and scale of an event or situation in an immediate accessible way, as static objects. We have come a long way since Duchamp's Readymades first appeared and are now competent in moving ideas from the virtual into the real world with the affordance of new digital technologies and new materials. However, if we are to advance our thinking to a more hybridized and symbiotic relationship with the digital, we need to look beyond his Readymades to Duchamp's *Large Glass*.

Towards the *Large Glass*

As with a number of his contemporaries, Duchamp was immersed in the rapidly developing scientific understandings and new technologies of his time (1887–1968). Through his participation as a young artist in the regular meetings at Puteaux, a suburb of Paris, he came into discussion with scientists, mathematicians and medics, and later with Cubist painters including Léger, Metzinger and Delauney who privileged conception over vision. This group expanded to bring in writers such as Apollinaire and artists such as Picabia and Gris, they discussed literature, Bergsonian philosophy, science, technology, mathematics and the notion of the fourth dimension which, according to Linda Dalrymple Henderson (1998, p. 38), 'signified a higher special dimension beyond visual perception and became a prominent element of Cubism theory'. The early 1900s was an exciting period for the history of science, a time of rapidly developing theories and findings concerning the nature of matter and energy which were continually published in the popular press. Discoveries such as X-rays, cathode rays, radioactivity, wireless telegraphy, invisible alpha, beta and gamma rays, non-Euclidean geometry and the fourth dimension, all informed new understandings of a de-materialization of matter. Duchamp's grounding in the topics of his day led him to investigate the invisible reality of matter itself and his 'Readymades' subsequently led to the dematerialization of the art object in the 1960s (Harrison 2013). The Readymades were no longer concerned with the visual aesthetics of the (art) object but with the ideas, the concept, held within it. The Readymades ('assisted' by connecting some of them together, or plain) allowed Duchamp to reduce the idea of aesthetic consideration to the choice of the mind, not to the ability or cleverness of the hand which he objected to in many paintings.

Duchamp's body of artwork and understandings were encompassed in his 'Large Glass' entitled *La Mariée mise à nu par ses célibataires, même* or *The Bride stripped bare by her bachelors, even*. This piece, together with the accompanying green and white boxes of notes, and the later work *Étant Donnes*, is generally regarded to be both the culmination and the summation of his work, occupying his thoughts between 1912 and 1923 when he abandoned it as finally unfinished leaving us with an open work.

The *Large Glass*

The *Large Glass* ensemble completes a corpus of non-linear, semantically associated ideas, the encasement of a plethora of non-sequentially interconnected ideas, a big data set of multidimensional information which can be interrogated through different pathways and correlations. He wanted to portray his Bride in the fourth dimension and began with painterly abstractions of the figure culminating in the flatness of glass as a material nearing the state of no thickness or 'inframince' and therefore acting as a signifier to the fourth dimension. He replaced traditional (thick) paint and canvas as tools for picture making and renounced painting, declaring his *Large Glass* to be 'a three-dimensional physical medium in a fourth dimensional perspective'. Duchamp said that he 'first glimpsed the fourth dimension in his work' in his *Bride* of 1912 (Steefel 1977, p. 110) he later brought the notion of *L'inframince* in to play as a way of reaching her.

L'inframince

The elusive state of *l'inframince* or 'infra-thin' began to evolve when Duchamp was working on the scaled down replicas of his art pieces for the *Boîte-en-valise* around 1937 and made notes on this between 1935 and 1945. The term refers to barely perceptible differences, changes or forms of separation between objects leaving a trace of one in the other, a kind of displacement, an in-between state or interface. It is an adjective not a noun and can never exist in its own right. For example, iridescent cloth such as shot silk or that with a moiré effect which has a different colour or quality according to the fall of light could be considered as being infra-thin. According to Ades, Cox and Hopkins (1999) infra-thin indicates a condition of liminality on the threshold between inside and outside, the interface between two types of thing, a virtually imperceptible gap or shift existing as absolute, and a passage from one state or dimension to another. 'Infra-thin encompasses time and space as well as indefinable relations such as exchange and response, for example, that govern the reception of works of art' (Ades, Cox & Hopkins 1999, p. 183). Juan Antonio Ramírez (1998, pp. 192–3) prefers to use the term 'infrafine' over 'thin' and another translation as 'infra-delicate' which infers an absence of weight, while Duchamp himself states that it is something

> which escapes our scientific definitions. I have chosen the word *mince* deliberately because it is a human, emotional word and not a precise laboratory measurement. The sound or the music which corduroy trousers, like these, make when one moves, is pertinent to inframince. The hollow in the paper between the front and back of a thin sheet of paper ... To be studied! ... It is

a category with which I have been concerned for ten years now. I believe that we can pass from the second and third dimension through the inframince.
(de Rougemont, cited in Sanouillet & Peterson 1975, p. 194)

Although Michael Sanouillet translates this sentence choosing 'on purpose the word *slim*' (Sanouillet & Peterson 1975, p. 194) and offers one of Duchamp's Notes defining inframince as:

WHEN
THE TOBACCO SMOKE
ALSO SMELLS
OF THE MOUTH
WHICH EXHALES IT
THE TWO ODORS
ARE MARRIED BY
INFRA-SLIM

(Note 9, *L'infinitif*)

Duchamp acknowledged the impossibility of a definition of inframince admitting that 'one can only give examples of it' (Russell 2003). Other examples given are:

the warmth of a seat which has just/ been left is infrathin

(Note 8, *L'infinitif*)

The possible is/ an infra-thin -/ the Possibility of several/ tubes of colour/ becoming a Seurat is/ the concrete "explanation"/ of the possible is infra/ thin The possible implying/ the becoming – the passage from/ one to other takes place/ in the infra thin

(Note 1, *L'infinitif*)

The difference/ (dimensional) between/ 2 mass produced objects/ [from the same mold] is an infra thin/when the maximum?/ precision is/ obtained

(Note 18, *L'infinitif*)

In his Notes 9–10 Duchamp defines the infrathin as 'infrathin separation – better/ than screen, because it indicates/ interval (taken in one sense) and/ screen (taken in another sense) – separation has the 2 senses male and female –' (Matisse 1983, p. 258). However obtuse and playful as these notes are, they still convey an understanding of inframince as a condition of liminality, as a slippage between dimensions that can conceptually place the Bride in the fourth dimension. This can then be readily understood as the shift between real and virtual states when engaged with the interactive interface of the computer screen.

The Darwinian *Shift-Life* mixed-media installation

Within my own practice, it is this transitional threshold of hybridity that is of interest. The *Shift-Life* (2009) installation emerged from a mixed reality Art-Science collaboration project and was exhibited during Charles Darwin's bicentenary exhibition at the *Shift-Time Festival of Ideas*, Shrewsbury, England (3–12 July 2009) part of the celebrations centrally organized by the Natural History Museum in London. *Shift-Life* is part of an ongoing exploration into the parallels between the non-linear human thinking process and computation using semantic association to link items into ideas, and ideas into holistic concepts. This mixed reality piece was to facilitate a holistic grasp of the necessary adaptation of life-forms in their struggle for survival in a volatile environment.

Responding to Darwin's ideas in his publication *On the Origin of Species* (1859), the aim of this participatory artwork was to create an alternate biological life as a set of artificial or virtual organisms that possess similar biological processes to their real counterparts – growth, reproduction, competition and adaptation. The virtual life existed in a trophic relationship of predator and prey and included sessile (rooted) and vagile (free moving) organisms. Animal intelligence was programmed into the virtual organisms to allow them survival strategies. The piece involved the construction of an enhanced mixed reality-based environment, connected with wireless sensors with environmental manipulators for altering the 'climate' of the ecosystem. By bringing virtual 'living' creatures into the physical world where they would seemingly respond to audience activity, a liminal space occurred blurring the perceived virtual and real states to the point where their viewers might suspend the belief that these life forms were artificial, and thus engage with the work on a deeper level by perceptually shifting them into the real world (Ch'ng, Harrison & Moore 2017; Harrison et al. 2009). The mixed reality interface was essential in this artwork as a means of easing the slippage from on world to another, it also encouraged intuitive actions from visitors to which the virtual world could respond in real time. A mixed-reality interface removes the necessity of a computer screen through which to experience the machine constructed world and encourages *l'inframince* to occur. Participants could physically manipulate a set of everyday objects such as watering cans, to radically alter the living conditions of the virtual creatures in their mixed-reality habitat. The virtual agents and environment were projected onto white beads contained within a large shallow box (see Figure 2.1) to create a sense of reality in the physical space, as if the creatures actually existed in the physical world. Participants altered the living conditions of the environment by pouring liquids directly into the box to adjust the pH level and humidity of the soil, by varying the light conditions, and by hammering to create earthquakes, altering the conditions and reaction of the real-time agent simulation with immediate effect. The environmental change could either be detrimental to the survivability of a certain species, or promote their growth and reproduction. These responses were dependent on the adaptation of their genotype, which described their survival strategies and trophic networks.

Participant actions had an immediate affect on the creatures and their ecosystem proffering an understanding of how changes in environmental conditions induce reactive responses from living creatures. Through the hands-on approach participants had direct control on tipping the balance between

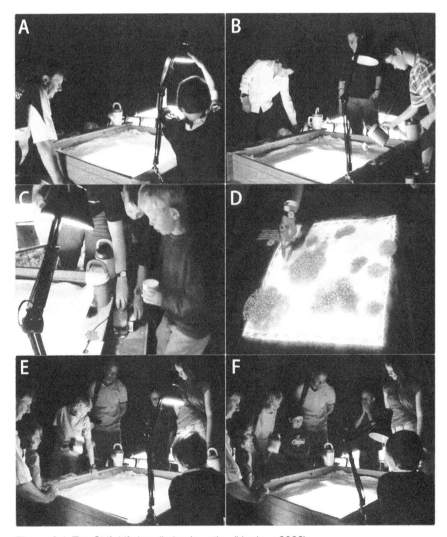

Figure 2.1 The *Shift-Life* installation in action (Harrison 2009).

survivability and total destruction of the virtual-real ecosystem. The algorithms implemented were self-sustaining and stable, without the need of intervention; as such, it was visually mesmerizing as noted by our participants who often remained in a state of reflection by passively observing others' actions, watching as 'life' took place in the virtual world (see Figure 2.1f). This allowed space for contemplation where the virtual world could be understood as an analogy for human activity and its effect on global climate change within our real world. As a form of live art, there were permutations of scenarios documented from the exhibition which demonstrated the many facets of events that could possibly happen in the ecosystem, including the following:

1. As someone poured in too much water, the humidity would alter and some plants may die back, this would mean less food for the green herbivore bugs, and consequently fewer bugs for the pink carnivores to eat.
2. Switching the lamp (sun) on would dry out an overly wet atmosphere and enable plants to grow again; however, too much sun might be detrimental to the point of causing a drought that would wipe out the carnivores entirely! They could become extinct due to their reproduction method of cloning, unlike the egg-laying herbivores. When this occurred the programme was restarted to reassure the smaller children that they weren't responsible for a complete genocide (see Figure 2.1a).
3. Pouring vinegar from a watering can would feed the poisonous plants, toxic to all the creatures, if they became too virulent this could be remedied by pouring baking soda liquid and restoring the plant balance, the herbivores' food (see Figure 2.1b).
4. Hammering on the box (earthquakes) sent the carnivores into panic mode and they would run for cover under the trees (see Figure 2.1e).

Once the piece was completed and on show, the viewers' slippage between virtual and real states became apparent, even though the setup was non-tech basic with plastic watering cans etc., and explained as such, and the creatures were comic brightly coloured line drawings, the viewers' talked about them as though they were alive (see Figure 2.1c). Their conversations illustrate their understanding of how the animals had to 'adapt to survive' in the climate changes that were being introduced into their ecosystem. But more interestingly, it showed how this piece worked on a higher level as a signifier for human activity, climate change and the earth:

1. 'What happens if you change the light, do the creatures disappear?' someone else requested that the lamp be brought nearer the box, 'Oh, they're all dying! Stop!'

2. 'So, if the Earth gets too close to the sun, we'll all die?' 'You've completely changed their planet, they're all dying; it's not in balance.' This meant that they were now extinct 'like the dinosaurs?' The participants asked us to restart the system to bring the creatures back into a sustainable environment, which we did. 'This could be the Earth that you've wiped out, we can't reboot the earth!'

The creatures programmed with simple rules produced a multiplicity of behaviours during the exhibitions, some of which were surprising and unpredictable in accordance with machine-learning.

The aesthetics of the piece, the rough look and feel of it, were important here to help elicit scientific principles to a non-science audience. The idea was to make hard science and complex technical details disappear for the participants, to allow for Ihdeian 'embodiment relations' (Ihde 1990) to take place where the perception of technology 'withdraws' into the body and the human experience through technology which is barely noticed by the users. The less challenging the interface, the easier it is to fully encounter the creatures in their world by perceptually joining them through *l'inframince* in this constructed hybrid space. This work, *Shift-Life*, manifests the data of evolution through direct interaction with physical implements. The creatures are data-objects with coded behaviours relating to their environment of data trees, water etc., they are only ever virtual characters but they appear to transition across into the material world through *l'inframince*, in the same way that digital data in any other form might pass over into the real.

Conclusion

In conclusion then, the varied forms of art practice in action this century display an investment in new technologies and the digitization of information. The examples given are testament to this shift away from the singular material art object and towards a hybridity within art making. This shift is the outcome of the changes in art thinking occurring over the last century and made apparent through the work of Marcel Duchamp (Readymades) and the rise of Conceptualism, leading to the de-materialization of the art-object. Postconceptualism re-contextualizes the physical art object and re-deploys its social relations through Internet media. Contemporary art thinking has therefore moved forward from Duchamp's Readymades to his Large Glass and l'inframince with a view to new media, and digital technologies now permit artists: to visualize digital data in material form, to collate objects as a physical realization of big data, to print art objects from code in new hybridized materials, and to create hybrid mixed-media installations of real/virtual states.

References

Adamson, G 2010, *The Craft Reader*, Berg, Oxford and New York.

Ades, D, Cox, N & Hopkins, D 1999, *Marcel Duchamp*, Thames & Hudson, London.

Atkinson, T & Baldwin, M 1968, 'Air show', in C Harrison & P Wood (eds), *1900–2000: An anthology of changing ideas*, pp. 868–73, Wiley-Blackwell, Oxford, 2003.

Beech, D 2009, *Words and objects after Conceptualism*, accessed 23 September 2019, http://www.art-omma.net/NEW/issue%2011/pages/dave_beech.pdf.

Buszek, ME (ed.) 2011, *Extra/Ordinary: Craft and Contemporary Art*, Duke University Press, Durham USA.

Chandler, J & Lippard, L 1968, 'The dematerialization of art', *Art International*, vol. 12, no. 2, pp. 31–6.

Ch'ng, E, Harrison, D & Moore, S 2017, 'Shift-Life interactive art: Mixed-reality artificial ecosystem simulation', *Presence: Teleoperators and Virtual Environments*, vol. 26, no. 2, pp. 157–81.

Duchamp, M 1917 - Editorial, The Blind Man, No.2, Beatrice Wood, New York, 1917. P5.

Duchamp, M 1934, *La Mariée mise à nu par ses célibataires, même* (The Green Box 1914), Edition Rrose Sélavy, Paris.

Duchamp, M 1956, 'The creative act', *Art News*, vol. 56, no. 4, pp. 28–9 (summer 1957; contents wrongly dated summer 1956). Reprinted in 'The Writings of Marcel Duchamp'.

Duchamp, M 1966, *L'infinitif* (The White Box), trans. C Gray, Cordier & Ekstrom, New York.

Duchamp, M 1983, *Notes*, trans. P Matisse (ed.), Centre National d'Art et de Culture Georges Pompidou, Paris; G.K. Hall, Boston.

Harrison, D, Ch'ng, E, Mount, S & Moore, S 2009, 'Experiencing the big idea', *Cognition and Creativity, Proceedings for 8th International Conference on Digital Arts and Culture*, University of California, pp. 199–204, https://escholarship.org/uc/item/9q6716gd.

Harrison, D (ed.) 2013, 'The re-materialisation of the art object', in *Digital media and technologies for virtual artistic spaces*, IGI Global, Hershey PA.

Henderson, LD 1998, *Duchamp in context: Science and technology in the Large Glass and related works*, Princeton University Press, Princeton.

Ihde, D 1990, *The Indiana series in the philosophy of technology*, Indiana University Press, Bloomington.

Lippard, L 1973, *Six Years: The dematerialization of the art object from 1966 to 1972: A cross-reference book of information on some esthetic boundaries: consisting of a bibliography into which are inserted a fragmented text, art works, documents, interviews, and symposia, arranged chronologically and focused on so-called conceptual or information or idea art with mentions of a such vaguely designated areas as minimal, anti-form, systems, earth, or process art, occurring now in the Americas, Europe, England, Australia, and Asia (with occasional political overtones)*, University of California Press, Berkeley, Los Angeles, London, 1997.

Ramírez, JA 1998, *Duchamp: Love and death, even*, Reaktion Books, London.

Russell, JD 2003, *Marcel Duchamp's readymades: Walking on infrathin ice*, accessed 23 September 2019, Docplayer.net.

Sanouillet, M & Peterson, E (eds) 1975, *The essential writings of Marcel Duchamp*, Thames & Hudson, London.

Steefel, LD Jr 1977, *The position of Duchamp's 'Glass' in the development of his art*, Garland Publishing, New York.

Veiteberg, J 2011, *Thing, Tang, Crash: Upcycling in contemporary ceramics*, Bergen National Academy of the Arts and Art Museums, Norway.

Artist websites

https://www.michael.eden.com
https://www.royalacademy.org.uk/exhibition/ai-weiwei-360
https://www.tate.org.uk›art›artworks›ai-sunflower-seeds-t13408
https://www.hrp.org.uk›tower-of-london›history-and-stories›tower-of…
http://wafaabilal.com/and-counting
http://www.stanscafe.co.uk/helpfulthings/essays-making-oatp.html
http://dougmccune.com/blog/2013/06/10/physical-maps/
https://semiconductorfilms.com/art/cosmos/

3
DATA AS ENVIRONMENT: PHYSICALIZATION STRATEGIES FOR COMMUNICATING ENVIRONMENTAL DATA

Laura Perovich and Dietmar Offenhuber

Introduction

A significant number of physical data displays and projects that situate visualizations in the environment address concerns such as climate change, pollution or the loss of biodiversity. In this chapter, we explore the questions of why artists and designers choose physical representations of data to address environmental issues and what are the advantages this medium claims to offer for this purpose.

The term 'environment' has different meanings. In early human-computer interaction (HCI) literature, the term appears mostly as an abstract concept describing a setting or a situation. In this sense, 'environment' means a representational space occupied by artefacts that serves as the site for interactions – either as a physical or simulated setting or as a metaphorical space. At the same time, 'environment' also means the natural world that we share and that acts upon us. In this meaning of the word it is not an abstract Cartesian space, but an active agent that affects our lives and is affected by them. Without question the exponential growth of digital technologies has had a significant impact on our environmental ecosystem; from the digital detection and more advanced mining of raw materials, to the chemical discharges of electronics manufacturing, and the energy consumption of data centres, server farms and cryptocurrency miners (O'Dwyer & Malone 2014; Røpke & Christensen 2013; Smith, Sonnenfeld & Pellow 2006). The characterization of digital information as abstract and virtual obscures the real impacts of their underlying technical infrastructures (Dourish 2017; Graham 2004).

Many designers and researchers have noted this disconnect and are beginning to embrace a more embodied, situated and more politically aware perspective on HCI (Harrison, Tatar & Sengers 2007). Others are inspired by cultural and environmental references, using the physical environment as a device for learning, reasoning and remembering – techniques that predate digital interfaces, modern technology and even literacy. In the early 1990s, the field of ubiquitous computing started to look at the natural world and the everyday environment as a metaphor and inspiration for novel digital interfaces. Concerned with the 'information anxiety' resulting from digital information overload, Mark Weiser and John Seely Brown (1996) noted that we are quite comfortable dealing with the infinite amount of analogue information that is constantly present in the physical environment. In Weiser's paradigm of ubiquitous computing, people interact with computers embedded in the physical environment like they would interact with their everyday surroundings (Weiser 1991). Building on Weiser and Brown's work, Hiroshi Ishii's concept of the *ambient display* emulates natural phenomena such as wind or the changing colour of the sky and uses them as metaphors for conveying data movement (Wisneski et al. 1998). Artists and designers have embraced the idea of tangible visualizations producing a wide range of data-objects and pixel-less displays (Gwilt 2013; Moere 2008). Influenced by these activities, the emerging field of data physicalization introduces the study of data-objects into the larger research framework of information visualization (Jansen et al. 2015, 2013; Jansen, Dragicevic & Fekete 2013).

Physical visualization techniques have also benefitted from the maker movement, the citizen science movement, and the sensing and digital fabrication tools associated with these new socio-technical systems (Jansen, Dragicevic & Fekete 2013). The development of cheap digital-to-physical prototyping tools and the spread of rapid prototyping practices and cultures have facilitated the quicker and easier creation of data physicalizations, and allow members of the community as well as researchers and creative practitioners to create complex objects and artefacts without requiring advanced craftsmanship skills. Moreover, citizen science has made environmental sensing accessible and familiar to more people, popularizing the low-cost environmental sensors that are often used for data physicalizations. These technologies invite more people to participate in the process of making data physicalizations and allow more people to experience data physicalizations which explore environmental data. However, ironically physical visualizations often rely heavily on environmentally harmful materials that may diminish any environmental aims of physicalizations created with these tools, something we return to later in the chapter.

Issues with materializing displays of environmental data

Considering the complexities of climate models, their data sources and their interpretation, what makes material visualizations attractive as a display modality? Climate and pollution are material phenomena often connected to a bodily experience, from the restricted breathing and heart issues caused by air pollution to the destructive flooding tied to climate change. In the process of measurement, however, they become statistical phenomena. It seems sensible therefore, to transform these abstract values back into visceral displays that engage all senses, as a way of making sense of this complex data (Gwilt, Yoxall & Sano 2012). Placing data into a real-world context may also help to emphasize the urgency of the underlying patterns of concerns. Another complicating aspect is the representational problem of climate change (Morton 2013). The large spatial and temporal scale at which phenomenon unfolds often makes it hard to observe on a human scale and calls for new visualization strategies. The creators of physical visualizations are often motivated by the desire to create a participatory and collaborative experience of sensemaking and exploration, one which can foster a collective action and sense of ownership.

Since research into these approaches is just beginning, there is little evidence and few definitive answers as to their effectiveness in communicating environmental or other sources of data. For many environmental issues, images, documentaries and visualizations have been effective in changing the public opinion – often through spectacular visual material that Greenpeace co-founder Bob Hunter described as 'mindbombs' (Hunter 1971). In the case of climate change, however, successes have been more modest. Critics have described the genre of 'climate change art' as rich with failures – to adequately represent climate change and its impacts – or to engage an audience, and to instigate change (Smith & Howe 2015). Participatory projects designed to generate discourse often remain deserted. Visualizations of climate models are perceived as abstract and distant rather than urgent. And most importantly, abstract information, even if understood and accepted, often does not seem to translate into action and public pressure. In the light of such disappointments, the search for new modes of expression seems like a good idea. But how can we ensure that the emerging field of data physicalization does not fall into the same traps of inflated expectations?

Approach and context

While empirical studies into the perceptual qualities of physical information visualizations are still rare, the main claims from literature from tangible media, contextual and embedded displays, and data physicalization can be summarized in the following table:

1	***Physical visualization*** makes environmental data tangible and/or contextual (Ishii & Ullmer 1997; Jansen et al. 2015; Moere 2008).
2	***Tangible*** means here that data sets can be explored with the hands rather than just the eyes – it can be manipulated, acted upon, individually or collectively. It has weight, texture, smell, taste, and creates a sound when struck (Ishii & Ullmer 1997; Jansen et al. 2015; Jansen, Dragicevic & Fekete 2013).
3	***Contextual*** means here that data are experienced in relation to the world instead of on the screen. Contextual data may also be 'situated' or 'embedded', meaning that the data are experienced precisely where and when it matters – in the actual lived experience of the environment that the data set corresponds to. Through many connections between the data and site, the physical data display can highlight implications and causalities (Dourish 2017; Jansen et al. 2015; Vande Moere & Offenhuber 2009; Willett, Jansen & Dragicevic 2017; Wisneski et al. 1998).
4	***Tangible and contextual*** engagement with data is especially useful in collaborative situations. While a purely visual analysis requires language to communicate tentative insights, physical data displays allow for exploring data by acting together and thus facilitate collaborative sensemaking and discourse (Brewer et al. 2007; Jansen et al. 2015; Schneider et al. 2011).
5	The ***material engagement*** with the production and exploration of data can facilitate modes of critical thinking about data and the world that are less supported by a purely visual exploration (Offenhuber 2019).

The implied advantages of tangibility over on-screen representations of data have played an important role from the beginning of physicalization research (Jansen, Dragicevic & Fekete 2013; Moere 2008). This idea is supported by work in experimental psychology that emphasizes the central role of action for perception and cognition (Tversky 2019). As summarized by the philosopher Alva Noë (2004), visual perception has more similarities with the sense of touch rather than the function of a camera – a staple metaphor of representationalist philosophy. Vision, along with the rest of the bodily senses, explores by moving, probing and interacting with the surroundings, rather than contemplating a static picture projected into the mind, hence Tversky's notion of 'action' for perception and cognition. Any form of data manifestation that engages multiple senses should therefore be advantageous for perception, cognition and sensemaking.

How to 'embed' data representations into everyday environments has equally been a longstanding concern. Much like traditional diagrams on paper, digital screens have a border that isolates the representations from their environment, which subsequently tends to be ignored. Physical displays can add to this understanding as they are inherently contextual, they take up space, are perceptually located in the environment and can be affected by environmental influences.

A switch from visual representation to embodied cognition can offer a way to address the familiar complaint about the gap between understanding and action. Addressing this perennial concern of environmental groups and non-governmental organizations (NGOs) could make data physicalizations especially attractive for environmental issues. The goal here would be to help participants experience the implications of 'data in the world' together rather than individually in an abstract informational space.

This last claim is perhaps the most ambivalent. One could also argue that interacting with a data physicalization makes participants actually *less* critical, by offering an aesthetic object whose exact relationship with the underlying data set is not always immediately clear and that can distract by drawing attention to qualities of the object rather than the underlying data. This sense of ambivalence or lack of ownership might be different, however, in a citizen science scenario, wherein participants engage in the physical process of data collection, for example, by collecting soil samples from a polluted site and aggregating them into a material display.

Common themes and formats in environmental data visualizations

Within the large number of art installations, speculative design projects, information campaigns and research projects that use the physical environment to address environmental concerns, we can begin to identify a range of common approaches. While many environmental data displays are ostensibly concerned with data communication, the setting and materiality of the display can create a strong emotional impact. Such emotional experiences may be particularly relevant where individual or collective action on environmental issues is a desired outcome. The following table describes some of the more common approaches used:

Marks of past environmental events

The practice of inscribing markers of past environmental events and disasters are widespread. The cataclysmic tsunami of 2011 brought back attention to the century-old Japanese tsunami stones that mark the high-water line as a warning to descendants. Many European churches and public buildings close to rivers have similar inscriptions that show the water levels of past flood events. Many artists have used a similar notational strategy to show the impacts of future events based on anticipated sea level rise: as new coastal lines painted into the streets or light installations that submerge buildings into virtual water (Callahan 2019; Mosher 2014).

Staging material traces and autographic phenomena

A second approach calls attention to existing traces of changes in the environment that are often overlooked (Offenhuber 2019). This can include highlighting signs of erosion on the windward side of buildings and attaching scales that make these changes observable over time. It also includes performative formats such as soundwalks or climate walks that focus on the development of sensory skills to detect changes in the environment or toxic tours that draw attention to pollution sources and the marks they make on the people and the environment around them (Communities for a Better Environment 2019; Pezzullo 2009).

Recreating environmental processes

Closely related to the previous approaches are projects that stage environmental processes as artificial models. In his *Ice Watch* series of work artist Olafur Eliasson has placed blocks of glacial ice into public space, where they melt away and surprise visitors with the rich tactile, auditory and visual experience afforded by the process (Weber, Bauman & Eliasson 2014). Other artists combine virtual reality with haptic feedback to create an environmental experience that isn't possible in the physical world, such as *Tree* led by Milica Zec and Winslow Porter, which gives people the experience of being a tree and living an accelerated life as part of a forest (Zec & Porter 2017).

Staging instrumentation

A variation of the previous approach involves staging experimental setups to investigate phenomena rather than the phenomena themselves. The approach has a long history dating back to the public experiments performed during the enlightenment making people familiar with physical phenomena and the design of experiments. The tradition is continued in contemporary citizen science approaches to collect data together with participants, the use of bioindicators for community-based sensing of pollution and the use of trained observers to characterize plumes from smokestacks and other air pollution sources (Fishman, Belina & Encarnación 2014; US EPA 2016; Wylie et al. 2017). Some artists bring forward the performative nature of these approaches by creating mediagenic sensors that display information in real time, such as Natalie Jeremijenko's Feral Robotic Dogs that move towards areas of higher air pollution, or air quality balloons that can be moved around the city and change colour based on air pollution data (Kuznetsov et al. 2011; Lane et al. 2006).

Narrative environments

The use of the physical environment as a device for explaining and remembering has a long history. Calvary paths on local hills that include representations of the stations of the cross are a familiar feature in many catholic areas. Scale models of the solar system in public parks are another example, conveying the distances between celestial bodies in relation to their size (NASA 2006). Evacuation paths make evident the structures of our cities and may be further interrogated by documenting the physicality of running them, through capturing and re-displaying the breaths needed for this task (D'Ignazio 2009). Arboretums and zoos can be seen as spatial representations of biological taxa. An artificial forest in a stadium in Austria, *For Forest* further displaces the environment from its expected context and suggests to us a possible environmental future where 'natural' environments only survive within curated human infrastructure (Littmann 2019).

Public projections and murals

Many projects use public projections to contextualize environmental data with the urban or natural environment. A data visualization projected on a building can have a very different effect compared to a chart on paper or screen. While the latter removes real-world context and forces the viewer to focus on the internal logic of the chart, a projection can turn the building itself into an element of the visualization that maintains its contextual relationships with the surroundings. Examples include the augmentation of a forest in Japan and projections on buildings that target urban air pollution, including Andrea Polli's *Particle Falls* and *In the Air* by Nerea Calvillo (Calvillo 2017; Polli 2016; teamLab 2019). Environmental data may also be representing on public buildings through more static displays, such as environmental data murals or through the use of living or natural materials (Ackroyd & Harvey 2019; Bhargava et al. 2016).

Recreations of environmental phenomena

Under a broader perspective, projects that are inspired by environmental phenomena and recreate their experience can be included in this list, since these projects can raise awareness to the beauty and complexity of natural phenomena. A popular example includes the rain room, an indoor installation which lets participants walk dry through a downpour thanks to sensors and actuated nozzles. Early examples include Ken Goldberg's 1995 installation *Telegarden*, a robotic garden that allowed participants to nurture plants over the internet (Goldberg et al. 1995). Many of these projects may be seen as extensions of science education practices that give experiential but highly contained understandings of natural phenomena, such as grow your own frog kits or terrariums.

Public data sculptures

A very simple but effective display strategy focuses on the sensory impact of mere material presence. The Spanish group Basurama collects trash on beaches and festival locations and turns it into large-scale sculptures that persuasively convey the magnitude of garbage generation and its overwhelming physical presence (Scott Brown, Turina & Handford 2006). Similarly, Mark Dion's *Thames Dig* gathered human materials from the shore of the river at low tide and publicly arranged and examined them to understand both the extent of their impact and the nature of the materials we leave behind (Tate 1999).

Climate protests

As a final point, protests such as the Fridays for Future[1] and the Extinction Rebellion[2] climate strikes can be seen as a performative visualization that represents the urgency and concerns of constituents. Climate protests are

> not just displays targeted at governments or the larger public, but also act as a stage for the protesters themselves, on which many forms of creative expression are presented. These protests are not only about *sending a message*, but constitute an improvisational space of learning and discourse. By disrupting infrastructures (intentionally or not), protests also have material impacts on a city, its economy or educational systems. Groups involved in the Extinction Rebellion were particularly creative in their development of performative displays and public installations as part of their acts of civil disobedience.

Data materiality and insights for the design of physical data displays

Data are not just material for analysis, they serve many different purposes. A sign on a construction site counting the days since the last accident is more than a quantitative measure; it is meant to raise safety awareness in the team. Citizens reporting a broken streetlight to the city are not just stating a neutral fact; they voice their dissatisfaction or express their willingness to participate in the maintenance of the city. In short, data are not just representations, they are enactments of social relationships, sentiments and attitudes. Data emerge from a multitude of relationships between displays, people and the policies and economics that shape our surroundings. They can materialize everything from the wear patterns of physical infrastructure, trends in melting ice, to the spatial relationships of stocks and shares.

The role of data enactment (e.g. the participation in creating, interpreting or giving mean to data) is central, but often overlooked in physical visualizations. Based on the effectiveness or the lack of effectiveness in engendering behavioural change through the communication of environmental data in the data visualizations strategies described in the previous section, one might be forgiven for suggesting that we stick with using bar charts and diagrams. But as we have discussed data, of course, are never isolated, decontextualized, indisputable facts. Material displays of data bring back some of the uncertainties and contextual relationships that are masked by the apparent accuracy of traditional charts and graphs. The design of physicalizations is therefore not just about translating data into matter, but about re-establishing relationships and resonance with the production of data and notions of uncertainty. For example, when physicalizations in public space become subject to the environmental conditions that produced them, as in the display of autographic phenomena such ice-cores,[3] the entanglement of data production and environmental conditions is expressed through the artefact itself. Experiencing causality in a material rather than symbolic visualization may create a different understanding of the connections, complexities and uncertainties of environmental systems. Gwilt, Yoxall and Sano (2012) talk about the contestation which is often generated through physicalizations of data and how this is an important element in creating discourse and understanding.

The process of collecting trash for Basurama's data sculptures is another example of data enactment. It requires the participants to consider each piece of trash individually and experience the time and effort required to remove it. Through their labour, the creators of the piece may have had a more powerful, lasting and nuanced experience than those who are only viewing it. In either case it is important to consider how the act of fabricating a physical data display in itself impacts the author, the viewers of the work and other stakeholders with influences in the world.

Projects like Jeremijenko's *Feral Robotic Dogs* or Kuznetsov's *Air Quality Balloons* allow for hands on interaction through the experience of the piece, situate air quality sensors and provide real-time physical manifestations of the data. They contextualize environmental data while also providing an interactive way to explore and test hypotheses; how does the path taken by the robotic dog change when I place it near a car exhaust pipe or other suspected pollution sources? How consistent is its behaviour? These experiences also resonate with the physical complexities of measuring air pollution, such as wind patterns and microenvironments, or failures of the sensors that cause the data outcomes to be different than expected. Whether observers connect these unexpected outcomes to the issues of data collection or whether they just cause confusion is up for debate.

Many projects benefit from the involvement of domain experts in a respective field and few artefacts can clarify a complex situation without additional explanation. Many physical visualizations therefore work best when they facilitate conversation with scientists or amateur experts. For example, in the case of water quality, ecologists have extensive knowledge of local water systems and can point out environmental indicators that can complement, confirm or complicate information from sensors. Bioindicators such as plants, insects and animals can help identify an ecosystem, provide expectations on its behaviour and indicate its health. The plants in a salt marsh are indicators of freshwater sources and show changes to the tidal patterns associated with climate change. The make-up of an insect population in a stream can be a sufficient indicator of its health – sometimes more complete than data from individual digital sensors. The combination of expert knowledge, participatory sensing and the production of artefacts are interesting settings for physical visualizations. The physical visualization is not just the artefact, but includes all circumstances that led to its creation.

A wider view of materiality and enactment also raises questions for traditional data sculptures and physicalizations – the materials used in digital fabrication are not always environmentally benign and may contribute to the environmental harms it seeks to reveal. It is difficult to compare the environmental impacts of material data displays to the environmental impacts of digital visualizations that rely on energy use and our computing systems. Yet, many environmental physical data displays rely on rapid prototyping tools, acrylic and other plastics, or consumer electronics which add to an increasing waste stream. People have also pointed to the environmental costs of large-scale installations that use natural materials. The *For Forest* artist estimated that relocating the trees for the installation released up to 55 tons of CO_2 and *Ice Watch* required considerable energy to transporting 100 tons of ice from Greenland to Copenhagen (Marshall 2019; Weber, Bauman & Eliasson 2014). It is difficult to balance the harms and benefits of such large public installations, after all, every significant activity requires energy. Nevertheless, it is an important question to consider: When do the potential harms of physical visualizations undermine the good intentions of their designers? And what approaches could be used to minimize contributing to environmental harm while taking advantage of the benefits that physical data displays may offer?

Having explored a wide range of environmental data projects and approaches we conclude with a series of questions to be considered when designing environmental physical data displays:

- How is the piece situated in the world? In which ways does it establish relationships with its surroundings and its audience?
- Does the piece engage multiple senses?
- How does it facilitate collaborative exploring, learning, and sensemaking that is less accessible in digital visualization techniques?
- Does the piece leverage existing sources of environmental information, from bioindicators to expert knowledge in reading ecosystems?
- Does the piece connect directly or indirectly to possible action or real-world impact on environmental issues? Is it intended to increase awareness, create emotional impact, change public perception or attitudes, create policy change, point towards new futures, or something else?
- Is it possible to evaluate the impacts assumed by the designer?
- In which ways do the choice of material and treatment for the display relate to the physical phenomena or data it represents?

- Does the material, fabrication, or maintenance of the piece incur environmental costs in the world? How does that cost compare to digital or other physical approaches to visualizing or communicating the environmental data? Is there another approach that offers similar potential benefits for fewer environmental harms?

And perhaps the most important point:

- What is the role of the participant in the project? What does she do, walk around, touch, manipulate? How does the piece change through the participants? Does the relationship between piece and participant resonate with the underlying matters of concern?

Conclusion

In 2008, Andrew Vande Moere speculated about physical data visualizations: 'what a pixel-less display might lose in resolution and information bandwidth, it could make up in a richer, more intriguing and memorable experience that nonetheless communicates complex information and insight' (2008, p. 469). Offering a rich, emotionally engaging experience without losing nuance has been a goal and motivation for many projects dealing with the climate crisis and other environmental threats we face today. These projects face a common dilemma: many environmental problems can only be measured through statistical means, which makes them seem abstract and unconvincing as evidence for a non-expert audience. Researchers and artists have tried to address this dilemma by bringing environmental data and models back into the physical world and re-establishing relationships with the phenomena they are concerned with.

By identifying common themes in existing environmental data displays, exploring the material and performative nature of data, and suggesting guiding questions, we hope to provide preliminary guideposts for those exploring this area. We argue that physical visualizations should not just be seen as a display modality – as one of many arbitrary transformations of data into spatial form. Successful projects don't just represent, they enact data: they require participants to actively connect the dots, involve them in the production of data or establish a connection to the material circumstances of data collection. In other words, successful projects allow us to experience the material underpinnings and implications of data rather than simply understand their statistical properties. Increasingly successful projects also reflect on their own materiality and explore ways to include sustainable approaches in their design and actualization.

We conclude with the obvious point that no visualization exists in a vacuum: they are used in arguments, lead to conversations, are promoted in newspapers, are used by teachers and scientists to explain an issue. They emerge from material practices that have environmental impacts themselves and become effective through their social context, which therefore have to be considered as parts of the endeavour. The recent global emergence of climate strikes is a reminder that we should not hope that visualizations lead to action, but consider action a central part of visualization.

Notes

1. https://www.fridaysforfuture.org
2. https://rebellion.global/
3. For example, see Keith Hartwig's *cryosphere* and *cold chain* https://keithhartwig.com/cryosphere

References

Ackroyd, H & Harvey, D 2019, 'Works | Ackroyd & Harvey', https://www.ackroydandharvey.com/category/works/.
Andreu-Perez, J, Poon, CCY, Merrifield, RD, Wong, STC & Yang, G-Z 2015, 'Big data for health', *IEEE Journal of Biomedical and Health Informatics*, vol. 19, no. 4, pp. 1193–1208, https://doi.org/10/gc92fz.
Bhargava, R, Kadouaki, R, Bhargava, E, Castro, G, & D'Ignazio, C 2016, 'Data murals: Using the arts to build data literacy', *The Journal of Community Informatics*, vol. 12, no. 3, pp. 197–216.
Brewer, J, Williams, A & Dourish, P 2007, 'A Handle on What's Going on: Combining Tangible Interfaces and Ambient Displays for Collaborative Groups', in *Proceedings of the 1st International Conference on Tangible and Embedded Interaction*. TEI '07. New York, NY, USA: ACM, pp. 3–10. https://doi.org/10/ck2x5q.
C+arquitectos/In the Air 2017, *Yellow Dust*, http://yellowdust.intheair.es/.
Callahan, M 2019, 'Signs of the times: New public art installation brings climate change home', *Northeastern News*, October 15, 2019, https://news.northeastern.edu/2019/10/15/northeastern-professors-new-public-art-installations-throughout-new-england-bring-climate-change-home/.
Calvillo, N 2017, *In the air*, http://intheair.es/index.html.
Communities for a Better Environment 2019, *Toxic tours*, https://www.cbecal.org/get-involved/toxic-tours/.
D'Ignazio, C 2009, 'It takes 154,000 breaths to evacuate Boston', *Catherine D'Ignazio | Kanarinka* (blog), 1 November 2009, http://www.kanarinka.com/project/it-takes-154000-breaths-to-evacuate-boston/.
Dourish, P 2017, *The stuff of bits: An essay on the materialities of information*, MIT Press, Cambridge, MA.
Eagle, N & Pentland, AS 2006, 'Reality mining: Sensing complex social systems', *Personal and Ubiquitous Computing*, vol. 10, no. 4, pp. 255–68, https://doi.org/10/cc9spv.
Fishman, J, Belina, KM & Encarnación, CH 2014, 'The St. Louis ozone gardens: Visualizing the impact of a changing atmosphere', *Bulletin of the American Meteorological Society*, vol. 95, no. 8, pp. 1171–6, https://doi.org/10/gf6499.

Gibson, JJ 1979, *The ecological approach to visual perception*, Houghton Mifflin, Boston.

Goldberg, K, Santarromana, J, Bekey, G, Gentner, S, Morris, R, Wiegley, J & Berger, E 1995, 'The Telegarden', in *Proceedings of ACM SIGGRAPH 95*, pp. 135–40.

Graham, S (ed.) 2004, *The cybercities reader*, Routledge, London.

Gwilt, I 2013, 'Data-objects: Sharing the attributes and properties of digital and material culture to creatively interpret complex information', in D Harrison (ed.), *Digital media and technologies for virtual artistic spaces*, IGI Global, Hershey, pp. 14–26, DOI:10.4018/978-1-4666-2961-5.ch002.

Gwilt, I, Yoxall, A & Sano, K 2012, 'Enhancing the understanding of statistical data through the creation of physical objects', *Design Society 73-1 Proceedings of the 2nd International Conference on Design Creativity vol.* pp. 117–26, https://www.designsociety.org/publication/32468/Enhancing+the+Understanding+of+Statistical+Data+Through+the+Creation+of+Physical+Objects.

Harrison, S, Tatar, D & Sengers, P 2007, 'The three paradigms of HCI', in *alt.chi session at the SIGCHI Conference on Human Factors in Computing Systems*, San Jose, California, USA, 1–18, https://research.cs.vt.edu/ns/cs5724papers/3paradigms.pdf.

Hill, WC, Hollan, JD, Wroblewski, D & McCandless, T 1992, 'Edit wear and read wear', in *Proceedings of the SIGCHI Conference on Human Factors in Computing Systems*, pp. 3–9, https://doi.org/10.1145/142750.142751.

Hunter, R 1971, *The storming of the mind*, McClelland and Stewart, Toronto.

Ishii, H & Ullmer, B 1997, 'Tangible bits: Towards Seamless interfaces between people, bits and atoms', in *Proceedings of the ACM SIGCHI Conference on Human Factors in Computing Systems*, ACM, 234–41.

Jansen, Y, Dragicevic, P & Fekete, J-D 2013, 'Evaluating the efficiency of physical visualizations', in *Proceedings of the SIGCHI Conference on Human Factors in Computing Systems*, pp. 2593–602, https://doi.org/10/gf65hg.

Jansen, Y, Dragicevic, P, Isenberg, P, Alexander, J, Karnik, A, Kildal, J, Subramanian, S & Hornbæk, K 2015, 'Opportunities and challenges for data physicalization', in *Proceedings of the 33rd Annual ACM Conference on Human Factors in Computing Systems*, ACM, pp. 3227–36.

Jememijenko, N 1997, *Technology in the 1990s*, Database Politics and Social Simulations, http://tech90s.walkerart.org/nj/transcript/nj_01.html.

Kitchin, R 2014, 'The real-time city? Big data and smart urbanism', *GeoJournal*, vol. 79, no. 1, pp. 1–14, https://doi.org/10/7ds.

Kuehr, R & Williams, E (eds) 2003, *Computers and the environment: Understanding and managing their impacts*, vol. 14, Springer, Dordrecht, https://doi.org/10.1007/978-94-010-0033-8.

Kuznetsov, S, Davis, GN, Paulos, E, Gross, MD & Cheung, JC 2011, 'Red balloon, green balloon, sensors in the sky', in *Proceedings of the 13th International Conference on Ubiquitous Computing*, pp. 237–46, https://doi.org/10.1145/2030112.2030145.

Lane, G, Brueton, C, Roussos, G, Jeremijenko, N, Papamarkos, G, Diall, D, Airantzis, D & Martin, K 2006, 'Public authoring & feral robotics', *Proboscis: Cultural Snapshot*, no. 11, http://proboscis.org.uk/publications/SNAPSHOTS_feralrobots.pdf.

Littmann, K 2019, *For forest*, For Forest, https://forforest.net/en/.

Marshall, A 2019, 'Forest in a soccer stadium outrages Austria's far right', *The New York Times*, 24 September, https://www.nytimes.com/2019/09/24/arts/design/forest-stadium-austria-klagenfurt.html.

Milica, Z, & Porter, W 2017, *Tree Official*, https://www.treeofficial.com/.

Moere, AV 2008, 'Beyond the tyranny of the pixel: Exploring the physicality of information visualization', in *IEEE International Conference on Information Visualisation (IV'08)*, London, UK, pp. 469–74, DOI:10.1109/IV.2008.84.

Morton, T 2013, *Hyperobjects: Philosophy and ecology after the end of the world*, Univ Of Minnesota Press.

Mosher, E 2014, *HighWaterLine*, HighWaterLine: Visualizing climate change, blog, http://highwaterline.org/.

NASA 2006, *Solar system walk*, NASA, https://www.nasa.gov/centers/glenn/events/solrwalk.html.

Noë, A 2004, *Action in perception*, MIT Press, Cambridge, MA.

O'Dwyer, KJ & Malone, D 2014, 'Bitcoin mining and its energy footprint', https://doi.org/10/cvqm.

Offenhuber, D 2019, 'Data by proxy – material traces as autographic visualizations', in *IEEE Transactions on Visualization and Computer Graphics (Proceedings of InfoVis 2019)*, pp. 1–3, https://doi.org/10/gf649f.

Pezzullo, PC 2009, *Toxic tourism: Rhetorics of pollution, travel, and environmental justice*. University of Alabama Press, Tuscaloosa.

Polli, A 2016, *Particle Falls*, Science History Institute, 22 July 2016. https://www.sciencehistory.org/particle-falls.

Røpke, I & Christensen, TH 2013, 'Transitions in the wrong direction? Digital technologies and daily life', in E Shove & N Spurling (eds), *Sustainable practices: Social theory and climate change*, pp. 49–68. Routledge, Abingdon, Oxfordshire, UK.

Schneider, B, Jermann, P, Zufferey, G & Dillenbourg 2011, 'Benefits of a tangible interface for collaborative learning and interaction', *IEEE Transactions on Learning Technologies,* vol. 4, no. 3, pp. 222–32. https://doi.org/10/fqwrcn.

Scott Brown, D, Turina, AF-C & Handford, NG 2006, *Basurama: Distorsiones urbanas = Urban distortions*, La Casa Encendida, Madrid.

Smith, P & Howe, N 2015, *Climate change as social drama: Global warming in the public sphere*, Cambridge University Press, New York.

Smith, T, Sonnenfeld, DA & Pellow, DN (eds) 2006, *Challenging the chip: Labor rights and environmental justice in the global electronics industry*, Temple University Press, Philadelphia.

Tate 1999, *'Tate Thames Dig', Mark Dion, 1999*, Tate, https://www.tate.org.uk/art/artworks/dion-tate-thames-dig-t07669.

teamLab 2019, *Digitized Forest at the World Heritage Site of Shimogamo Shrine, Kyoto*, https://www.teamlab.art/e/shimogamo/.

Tversky, B 2019, *Mind in motion: How action shapes thought*, Basic Books, New York.

US EPA 2016, *Method 9 – visual opacity*, US EPA, 20 June 2016. https://www.epa.gov/emc/method-9-visual-opacity.

Vande Moere, A & Offenhuber, D 2009, 'Beyond ambient display: A contextual taxonomy of alternative information display', *International Journal of Ambient Computing and Intelligence*, vol. 1, no. 2, pp. 39–46.

Wang, Y, Segal, A, Klatzky, R, Keefe, DF, Isenberg, P, Hurtienne, J, Hornecker, E, Dwyer, T & Barrass, S 2019, 'An emotional response to the value of visualization', *IEEE Computer Graphics and Applications*, vol. 39, no. 5, pp. 8–17.

Weber, E, Bauman, I & Eliasson, O 2014, 'Can art inspire climate change action? An ice installation aims to do just that', *Guardian*, 23 October, http://www.theguardian.

com/sustainable-business/2014/oct/23/climate-change-ice-watch-installation-art-greenland-copenhagen-ipcc.

Weiser, M 1991, 'The computer for the 21st century', *Scientific American*, vol. 265, no. 3, pp. 94–104.

Weiser, M & Brown, JS 1996, 'Designing calm technology', *PowerGrid Journal*, vol. 1, no. 1, pp. 75–85.

Willett, W, Jansen, Y & Dragicevic, P 2017, 'Embedded data representations', *IEEE Transactions on visualization and computer graphics*, vol. 23, no. 1, pp. 461–70, https://doi.org/10/gfz688.

Wisneski, C, Ishii, H, Dahley, A, Gorbet, M, Brave, S, Ullmer, B & Yarin, P 1998, 'Ambient displays: Turning architectural space into an interface between people and digital information', in NA Streitz, S Konomi & H-J Burkhardt (eds), *Cooperative buildings: Integrating information, organization, and architecture*, Springer, Berlin, pp. 22–32, https://doi.org/10/fj6n8z.

Wylie, S, Wilder, E, Vera, L, Thomas, D & McLaughlin, M 2017, 'Materializing exposure: Developing an indexical method to visualize health hazards related to fossil fuel extraction', *Engaging science, technology, and society*, vol. 3, pp. 426–63, https://doi.org/10/gf65bj.

4
DESIGNING EXPLANATIONS OF DATA-BASED INTERACTIONS IN SOCIO-TECHNICAL SYSTEMS

Aaron Fry

Introduction

In recent years problems have arisen through the use and sometimes exploitation of personal user data and large technology companies have been called to account for their business models, policies and safeguards around personal privacy and use of these data. Governments, journalists and academics have made attempts to grasp often unforeseen social consequences resulting from the transactions within computers, their internal processes and the transactions external to computers. Trist and Bamforth (1951) (here termed the 'Tavistock scholars') wrote a seminal paper while researching at Tavistock Institute in which they developed the theory of Socio-Technical Systems, or STSs. Their work is powerful because it nullifies functional distinctions between internal and external interactions; STSs' occur when technical and social factors interact, generating the conditions for organizational performance. These ideas are important in understanding technologies as inseparable from social systems as the continuum of both internal and external interactions can be understood as designed entities.

Understanding of the interaction of algorithm, data structure and program are derived from Wirth (1975) and grounded in an assumption that both code and the infrastructures of digital systems are always physical and material, an idea that references computer scientist/sociologist Paul Dourish (2016,

2017) and sociologists such as MacKenzie (2009), who analyse the material sociology of markets. These arguments are also indebted to organizational and management scholars such as Orlikowski and Scott (2008, p. 434) who define 'sociomateriality', as 'an inherent inseparability between the technical and the social', they contextualize the ideas of the Tavistock scholars within twenty-first-century technology, work and organizations. The literature on how the digital or virtual might be materially manifested ranges from descriptions of new media art (Paul 2007), to analysis of consumption practices (Magaudda 2013). In design, perhaps the scholarship most closely associated to practices of design thinking in relation to computer systems comes from the Special Interest Group on Computer–Human Interaction (SIGCHI), notable here is the work of Jeffrey Heer and the Interactive Data Lab at the University of Washington, in their visual explanation of systems via infographics and data visualizations (Hoffswell, Li & Liu 2020). Although design is framed here within computer science, their work discusses and analyses visual explanation.

The increasing pervasiveness and permeability of digital information with social system makes the task of distinguishing internal-from-external, in a given socio-technical situation, much less relevant than seeking to create better explanations for how algorithms, data structures and programs affect human societies. This directive pays attention to the kinds of maps, models, explanations and stories that societies will need in coming years and shifts emphasis from how systems work towards what they do. To illustrate the current deficit of sufficient explanation, two recent and connected cases concerning Cambridge Analytica and Facebook are instructive. The first demonstrates the mutability of data's value, while the second illustrates the complexity and opacity with which data interactions confront those who seek explanation.

Goodman and Flaxman (2017) propose the 'right to explanation' as an extension of a provision of the EU's General Data Protection Regulation of 2016–8, which requires data processors to ensure data subjects are notified about the data they collect. They argue that explanation is not a question of addressing the how but rather the why of data collection. The 'why' of data collection might be best understood through learning from instances of failure in explanations of a given STS. Typically, when failures occur, the damage has already been done. Hearings and enquiries may determine how a given crisis occurred, but are retrospective and often achieve little in anticipating and preempting future troubles. Facebook's example explains the problem of deficient explanation, and upon review of the work of Facebook's 'Data for Good' program, it appears as though the company has an opportunity to deploy its data for the betterment explanation of current- and-future interactions within its own STSs. Visually based tools and methods of design thinking hold promise in engaging stakeholders to develop better solutions around these interactions. While these explanatory tools and methods are not currently sufficiently fit-to-purpose, versions of these may ultimately help those outside of the computer science and engineering communities, to work together to redesign our digitally embedded STSs.

Data as asset, data as system

In 2006 in a lecture, British data scientist Clive Humby coined the maxim that 'data is the new oil', as an analogy this aphorism usefully captures the general notion that fortunes can and have been made through the use of data, especially personal user data or business and trading data. However, in terms of its materiality, in a monetary transactional capacity, data does not, strictly-speaking behave like oil, which is a liquid, fungible and transportable commodity (Danes 2016). Oil's utility is the same for Amazon founder, Jeff Bezos as it is for anyone else; it produces the same amount of energy per unit and all, theoretically, have equal access to oil's utility. Arguably Bezos can use it in rockets or to power his servers, but the distinction in utility value, unit-for-unit, is very similar. In the case of data, however, most individuals have much less ability to utilize it in a transactional capacity than does Mr. Bezos. Using a hypothetical situation in which one comes into possession of a year's worth of Amazon's purchase data, Martínez (2019) states:

> Accounting rules don't call (yet) for tech companies to specify their data as a separate asset on the balance sheet, but by any reasonable valuation, Amazon's purchase data is worth an immense fortune ... *to Amazon.*

Worth an immense fortune to Amazon and possibly to Amazon's business competitors, the fungibility, utility and business value of the data depend on Amazon's comprehensive STS of employees, logistics hubs, retail outlets, loyalty programs and more. Understanding that data behaves differently as an asset, from oil, is key to developing a viewpoint on current debates around data ownership and the value of data explanation, relative to data ownership.

The movement towards personal ownership of one's data and the concept of a 'data dividend' is alluded to in the 2019 documentary The Great Hack (Amer & Noujaim). One of its protagonists, David Carroll, in his process of suing Cambridge Analytica for the return of his personal data, states, that he:

> knew that the data from our online activity wasn't just evaporating, and as I dug deeper, I realized that these digital traces of ourselves are being mined into a trillion dollar a year industry; we are now the commodity.

The common metaphor of mining, invoked by Carroll, is interesting to consider in the case of data. Some mined minerals, such as gold, carry inherent value similar to that of oil, whereas others, such as rare earth minerals, have value to the companies, such as Apple or Samsung, that incorporate them into production systems that result in smart phones. While we might lament social and environmental costs of these supply chains, we cannot deny the utility value that a computer in our hand affords us. Jaron Lanier (2013, p. 66), an advocate for models of data ownership, raises questions about data privacy, he contends that:

> If the state must be able to analyze everyone's personal information to catch terrorists before they act, then individuals cannot be entitled to both privacy and safety. Or at least this is the way the trade-off is often framed. Something is askew in thinking about privacy this way. Considered in terms of trade-offs, privacy inevitably ends up being framed as a culturally sanctioned fetish – an adult security blanket. How much privacy are people 'willing to give up' for certain benefits?

While it is easier for consumers of data driven platforms and apps to identify clearly nefarious abuses of privacy, the nuance of Lanier's question will remain with us and will ultimately require an equally nuanced account. In the following section two moments in the Cambridge Analytica/Facebook scandal are highlighted; these illustrate data's interactional and transactional agency and point towards the complexity of attempting to grasp how data behaves within STSs.

The first case is the 17 March 2018 publication of a news story detailing the acquisition by Cambridge Analytica of the data of up to 87 million Facebook users (Wichter 2018).

Cambridge Analytica's psychometric framework and data analytics were used to identify 'persuadable' voters which informed the design of targeted messages for them. This technique is thought to have provided a significant advantage to the 2016 US Presidential Trump-Pence campaign through enhanced ability to precisely identify undecided voters in the swing states of Pennsylvania, Michigan and Wisconsin and influence them with messages customized to their motivational triggers. In its raw form, the aggregate value, globally, of data in the marketplace, is estimated, in 2020, to be $250 million (Valentino-de Vries et al. 2018). They are describing the market value of data that is traded between companies using platforms such as Microsoft's Azure or DataMarket.com. By contrast, obviously, the monetary value of Facebook's user data targeted toward influencing the US election is incalculable. This shifts the conversation from the societal value of personal ownership over one's data towards how, why and for whom value is generated by large aggregated datasets. How do these 'raw data' intersect with algorithms, data structures and programs to create and direct actionable strategy? What collective societal benefits and risks may result from data's deployment in this form?

Current understanding of the value of data-as-strategic insight are notoriously difficult to describe, a point evident in our second case, that of Facebook CEO Mark Zuckerberg's 10 April 2018 testimony to US Senate congressional committee in the wake of what had by this time been coined the 'Cambridge Analytica scandal'. In addressing the application 'This Is Your Digital Life' and its ability to harvest data from those who had released it as well as those who had not, Facebook's CEO and founder admitted that, even from a technical and legal standpoint, the company had not anticipated how data might be mobilized through Facebook's ecosystem of applications. He (2018) stated that:

> [We are] investigating many apps, tens of thousands of apps, and if we find any suspicious activity, we're going to conduct a full audit of those apps to understand how they're using their data and if they're doing anything improper. If we find that they're doing anything improper, we'll ban them from Facebook and we will tell everyone affected.

Zuckerberg's words here highlight three connected problems concerning data-as-interaction/transaction in the permeable space of digitally embedded STSs. The first is the complexity of defining what the various interactions are within a computer program and what these mean when deployed within a STS, how does one identify 'suspicious activity?' The second concerns current deficits of explanatory power when confronted with these complexities, for example, how and exactly why, is the use 'improper?' The third concerns a lack of attention to consequences or whether the incentive structures, ethical guidelines and remedies that currently exist are commensurate with the impact that misuse has on societies. Does 'telling everyone affected' constitute a satisfactory remedy?

In the development of their STS theory, the Tavistock scholars analysed the 'responsible autonomy' of coal miners working in pairs or small groups in pits contrasted with the new work dynamics necessary as a result of a transition from this to the industrialized 'long wall' coal extraction method. Trist and Bamforth (1951, p. 10) state that:

> It is only since the morale changes accompanying recent face-work innovations have begun actually to be experienced in working groups that the nature of longwall troubles is becoming manifest. That they require understanding in social and psychological terms is something that still remains largely unrecognized. Accounts so far have presented recent changes almost exclusively in engineering terms.

The Tavistock scholars' work helps considerably in explaining some of the effects of the innovation of increased interaction between computer and societal systems, particularly when these are framed primarily as engineering concerns.

STSs do not make a binary distinction between the engineered system, for example, long wall coal extraction, and the social and psychological effects of that system on working groups of miners. The issues they are primarily concerned with are deficits in the quality of work, workplace safety and the morale of work groups resulting from the introduction of this new technology. Long wall extraction introduced a mass production system into a social and spatial system, to which, they argue, it is not conducive. In the Cambridge Analytica case, a parallel can be drawn between the situation of long wall methods and the effects of a new process of personal user data being used to target persuadable voters based on psychometric profiling. While the practice of data driven psychometric profiling arguably has more benign social consequences as used in a commercial marketing context, this is not the case when it is deployed to influence political outcomes in a large democracy. Both cases share the quality of being technical innovations that involve new process combinations and/or contexts of application, deployed without consideration to attendant social effects, and resulting in societal consequences. The second reason is that STS's attend to the materiality of this entire system. We understand that systems contain material elements of greater or lesser tangibility (e.g. such as servers and code, human actors and more) and we therefore understand that data does not need to be re-materialized insofar as data and virtuality are correctly understood as instantiations of material interactions (Dourish 2016, 2017). Further, these materially grounded definitions support the hypothesis that STSs are designed and can therefore be understood through design.

Explanation requires design

Returning to issues surfaced by the Cambridge Analytica scandal, Burrell (2016, pp. 1–2) defines three barriers to transparency in machine learning algorithms, distinguishing between:

> (1) opacity as intentional corporate or institutional self-protection and concealment and, along with it, the possibility for knowing deception; (2) opacity stemming from the current state of affairs where writing (and reading) code is a specialist skill and; (3) opacity that stems from the mismatch between mathematical optimization in high-dimensionality characteristic of machine learning and the demands of human scale reasoning and styles of semantic interpretation.

This analysis poses important questions: 'first, what degree of explanation can successfully "explain" results, and, perhaps more pertinently, how the production of such an explanation – which must, of course be generated algorithmically – can be itself explained' (Dourish 2016, p. 8). Although I disagree that explanation may *only* occur by way of algorithm, Dourish raises an important question; what constitutes a sufficient or satisfactory explanation, and for whom? Of the three barriers to transparency, the first may be a matter for regulatory bodies but the answer may not be this simple. Algorithms and datasets have been found, for example, to reflect and amplify racism and hate speech (Noble 2018), and, while this may be unintended, deployment of AI-generated 'deepfake' technologies, for example, constitutes deliberate and directed misinformation (Sample 2020). For societies, governments and judicial bodies, both uses have clearly deleterious results, and it is not easy to separate intent from result. It is also difficult to separate intent and result from problems of technical literacy and of human-scale reasoning. The second of the three points, that of gaps in technical literacy, can be illustrated by the instances in which legislators have struggled to understand the role that complex financial products, such as Collateralized Debt Obligations (CDOs) and derivative financial products, played in the 2008–9 financial crisis. The demands for explanation that ensued from the crisis were often less-than-complete, and importantly, they occurred retrospectively rather than preemptively. Colander et al. (2009, p. 258), argue that economic models need to anticipate escalation of systemic risk by capturing the micro-interactions that may be benign, in isolation, but are cumulatively consequential as system interactions:

> Economist's micro foundations should allow for the interactions of economic agents since economic activity is, essentially, interactive ... only a sufficiently rich model of connections between firms, households and a dispersed banking sector is likely to allow us to get a grasp on 'systemic risk.'

In this light, technical literacy may be equally well understood as systemic literacy. This literacy extends beyond understanding the specifics of the code-based operation of algorithm, to the interactions between constituent elements within a STS. We assert that current deficits in system-oriented understanding have hampered our ability to proactively design STSs towards collective political and social ends. These deficits leave us only with reactive 'what happened and why?' hearings and reports. The causes of these deficits may be an imaginary failure, or attributable to calculation and business strategy, sometimes both. Addressing the latter obstacle, information asymmetry is a key factor in transactional advantage between a buyer and seller (Akerlof 1970; Samuelson 1984). Célérier & Vallée (2014) found the transactional advantage obtained through information asymmetry to be a motive for the creation of financially complex products. Their study of 55,000 structured retail financial products found that complexity had significantly increased in the period 2002–10 and that relatively more complex financial products positively correlate with higher markups by financial service providers. One of their conclusions is that 'the design of retail structured products is more consistent with banks catering to households seeking high yield in a low interest environment and with an obfuscation motive for financial complexity' (Célérier & Vallée 2014, p. 4). The framing of a financial product's cost/benefit in complex technical language is part of many bank's business models. It is clear then that technical language can be used deliberately to create and maintain information asymmetries, or, as Burrell (2016) suggests, to support intentional concealment. Technical language may also exist because the processes themselves are legitimately complex, detailed and precise, but regardless of whether the intention is to conceal or to better-define, human-scale explanation has a highly relevant role to play in consumer protection (Lusardi & Mitchell 2009), it also invites the perspectives of diverse stakeholders into the redesign of STSs.

Burrell's third point addresses mismatches between the representational style of machine transactions, expressed in code, and human-scale reasoning and styles of interpretation. Broadly this latter point addresses a given explanation's comprehensibility, or the popular reach of a given explanation. Comprehensibility and accessibility are crucial to the functioning of a democratic political system, a role that the press has traditionally played. This suggests that today's complex digital data and STSs interactions may require supplemental explanations and tools, and these may have additional and alternate uses from those of the fourth estate. It is revealing, for example, that, with reference to the US financial crisis, the Wikipedia entry for 'CDO', prominently features a graphic explaining how one works. This graphic is part of the Federal Government's 633-page Report of the National Commission on the Causes of the Financial and Economic Crisis in the United States (Financial Crisis Inquiry Report 2011, p. 128). In searching for explanation, lay readers may quickly default to such graphical explanations, and the wiki platforms that feature them, as their primary, and often only, explanation.

Transactional interactions within and between algorithm, data structure, program, societal contexts and financial instruments increasingly converge around the effects of algorithmic trading and around digital currencies and blockchain-enabled products and services. In these explanations there are the complexities and technical terms associated with financial transactions, for example, structured finance, those associated with their enabling technologies, for example, blockchain, and those associated with socio-technical spheres, for example, ethics, competition, monopoly, security and trust. This perfect storm of explanatory complexity is on display during Mark Zuckerberg's second congressional testimony on 23 October 2019, entitled 'Facebook and an Examination of its Impact on the Financial Services and Housing Sectors' (U.S. House Committee on Financial Services 2019). Ostensibly this was primarily intended to be an explanation of the privacy and security implications of Facebook's development of its cryptocurrency Libra, and separate digital wallet, Calibra. However, it expanded into a wide-ranging discussion of Facebook's exposure of the US' electoral system to vulnerability, its automation and delegation of important curatorial and fact-checking roles, its privacy provisions for user data and its use of algorithms that generate discriminatory consequences. During testimony, Facebook's founder and CEO often framed questions about the trustworthiness, credibility and ethical integrity of the company in terms of policy and technical solution. As a result, it was clear that congressional representatives, and those watching the hearing, were left without adequate human-scale reasoning and a style of interpretation that came close in meeting the complexity of the questions asked.

When evaluating the efficacy of an explanation of data-based transactions in STSs, and in light of the case of Zuckerberg's 2019 testimony, I recast Burrell's barriers to transparency serve as *opportunities* for transparency with three key measures of explanatory success: (1) explanatory motivation, (2) quality of explanation and (3) explanatory comprehensibility. Explanatory motivation refers to the ethical and moral dimension: Is the explanation setting out to increase understanding or to obfuscate? Quality of explanation refers to whether the explanation addresses the STS: does the explanation address this holistically? If not, any explanation will be partial or incomplete. Explanatory comprehensibility refers to human-scale reasoning and style of interpretation: what human is the explanation designed for? Is it designed for that human's capacity to reason and interpret?

Designing explanation

One of key points made by the Tavistock scholars' analysis of STSs was that asymmetrical optimization of either the social or the technical leads to unpredictable and un-designed relationships which may be injurious to the whole. The effects of such un-designed relationships can be readily discerned, but the corollary of these is the question of how *designed* relationships might occur.

The first of a number of published reports from Facebook's Data for Good (2016) program was titled 'A New Paradigm for Personal Data, Five Shifts to Drive Trust and Growth'. This report describes shifts which cover many of the same problems outlined in this chapter.

It is clear that, by 2016, voices, within Facebook, had developed a nuanced view of how data intersects with STSs and charted an optimistic course for future development. Much of the project's research is in partnership with academics and it attends to public policy and public health issues that Facebook's immense datasets may usefully support. These reports and presentations feature analyses accompanied by data tables and visualizations. Sometimes the reports intersect with Facebook's business interests and public relations objectives, for example, the program's report on Patterns of Trade Restrictiveness in Online Platforms (Ferracane & van der Marel 2019), others engage with issues of acute public concern such as their production of population density and disease prevention maps and tools to assist public health professionals during the Covid-19 pandemic. In re-discovering its original purpose, the Data for Good program may consider operating as a real-time explanatory window into the socio technical interactions of Facebook itself.

Management scientist Herbert Simon (1970, p. 111) wrote the now widely quoted aphorism that, 'Everyone designs who devises courses of action aimed at changing existing situations into preferred ones'. Simon's 'science of design' was aligned with the roughly contemporaneous Design Methods movement, both shared foundations in systems analysis, quantitative methods, and use of computers to aid the design process, ideas related to RAND's cold war era development of system thinking, game theory etc. In the 1950s, while based at Hochschule für Gestaltung (HfG Ulm), Horst Rittel began applying ideas from cybernetics and operational research to design before moving to Cal Berkeley in 1963 to help found the Design Methods Group and journal. In England, L. Bruce Archer's establishment of the Design Research Unit, at London's Royal College of Art in 1964, followed by a series of conferences and the foundation of the Design Research Society in 1966, were further attempts to apply scientific methods to design. When applied to management, figures such as Bruce Henderson and Bill Bain began to integrate design-derived methods into their consulting practices. These concurrent developments in design and business set the stage for David Kelley's company IDEO and its codification, by the early 2000s, of design thinking into transferrable toolkits and methods (Huppatz 2015). IDEO's popularization of design thinking has contributed to its increased adoption, and the related-practice of Service Design, into product development and business strategy over the past decade. Many companies, NGOs and government agencies are motivated in this by a desire to make their products, services and systems more 'human centred' and the appeal of method-based approaches to design thinking lies in promise that out-of-the-box applications can yield positive outcomes, or at minimum, new ways of reframing familiar business problems. Workbooks such as those of Stickdorn and Schneider (2010), Stickdorn et al. (2018), IDEO (2011), Liedtka and Ogilvie (2011) and Kumar (2012) proliferate in these settings.

In this discussion of explanation, the focus within design thinking is on its mapping and visualization methods and how these connect with my discussion of STSs' interactions with digital data. The Tavistock scholars used two visualizations of the long wall process to demonstrate how the physical space of labour, and the equipment used in the process of coal extraction, contributed to social and psychological effects. Their visualizations were used, in much the same way that scientific articles may use graphics, to elucidate text and provide supplementary explanation of phenomena. Visualization is used very effectively by environmental scientist, Donella Meadows (2008) in her description and depictions of systems through use of pipes, steam and faucets to explain system stocks and flows. The Visualizing Finance Lab (Fry, Wilson & Overby 2013) have discussed the effectiveness of metaphor in explanatory infographics. Bresciani's (2019) review of visualization literature includes Goldschmidt's (1994) research on what visual thinking means to designers and the development of a discourse on the production of thought via visual imagery. Suwa and Tversky (1997) elaborate on the role of visualization in support of design, while Atilola, Tomko and Linsey (2016) and van der Lught (2005) explain visualization's role in processes for enhancing idea generation and creativity. Kokotovich (2007) describes how visualization structures thinking, while Goldschmidt and Smolkov (2016), Larkin and Simon (1987) and Suwa and Tversky (2009) discuss the ways in which visualization augments problem-solving abilities. This body of theory may be elaborated to better understand the role of visualization in supporting dynamic media, such as animation with voiceover, support other kinds of explanation and relationship between narrative and visualization. Kress and van Leeuwen (1996) and multimodal design scholarship, specifically addresses these interactions. Returning to the 2008–9 financial crisis, the kind of multimodal explanation that became a viral artefact at the time was Jonathan Jarvis' The Crisis of Credit Visualized (2009). By contrast, although design thinking methods similarly use spatialized mapping methods, there are key differences, first design thinking processes are necessarily collaborative, interactive and remain provisional for long periods of time. In these processes it is common to see post-it notes with various attributes being grouped, relocated, categorized, re-labelled. These maps focus on the interdependencies between elements in an ecosystem, and are iteratively generated. Although any good visual explanation is also collaborative, it is not a necessary condition. Figure 4.1 below shows the early

Figure 4.1 Working toward an 'Affinity Map' in a design thinking session for the Visualizing Finance Lab. Parsons School of Design, NYC. February 2019. Photo by author.

stages of an affinity map with speculative clusters of concepts, these groupings and categories remain in flux through successive iterations of the same map, as more inputs are added and opinions sought.

Because design-thinking processes hold the possibility for participation with interdisciplinary teams, they offer potential for facilitated generative mappings and visualizations to be co-created by social scientists, policy analysts, computer scientists and others. Because maps are interactive, dynamic and provisional, they allow for the possibility of associations and understandings to emerge over time and in a reflective manner. The map in Figure 4.2, below, shows first and second-order effects, this would enable a collaborative team to extrapolate effects from a hypothetical future scenario, facilitating discussion, exploration and plotting of the implications of a decision or course of action as it may play out over time.

A second difference is that design thinking is a process that may never create a visually resolved outcome, and, in fact, is often used in service and

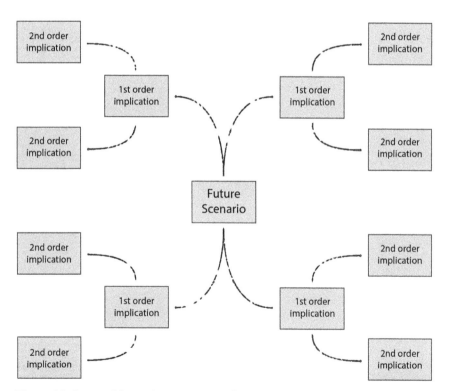

Figure 4.2 A map of first and second-order effects. Used for an innovation exercise within an American automotive company in March 2020. This is the author's version of a template derived from the collaborative whiteboard platform 'Miro'. Photo courtesy of Megan Staake.

organizational design roles in which the human-human or human-machine interactions themselves are intangible. A third difference is that design thinking processes may seek to understand a past, present or future state of a system but do not necessarily need to create the kinds of snapshots characterized by explanatory infographics. As previously mentioned this may confine an infographic's explanatory power to current states: what is happening and past states: what happened? The infographic explains, but is not a medium suited to reflection and conjecture.

Returning to the Data for Good thought experiment, design thinking's widespread and growing adoption in corporate strategy contexts makes it plausible that Data for Good is familiar with such approaches and may be using them. An open question is whether design thinking methods, processes, tools and practices are collectively up to the task of addressing gaps in technical literacy and the demands of human-scale reasoning and styles of interpretation produced by data-based transactions or interactions in STSs, particularly on the magnitude of complexity and scale with which a company such as Facebook operates.

Conclusion

A case is made here for the importance of developing better *explanations* about data interactions in STSs. The Tavistock scholars' work on technical innovation and social-psychological interaction, and the work of Dourish (2016, 2017), Burrell (2016) and on digital systems, address digital systems as designed material; their descriptions confront the opacity and vagueness which often accompanies complexity and they seek to undo its accompanying rhetoric of virtuality or immateriality. Once systems are understood materially, as designed entities. Design Thinking holds obvious potential, through its ability to show, map and explain and ultimately to facilitate redesign of systems. I anticipate that more work on the theory and practice and cases of design thinking, in the kinds of complex applied settings described here, will advance understanding of its feasibility and efficacy in providing explanations for future technicians and engineers of these systems, and for the citizens who use them. Additional research and practice are needed to ascertain whether the promise of design thinking can help to provide such explanations and whether and how they are superior to current explanations. A subset of this enquiry is an examination of the problem of the dynamic system. How does an explanation evolve, in real-time, with sufficient human input and reflection? How can explanation adapt to and keep pace with changes in the interactions of algorithm, data structure, program and society? A separate-but-related direction of inquiry concerns the question of whether design thinking could support broader stakeholder participation and diversity of viewpoints in the design of digital interactions in the STSs of tomorrow.

References

Akerlof, GA 1970, 'The market for "lemons": Quality uncertainty and the market mechanism', *The Quarterly Journal of Economics*, vol. 84, no. 3, pp. 488–500.

Atilola, O, Tomko, M & Linsey, J 2016, 'The effects of representation on idea generation and design fixation: A study comparing sketches and function trees', *Design Studies*, vol. 42, no. 3, pp. 110–36.

Amer, K (dir.) & Noujaim, J (dir.) 2019, *The Great Hack*, Netflix.

Bresciani, S 2019, 'Visual design thinking: A collaborative dimensions framework to profile visualisations', *Design Studies*, vol. 63, pp. 92–124.

Burrell, J 2016, 'How the machine "thinks": Understanding opacity in machine learning algorithms', *Big Data & Society*, vol. 3, no.1, pp. 1–12.

Célérier, C & Vallée, B 2014, 'The motives for financial complexity: An empirical investigation', SSRN 2289890, University of Zurich.

Célérier, C & Vallée, B 2015, 'The motives for financial complexity: An empirical investigation', SSRN 2289890, University of Zurich.

Colander, D, Goldberg, M, Hass, A, Juselius, K, Kirman, A, Lux, T & Sloth, B 2009, 'The financial crisis and the systemic failure of the economic profession', *Critical Review*, vol. 21, no. 2–3, pp. 249–67.

Ctrl-Shift 2016, *A new paradigm for personal data: Five shifts to drive trust and growth*, https://www.ctrl-shift.co.uk/wp-content/uploads/2017/03/Report-3-A-new-paradigm-for-personal-data-3-11.pdf.

Data for Good 2020, *Our work on COVID-19*, Data for Good, https://dataforgood.fb.com/docs/covid19/.

Danes, R 2016, *Questioning the 'Big' in Big Data: Is it the size of data in the fight, or fight in the data?* Silicon Angle, https://siliconangle.com/2016/09/22/questioning-the-big-in-big-data-is-it-the-size-of-data-in-the-fight-or-fight-in-the-data-wikibonboston/.

Dourish, P 2016, 'Algorithms and their others: Algorithmic culture in context', *Big Data & Society*, vol. 3, no. 2, pp. 1–11.

Dourish, P 2017, *The stuff of bits. An essay on the materialities of information*, MIT Press, Cambridge, MA.

Ferracane, MF & Van Der Marel, E 2019, 'Patterns of trade restrictiveness in online platforms: A first look', European Center for International Political Economy (ECIPE), https://doi.org/10.1111/twec.13030.

Financial Crisis Inquiry Report 2011, *Final report of the National Commission of the causes of the financial and economic crisis in the United States*, https://www.govinfo.gov/content/pkg/GPO-FCIC/pdf/GPO-FCIC.pdf.

Fry A, Wilson & Overby, C 2013, 'Teaching the design of narrative visualization: Using metaphor for financial literacy and decision making', in *Proceedings of the 2nd International Conference for Design Education Researchers*, DRS // CUMULUS, Oslo, 2013.

Goldschmidt, G 1994, 'On visual design thinking: The vis kids of architecture', *Design Studies*, vol. 15, no. 2, pp. 158–74.

Goldschmidt, G & Smolkov, M 2016, 'Variances in the impact of visual stimuli on design problem solving performance', *Design Studies*, vol. 27, no. 5, pp. 549–69.

Goodman, B & Flaxman, S 2017, 'European Union regulations on algorithmic decision making and a "right to explanation"', *AI Magazine*, vol. 38, no. 3, pp. 50–7.

Hoffswell, J, Li, W & Liu, Z 2020, 'Techniques for flexible, responsive visualization design', in *CHI '20: Proceedings of the 2020 CHI Conference on Human Factors in Computing Systems*, pp. 1–13, https://doi.org/10.1145/3313831.3376777.

Huppatz, DJ 2015, Revisiting Herbert Simon's 'Science of Design', *Design Issues*, vol. 31, no. 2, pp. 29–40.

Jarvis, J 2009, *The crisis of credit visualized*, Crisis of Credit, http://crisisofcredit.com/.

Kokotovich, V 2007, 'Problem analysis and thinking tools: An empirical study of non-hierarchical mind mapping', *Design Studies*, vol. 29, no. 1, pp. 49–69.

Kress, G & Van Leeuwen, T 1996, *Reading images, the grammar of visual design*, Routledge, London and New York.

Kumar, VR 2012, *101 design methods: A structured approach for driving innovation in your organization*, Wiley, New York.

Lanier, J 2013, 'How should we think about privacy? Making sense of one of the thorniest issues of the digital age', *Scientific American*, vol. 309, no. 5, pp. 64–71.

Larkin, J & Simon, H 1987, 'Why a diagram is (sometimes) worth ten thousand words', *Cognitive Science*, vol. 11, no. 1, pp. 65–100.

Liedtka, J & Ogilvie, T 2011, *Designing for growth: Thinking toolkit for managers*, Columbia University Press, New York.

Lusardi, A & Mitchell OS 2009, *How ordinary consumers make complex economic decisions: Financial literacy and retirement readiness*, http://www.nber.org/2009rrc/Full/2.1%20Lusardi,%20Mitchell.pdf.

MacKenzie, D 2009, *Material markets: How economic agents are constructed*, Oxford University Press, Oxford.

Magaudda, P 2013, 'What happens to materiality in digital virtual consumption', in M Molesworth and JD Knott (eds), *Digital virtual consumption*, Routledge, New York, pp. 118–33.

Martinez, AG 2019, 'No, data is not the new oil', *Wired*, https://www.wired.com/story/no-data-is-not-the-new-oil/.

Meadows, DH 2008, *Thinking in systems: A primer*, Chelsea Green Publishing, White River Junction, VT, USA.

Noble, SU 2018, *Algorithms of oppression: How search engines reinforce racism*, NYUPress, New York.

Orlikowski, WJ & Scott, SV 2008, 'The entanglement of technology and work in organizations', *LSE Working paper series* (168), Information Systems and Innovation Group, London School of Economics and Political Science, London, UK.

Paul, C 2007, 'The myth of immateriality: Presenting and preserving new media', in O Grau (ed.), *Media art histories*, MIT Press, Cambridge, MA, pp. 251–74.

Samuelson, W 1984, 'Bargaining under asymmetric information', *Econometrica*, vol. 52, no. 4, pp. 995–1006.

Sample, I 2020, 'What are deepfakes – and how can you spot them?', *Guardian*, 13 January, https://www.theguardian.com/technology/2020/jan/13/what-are-deepfakes-and-how-can-you-spot-them.

Simon, H 1970, *Sciences of the artificial*, 3rd edn, MIT Press, Cambridge, MA.

Stickdorn, M & Schneider, J 2010, *This is service design thinking: Basics – tools – cases*, BIS Publishers, Amsterdam.

Stickdorn, M, Hormess, M, Lawrence, A & Schneider J 2018, *This is service design doing: Applying service design thinking in the real world. A practitioner's handbook*, O'Reilly Media, Sebastopol, California.

Suwa, M & Tversky, B 1997, 'What do architects and students perceive in their design sketches? A protocol analysis', *Design Studies*, vol. 18, no. 4, pp. 385–403.

Suwa, M & Tversky, B 2009, 'Thinking with sketches', in AB Markman & KL Wood (eds), *Tools for innovation: The science behind the practical methods that drive new ideas*, Oxford University Press, Oxford, pp. 75–84.

Transcript of Mark Zuckerberg's 2018 Senate hearing. Retrieved from https://www.washingtonpost.com/news/the-switch/wp/2018/04/10/transcript-of-mark-zuckerbergs-senate-hearing/.

Trist, EL & Bamforth KW 1951, 'Some social and psychological consequences of the Longwall method of coal-getting', *Human relations*, vol. 4, no. 3, pp. 3–38.

U.S. House Committee on Financial Services 2019, *Facebook and an examination of its impact on the Financial Services and Housing Sectors*, https://financialservices.house.gov/calendar/eventsingle.aspx?EventID=404487.

Valentino-de Vries, J, Singer, N, Keller, MH & Krolik, A 2018, 'Your apps know where you were last night, and they're not keeping it secret', *New York Times*, 10 December 2018, https://www.nytimes.com/interactive/2018/12/10/business/location-data-privacy-apps.html

van Der Lught, R 2005, 'How sketching can affect the idea generation process in design group meetings, *Design Studies*, vol. 26, no. 2, pp. 101–22.

Wichter, Z 2018, '2 days, 10 hours, 600 questions: What happened when Mark Zuckerberg went to Washington', *New York Times*, 12 April, https://www.nytimes.com/2018/04/12/technology/mark-zuckerberg-testimony.html.

Wirth, N 1975, *Algorithms + data structures = programs*, Prentice-Hall Series in AutomaticComputation, Upper Saddle River, NJ.

5
MOVING DATA: VISUALIZING HUMAN AND NON-HUMAN MOVEMENT ARTISTICALLY

Michele Barker and Anna Munster

Introduction

How does data 'move'? How can we both feel data moving and feel movement through visualization techniques? How might specific visualization practices – both analytical and artistic – constrain or help us explore all kinds of movement, including that initiated by both human and non-human forces? This chapter proposes that artistic approaches using 'movement data' within experimental animation, experimental high-speed cinematography and some choreographic data visualization approaches, register a 'feeling' for and of moving data and image. This differs from conventional visual analytical methods, which locate 'patterns' in movement data, that might not be helpful for registering processes of movement as it actually occurs. Instead, visual analytical approaches are interested primarily in movement that has already taken place. Visual analytics then set about mining those occurrences of movement for their implicit or buried significance and form. But how might data visualization instead give us a sense of moving, *as it is happening* rather than when it has already formed?

Instead, following a line of practice-based thinking that comes out of radical choreographic theory (Forsythe, Palazzi & Shaw 2009; Manning 2009) and an understanding of the moving image inflected by Henri Bergson's philosophy, suggests that the felt registration of movement requires aesthetic strategies that go beyond visual representation and analytics. What, then, do we mean by conveying a felt registration of movement using imagistic techniques that do not fall back into simplistic notions of 'representing' data patterns? There are many media technologies for visually recording and capturing movement, running the gamut from traditional cinema through to motion capture and more; each has entire histories and techniques for representing and conveying motion and hence we are wary to not impossibly broaden the scope of our thinking here. We will need to put aside the many debates in cinema studies, for example, concerning the successes and failures of moving image's capacities to actually work with movement (for example Deleuze 1986, 1989).

However, we do want to immediately clarify that we are not concerned with whether data visualization of movement affects us emotionally but rather how the movement of data, and visual techniques that record and present movement generally, might be felt in their very moving. Another way to put this would be to first ask: how does time, changing in onscreen space, feel, given that it is actually impossible to see time? And following from this: what can data and moving image aesthetically offer in registering affectively 'moments' of time's imperceptible movements? Artistic efforts to work with movement data can bring a sensibility attuned to the relationality of movement and time to visualization. We also suggest – in our consideration of both our practice and in collaborative work that deploys data visualization to explore the choreographic practices of William Forsythe – that conventional movement data sets must be carefully reconfigured in their design and visualization if they are to afford a felt registration of movement. Instead, we will argue that this felt registration can be aesthetically composed for by creating work that itself sets up relational conditions among its visualization techniques and between other medial and/or nonmedial elements. These might include sonic, spatial, collaborative, corporeal and sculptural entities, among others. It is the differences among these entities' 'movement paths', speeds and intensities that combine and juxtapose to generate an emergent sensing of, as Erin Manning (2012, p. 14) puts it, 'movement moving'. Furthermore, contemporary visualization technologies and techniques have their own specific capacities (and limitations) for marking the passing of time and these must be taken into account when artistically composing for these relational conditions among elements so as to enable movement's felt registration. We will later elaborate upon how two techniques can be developed within, first, cinematic and then, second, data visualization using this relational sensibility. We discuss our own audiovisual installation work *pull* (Barker & Munster 2017) as a realization and exploration of such techniques. Finally, we gesture towards other examples such as William Forsythe's *Synchronous Objects* (2010) to indicate how other artists draw out a feeling for of movement in its very unfolding using data visualization, albeit in vastly different artistic practices.

Movement data, from the perspective of visual analytics ... and its limitations

The use of 'movement data' – typically geographical x, y coordinates accompanied by timestamp data – has been a strong focus of big data visual analytic research into geospatial movement of human, animal and inanimate objects tracked via GPS or positioning enabled devices. This transmitted data is captured, stored and analysed via the open source Geographical Information System (GIS), rendering it visually understandable.

One of the main reasons for developing a visual analytics approach to often massive movement data sets has been to enable representation of data as, for example, aggregated spatial flows. Data visualization in many historical accounts itself begins with Minard's famous 1869 aggregation of troop movement statistics using Sankey flow conventions (Friendly 2002). Sankey visual conventions represent flows of movement or energy via linear bands or arrows (indicating direction) whose widths are proportionate to each other. Minard used these conventions to visualize the decrease in aggregate Napoleonic troop quantities as variables such as weather, lack of food, disease and length of battle affected their failure to invade Russia in their 1812–13 campaign. Visualization has, since then, been deployed for its capacity to draw the eye to, for example, intensifications of multiple and aggregated movement pathways within an image area (Andrienko et al. 2013, pp. 10ff). An area of data research and visualization where such aggregated movement pathways have flourished in the last two decades is in the study of animal behaviour and movement over time (see, for example, Spretke et al. 2011). The online data repository and project *Movebank* hosted by the Max Planck Institute began in 2007 to collect, aggregate and visualize the locations of individual animals over time. *Movebank* has an outward facing aspect to its research, *Animal Tracker*, which allows the public to see the trajectories of, for example, aggregated movements of migratory birds such as the white stork mapped against a 2D image of the earth over a year's worth of movement.

But – as visual analytical research itself is only too aware (Andrienko et al. 2013, p. 2) – movement data is a form of sampling, which extracts discrete information from activity or action that is continuous; that is, movement. This collecting and/or sensing of data points, in order to create a movement dataset, selects out movement instances leaving the *movement between* timestamped data points out of the set. The process of collecting or sensing data points to create a movement data set is a process of selection – not simply a process of formatting – in which the movement between timestamped data points, however miniscule, will have been omitted from the set (see Figure 5.1).

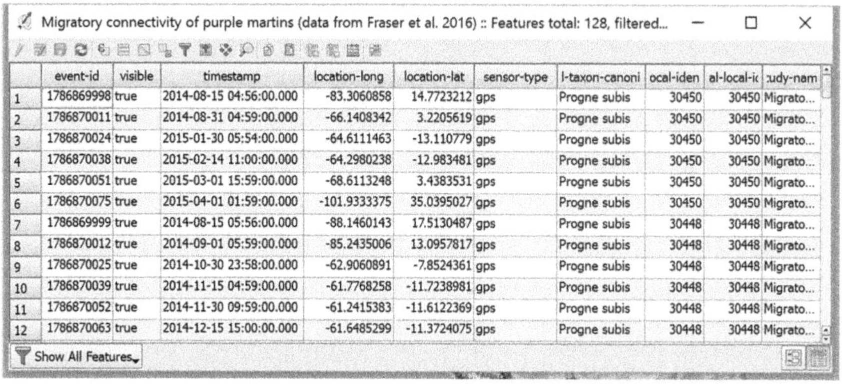

Figure 5.1 An example of typically formatted movement data containing x, y coordinates as longitude and latitude positions and timestamps. Fraser KC, Shave A, Savage A, Ritchie A, Bell K, Siegrist J, Ray JD, Applegate K, Pearman M (2016) Data from: Determining fine-scale migratory connectivity and habitat selection for a migratory songbird by using new GPS technology. Movebank Data Repository. doi:10.5441/001/1.5q5gn84d. Published under Creative Commons license, Universal Public Domain Declaration.

The data analytic approach to movement derives implicitly from Euclidean geometrical and linear/sequential visual frameworks. This seems reasonable in many ways, given that most tasks to be solved for movement in relation to, say, computer vision, require data rendering within the x, y, z coordinate spaces of 2D and 3D visual computation. Here movement is conceived as series of discrete positions occupied by moving objects, connected via the sequential unfolding of time. Space, time and moving object, then, give rise to discrete data that can be analysed and visualized either separately or together via various techniques. However, this approach runs into many classic philosophical problems: how to account for movement between time instances; and how to represent collective movement as heterogeneous rather than simply aggregated. These problems lie at the core of how to use visual means to register the way movement moves; the way it simultaneously continues and changes as it unfolds as a process.

Process-based approaches to movement

An entire field of thinking that has recently revived these issues via a reconsideration of the process-based philosophy of not only Bergson but Alfred North Whitehead and William James. Of concern here is the different way process-based philosophy approaches movement, which could be very loosely characterized as: first, a preoccupation with transition and the production of continuity in any temporal direction over the reduction to position and sequence; and second, acknowledging the non-linear multiplicity of any movement in process, over and above its causal attribution to either a subject or object at a discrete point in time. It is not that there are no discrete moments and that everything is constantly in flux – a somewhat confused criticism sometimes levelled at process-based thought. Instead, experience is considered as made up of complexes of actual occasions, to use Whitehead's terminology (1978, pp. 22ff), whose nature is only ever given as each occasion becomes or is in the process of unfolding what it is. One can only ever know how each actual occasion will come to be what is, as it is in process and in relation ('prehending') all other occasions in the 'complex' (nexus) in which it (and others) are unfolding.

To give a concrete example: the choreography of throngs of people walking through a city street, all taking different directions and positions as they converge at a pedestrian crossing, could easily be positionally captured and correlated with timestamps. Out of such a dataset, movement paths could be mapped and movement trajectories analysed. But what about that common and yet awkward experience of walkers approaching each other from opposite directions, abruptly stopping less than a metre apart and, then facing each other, attempting to shuffle against each other's potential onward movement so as to continue their own path down different streets and lanes? How might one visually present such a set of relational entanglements in which, somehow, the differing flows of movement are both cut and yet continue to keep forming? How is this felt interruption and yet continuing movement actually playing out in this minor choreographic event? What visually might be presented, in order to evoke, the mild frustration, embarrassment and sometimes humour of such everyday occurrences? What and how are the ways in which the forward movement of each walker will have both come to this and re-emerge out of it to be sensed? Here it is a question of what one might compose to register the shifting space-time between the walkers walking as this emerges in the actual event. How might it be possible to register such movement events using computational visual techniques?

Cinematically visualizing a feeling of movement

pull (2017) is a multi-channel audiovisual installation that focuses on one momentary experience (a nexus of actual occasions), asking us to sense its lived time as extraordinary. This experience is the moment a large wave forms and you dive deep as it breaks above. In this instant, everything changes: there is a calmness, a silence and an energy, transforming the sensing body in this submerged moment. In *pull* this is drawn out infinitely, suggesting not a discrete time or space that could be simply mapped, but rather a nexus of occasions simultaneously prehending their pasts (the moments that came before, such as diving under) and forever apprehending their future: how will the wave form; when will it crest and crash? The installation presents the experience of submergence from different perspectives – the filmic one, shot underneath a wave; and the capture of that experience as movement data. Without narrative and designed as two seamless replays of that moment, the visual dimension of the work is highly cinematic. *pull*'s audiovisual exploration of time and embodied perception uses water as a force outside humans' short 'moment' in geological time.

Underpinning the work is a challenge to the moving image's relationship to movement and temporality. Cinema's movement is generally understood in relation to frames per second (fps): both the speed of the camera's recording of a moment and the speed that successive frames pass through a projector or digital playback system. This understanding of the moving image is created through a series of discrete moments – frames – are held together as movement for the viewer through various systems of playback. It is the arc of moving images over a period of time that sets up the premise for movement to occur across the timespan of the film; that is, its total number of fps then calculated as the length and duration of the time it takes to watch the film unfold. *pull* challenges this logic through a series of interconnected techniques. These techniques – extreme slow motion, forward-reverse motion and seamless looping – operate as a perceptual machine to 'unhinge' the work from the progressive movement of discrete frames so as to enter a space where frames 'bleed' and linearity loses its grip on temporality (see Figure 5.2).

Bergson's theory of duration informs our understanding of time, movement and experience in this work. For Bergson, time needed to be thought outside the spatialized linear sequence of beginning, middle, end. Such vectors imply that time – and hence our experience of it and in it – is something that can be precisely mapped. To measure time (and, by implication, data) is to measure intervals across a specified distance which travel in a specified direction. Yet our experience of time, as previously argued – along with various technologies and techniques for measuring time such as timestamps – comprises transitions

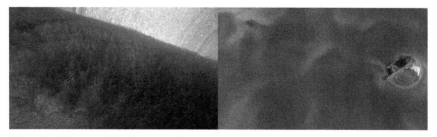

Figure 5.2 Screenshot of two moving image channels combined in *pull*, 2017, Michele Barker and Anna Munster, multi-channel audiovisual installation. The left shows high-speed cinematography; the right movement data rendered as 3D CGI.

and intervals between the intervals. Something is left out that is always 'in' time experienced: time measured is not time felt. As Bergson (1946, pp. 10–11) said, 'In between these simultaneities anything you like may happen'. Rather than the precise measurement of time – what Bergson calls a quantitative multiplicity – he offers us duration: a qualitative multiplicity where time can only be understood as what is experienced, what is felt as passing, as changing (Bergson 1960, p. 105). Here, movement, understood as changing through/across and because of time, cannot be expressed as sequential motion but rather is part of movement's experience. Later in this chapter, we point to the ways William Forsythe brings a form of visual data practices (rather than data visualization) to explore how a complex dance unfolds over time across a range of dancing bodies and movements. Forsythe's foray into visual data practices is useful because he starts from understanding choreography itself *not* as a sequence of movements over time but as the ways bodies come to organize each other and are organized by a particular environment (Forsythe cited in Spier 2011, p. 139). This means the visual data practices he uses to 'image' this dynamic field of bodies moving and environment organizing are less representations of a sequence of dance moves than traces of dynamic forces that emerge as the bodies organize each other in a specific space. In the *Synchronous Objects* project, discussed towards the end of this chapter, visual lines of 'traced' movement flash and unfold, pinging across the screen as if just registering a forcefield of exchanges that are movement emerging as it actually occurs. Yet rather than persisting as representations of a definite pattern that has taken place, these vectoral traces fade rapidly and become taken up by another group of movements/lines played out by dancers across a different (screen) corner. It is this emergent tracing-fading that registers the dynamics of the movement rather than putting into place a visualization of something that is embedded.

Things could be moving with respect to their past (memories), their present (whatever is actually unfolding) and their future, or multiple potential unfoldings of any time whatsoever and even all at once. The duration of an event moves as freely backward as it does forward. We see this in the technique of reversed motion in cinema. In the history of cinema, most instances of reversing footage operate more as a gimmick or device to create a visual cue for a flashback, although there are also other examples of the use of reverse editing in cinema (see Tohline 2015). In *pull* reverse motion of the wave breaking became a powerful effect that, when insinuated subtly into the cinematic channel of the piece during the editing process, thwarts the vector of forward progressive motion. Instead, time and the wave's movement both ebb and flow, like the force of the water. These altered directions are not evident when watching within the installation space: the shift from forward motion to reverse works seamlessly in conjunction with the endless looped structure of the piece. Such looping ensures cinema's desire for temporal ordering via beginning and end is likewise thwarted: it places the viewer in a changing yet strangely familiar landscape. This technique becomes a way to consider the experience of time/events durationally: these do not occur as abrupt shifts, for even the most pressing recollections still position themselves relatively seamlessly into the flow of experience. To recall the familiarity of the wave moving is equally a part of the present time of watching it. The capacity, within actual embodied experience, to inhabit different kinds of duration that are nonsequential, presents a challenge to linear data structures that tend to use sequential lists and trees. However, it should also be noted that such structures do not exist as isolated elements but are put into motion themselves by computation, which increasingly deploys processes that are recursive and hence nonlinear (see Hui 2018). Data *visualization* understood as simply *representing* patterns or relations in data fails to live up to the challenge of being a trace or even index of the dynamic processes of contemporary computation. Our interest, then, in using data *imagistically* is an attempt to move away from this representationalist and outdated conception of computing as well toward an exploration of how computational movements might also help us register different kinds of duration.

Most crucial to considering the wave breaking moment as qualitative multiplicity in *pull* was our use of extreme slow motion cinematography. The wave sequence was shot at 1,000 fps and slowed down even further in post-production. Played back at 25 fps, things ordinarily invisible are amplified to surreal proportions: details of water density; currents moving in multiple directions; air bubbles and micro-organisms. In working directly with vastly altered frame rates, the intention was to generate an experience of time appearing to 'almost stand still'. The focus is on bodily experiences of movement and duration in this moment. The aim is not to record a moment in time, but rather to be aware of time as the matter of experience.

High-speed cameras are used in a variety of biomechanically led scientific, as well as medical and sporting applications (Dalton 2002). And while this means it is now possible to forensically analyse the rich detail offered by these super-fast frame rates, it is also possible to learn a different cinematography by feeling into the force of movement through the image, rather than scraping to see its traces. Such scraping is never satisfied with even the most minute details – we can never see all that is unseeable because there will always be some 'quantity' leftover to divide and measure. Here we come to the heart of Bergson's critique of the illusion of motion in which time and movement are made to coincide as the divisible line that underlies both (Bergson 2005, p. 191). The paradox – famously known as Zeno's arrow of time – is that the more we see the subdivisions, the more the subdivisions keep coming. The subdividable line, rendered here as the increasing quantity of image data captured by increasing quanta of frame rates, never attains a state of total division or absolute visibility, since this very approach always leaves over a potential remainder to be subdivided or perceived. Instead, to feel imperceptibility, we require different techniques in the creation and stitching together of moving images that are both sustained by and create movement.

Toward data that moves, feeling its movement

pull cinematically strives to explore how to register the way movement moves, yet how can data participate in such movement moving? For this element of the project we took the x, y coordinates and timestamp data derived from a cinematographer while shooting the underwater wave sequences over several hours. Wearing a GPS enabled watch designed specifically for tracking the motion of surfers, data was collected on the cinematographer's movements – velocity and position – as he moved through the water. It was crucial to consider the data not as a representation of movement conceived as a series of discrete positions occupied by a moving object (the cinematographer's body), reconnected through interpolating each moment between the timestamp data captured as seconds. To follow this set of visualization techniques would mean space, time and object only giving rise to discrete data sets. Those sets would then be analysed and visualized either separately or together through various analytical means (see Figure 5.3).

Figure 5.3 Left: Cinematographer Chris Bryan filming under waves and wearing the GPS enabled watch capturing movement data. Right: Screenshot of the motion path produced by x, y coordinates of the cinematographer's geospatial location correlated with timestamp data over a 3-hour period taken from the visual interface on the GPS enabled watch.

Thus, like the filmic event of the wave forming and breaking, data had to participate in the event of moving, and hence it was not viable for us to simply animate an object moving along the motion path created by the dataset. As Bergson (1946, pp. 164–5) reminds us, rather than thinking about the line, we must consider the action itself and this requires us to think in more complicated ways about movement. *pull* required the creation of two kinds of movement within the animation scene. The first was the movement of the fluid simulation, which was created using a series of parameters taken from hydraulic information embedded in software packages that animated the fluid mechanics of reef breaks. The actual motion path created by the x, y and timestamp of the cinematographer's data while shooting was animated as a negative space moving through and against the fluid mechanics. This path was set up as a collider in relation to the fluid simulation so that the forces of the fluid against the continuity of the motion path constantly formed and reformed in relation with each other. Rather than appearing as a representation of a movement path, the negative space presents as a bubble that both has its own momentum and is also being formed as it moves in relation to the moving fluid simulation. The choice of 'negative space' was important since it suggests something whose form is implied – registering as felt form rather than spatially given.

The moving data here gains its traction from a set of occasions that are all actual yet not necessarily visualized per se. The movement of a (human) body bobbing around subject to non-human forces and yet also intent on a specific activity is felt right at the nexus of a set of relations, forms and forces that concresce; that is, come together in their multiple and qualitative changings in time, each also in relation with the other(s). Movement data gains (its) duration: 'A duration is a complete locus of actual occasions in "unison of becoming" or in "concrescent unison"' (Whitehead 1978, p. 320)

What is suggested here is a different approach to not only using cinematic and movement data artistically but to also considering what movement might be when thought visually with the help of process-based philosophy. Gesturing towards some other artistic approaches that rigorously reconfigure the relations between movement, data and the visual, suggests that a different aesthetic tendency might be emerging from these practices. We turn first to the project that grew out of the choreographic and dance work of William Forsythe's Company and culminated in the large project *Synchronous Objects* (2010). While focusing on only one aspect of this project – the use of multivariate datasets taken from recordings of Forsythe dance works to create visualizations of the choreographic thinking operative in this movement – it is important to also say a little about Forsythe's overall practice. His motivation for working on the *Synchronous Objects* project came from a desire to provide a visual resource that might respond to and provoke the question: what does physical thinking look like? (Forsythe 2010a). The 'data visualizations', which in myriad ways drew out complex patterns in the movement of a videoed dance piece, *One Flat Thing Reproduced* (Forsythe 2003), were responses to that question. They were not attempts to represent the movement of the dancers but rather to open a conversation about other modalities for relating to and engaging with the felt or embodied knowledge that dancing enacts.

Forsythe and his dancers already work in unconventional ways with movement, since their approach is not to learn dance positions, routines or sequences but rather to create fields of movement interrelations always open to change every time they are performed (see Manning 2009). They are, then, concerned with a conception and practice of movement in which positions and routines cede to change and the deployment of rigorously practised techniques of improvization. The emphasis is on movement as it arises both out of relational gesture and through its own moving or, as has characterized this above, change. In the *Synchronous Objects* project, Forsythe collaborated with visual designers, statisticians, dance theorists as well as his ensemble to create a series of visual objects from, among other quantitative and qualitative data, a large dataset captured from *One Flat Thing Reproduced* and from various other video recordings of rehearsals for this work. Importantly, the statisticians and designers took up the challenge of Forsythe's own choreography to understand movement. In their research emerging from the project, the data designers state that they adopted Forsythe's definition of dance as connective space between dancers, sets of choreographies and their dynamic interplay. Dance happens *between positions* not in the holding of and vector toward the next position (Alquvist et al. 2010, p. 549).

Interestingly, this required a rethinking of movement data as not simply delineated only by coordinate and timestamp values but rather by the necessity of engaging space and time themselves as dynamically interrelated. Traditional movement datasets were still used including: x, y and z coordinates (since the movement was itself a recording of dancers along depth axes as well), and 4-ms timestamps for all coordinates. Yet the designers had to think about how these datasets would dynamically relate in the visual objects produced. In some of the visual objects generated, a new technique was used that the designers call 'linked brushing' (Alquvist et al. 2010). In different visual objects, spatial data, time and other attribute data (dancer's name and so on) call each other up through a user interactively 'brushing', as if caressing, an object. This results in changes to the visual object and the generation of complex overlapping visual trajectories in which movement paths criss-cross to create vectoral topological spaces (for example, *Synchronous Objects* 2010b). These trajectories no longer represent where a dancer or even the dance moves in space throughout time but rather unfold the felt complex of the relations moving the dance as an entire event, while it is danced.

Although using quite different visualization methods, this relational approach has similarities to the way movement and movement data have been approached in *pull*. Both projects work with movement, space and time as processually brought in to being; all emerging in their actual unfoldings through complex series of interrelating and dynamic entities. Importantly these entities are also immanent to these processes. For Forsythe, the dancer is only an entity in relation – in counterpoint – with other dancers, with the space in which the dance takes place, with the actual performance taking place and with the techniques all bring to the ensemble. The question for visualization (data and other forms that depend upon sequentialism and the subdivision of movement) then becomes: how can visual composition engage with movement as this dynamic durational topology? This is not simply a question for artistic visualization but might also have approaches to offer a range of difficult visualization tasks such as situational awareness for computer vision in moving autonomous entities.

It is important to distinguish this approach from using a technology such as motion capture to demonstrate how a dancer or performer is moving or to even create an aesthetic visual depiction of this. There is important research being undertaken within this area in, for example, projects such as Thecla Schiphorst's *Moving Stories* (2012–2015). However, there is a tendency within even experimental motion capture visualization to continue to think of movement as that which necessarily proceeds from a moving subject – generally the body captured by the motion sensors as genesis of action. Having already set up the origin of movement by locating this in a subject, it is then difficult to understand movement as arising out of a field of relations whose time and space are also generated in the very moving set apace by this field. Nonetheless, there is nothing to prevent future artistic work that explores movement as processually emergent from being carried out via a wide variety of visualization practices and technologies.

Conclusion

But where this argument might conclude – with a provocation for work yet to be undertaken rather than to summarize what has already been discussed here – is with the plea that movement not be locked down by data or by any form of visualization. If movement datasets are indeed large this is not simply because movement takes place over time hence producing many data records. Nor is it that movement needs to be broken down precisely – in a kind of post-Muybridgean trajectory – in order to reveal the hidden depths that the now high-speed moving image might offer. While both forms of visualization incur large amounts of data, the reduction of movement to the 'patterns' within this data or to locating the 'invisible' will never resolve its rhythm or potential trajectories.

Movement, emerging in duration, will always gesture to its elsewheres: the movement just preceding this one, setting the next one up; the movement now unfolding towards a yet un-imaged future.

To watch thoughtful contemporary dance; to see crowds negotiate a seven-way intersection; to look at a wave cresting and crashing from above or below; all of these ask us to feel movement emerging in the middle. Let's see if we can also (data) visualize from this imperceptible space of the inbetween where movement multifariously unfolds.

References

Alquvist, O, Ban, H, Cressi, N & Shaw, NZ 2010, 'Statistical Counterpoint: Knowledge Discovery of Choreographic Information Using Spatio-temporal Analysis and Visualization', *Applied Geography*, vol. 30, pp. 548–60.

Andrienko, G, Andrienko, N, Bak, P, Keim, D & Wrobel, S 2013, *Visual Analytics of Movement*, Springer, Heidelberg and New York.

Barker, M & Munster, A 2017, *pull*, Audiovisual Installation, Exhibition Documentation', accessed 20 March 2018, http://experimenta.org/makesense/artists/barker-munster/.

Bergson, H 1946, *The Creative Mind: An Introduction to Metaphysics*, trans. ML Andison, Philosophical Library, New York.

Bergson, H 1960, *Time and Free Will*, trans. FL Pogson, Harper and Brothers, New York.

Bergson, H 2005, *Matter and Memory*, trans. NM Paul & WS Palmer, Zone Books, New York.

Dalton, Rex 2002, 'Caught on Camera', *Nature*, vol. 418, pp. 721–2.

Deleuze, G 1986, *Cinema One: The Movement Image*, trans. H Tomlinson & B Habberjam, University of Minnesota Press, Minneapolis.

Deleuze, G 1989, *Cinema Two: The Time Image*, trans. H Tomlinson & R Galeta, University of Minnesota Press, Minneapolis.

Forsythe, W 2003, *One Flat Thing Reproduced*, video, YouTube, accessed March 19 2018, https://www.youtube.com/watch?v=cufauMezz_Q.

Forsythe, W 2010a, *Synchronous Objects*, accessed 19 March 2018, http://www.synchronousobjects.org.

Forsythe, W 2010b, *Synchronous Objects*, http://www.synchronousobjects.org, accessed 19 March 2018, https://synchronousobjects.osu.edu/content.html#/StatisticalCounterpoint.

Forsythe, W, Palazzi, M & Shaw, NZ 2009, *Dance, Data, Objects Essays*, Ohio State University, accessed 19 March 2018, https://synchronousobjects.osu.edu/assets/objects/introduction/danceDataObjectEssays.pdf.

Friendly, M 2002, 'Visions and Re-visions of Charles Joseph Minard', *Journal of Educational and Behavioral Statistics*, vol. 27, no. 1, pp. 31–51.

Hui, Y 2018, 'Preface: The Time of Execution', in H Pritchard, E Snodgrass & M Tyzlik-Carver (eds), *Data Browser 6: Executing Practices*, Open Humanities Press, pp. 23–31.

Manning, E 2009, 'Propositions for the Verge: William Forsythe's Choreographic Objects', *Inflexions*, no. 2, accessed 18 March 2018, http://www.inflexions.org/n2_manninghtml.html.

Manning, E 2012, *Always More than One*, Duke University Press, Durham and London.

Schiphorst, T 2012–15, *Moving Stories*, accessed 19 March 2018, http://movingstories.ca/movingstories/.

Spier, S 2011, 'Choreographic Thinking and Amateur Bodies', in S Pier (ed.), *William Forsythe and the Practice of Choreography: It Starts from Any Point*, Routledge, London, pp. 139–50.

Spretke, D, Bak, P, Janetzko, H, Kranstauber, B, Mansmann, F & Davidson, S 2011, 'Exploration through Enrichment: A Visual Analytics Approach for Animal Movement', in *Proceedings of the 19th ACM SIGSPATIAL International Conference on Advances in Geographic Information Systems*, pp. 421–4, https://doi.org/10.1145/2093973.2094038.

Tohline, A 2015, 'Towards a History and Aesthetics of Reverse Motion' PhD diss., Ohio University, Ohio.

Whitehead, AN 1978, *Process and Reality*, The Free Press, New York.

SECTION TWO
MAKING DATA: PRACTICES

In this section we focus on a range of exemplar forms and contexts for the application of data-objects. Examples where data-objects have been used in education, in the capturing of cultural and heritage interactions, and the making sense of and valuing of personal biometric data are described. The creative practices of translating hard to comprehend climate change data into forms and experiences ordinary people can relate to is also explored in this section.

6
UNCANNY LANDSCAPES: TACTILE AND EXPERIENTIAL ENCOUNTERS WITH ECOLOGICAL DATA

Zoë Sadokierski, Monica Monin and Andrew Burrell

Introduction

Communicating complex ecological issues such as anthropogenic climate change and the effects of capitalist culture on diverse ecologies is difficult. Challenges include communicating phenomena that occur over unimaginable timescales and are often invisible to the naked eye; making these global phenomena relatable on a local and individual scale; and, instilling an understanding of the human species as *enmeshed* (Morton 2012) and *entangled* (Tsing et al. 2017) within complex ecologies, in order to foster attention and care for the world. Moreover, coming to terms with such issues can lead to despair and hopelessness. Glenn Albrecht (2007) coined the term 'solastalgia' to describe a form of existential distress caused by facing environmental change at a local scale. Beyond individual distress, psychologist Per Espen Stoknes (2015) describes a 'psychological climate paradox', a form of political inertia in which voter concern for climate change in wealthy democracies falls as scientific evidence mounts, due to psychological barriers triggered by current science communication. Like many other scholars, scientists and journalists addressing the climate paradox, Stoknes identifies an urgent need for new kinds of ecological narrative if we, as a species, are to demand and enact the systemic economic, cultural and political changes required to transition to more sustainable ways of being in the world.

Environmental humanist Rob Nixon (2011, p. 3) frames the narrative problem at the heart of the current, anthropogenic ecological crisis:

> How can we convert into image and narrative the disasters that are slow moving and long in the making [...] How can we turn the long emergencies of slow violence into stories dramatic enough to rouse public sentiment and warrant political interventions, these emergencies whose repercussions have given rise to some of the most critical challenges of our time?

Traditional science communication relies on visualizations such as charts, graphs and maps, which aim to accurately represent data but often fail to clearly inform or engage non-expert audiences. In turn, these scientific methods of communication are utilized by journalists, activists and lobbyists alike as they seek to engage this non-expert audience, yet they often still miss their mark. At its core this failure may relate directly to a mismatch in an understanding of scales; for example, a scientific understanding of geological timescales differs significantly to a non-expert's phenomenological understanding of a lived human-historical timescale.

One way that science communicators are addressing this narrative problem is by embedding human stories into empirical information visualizations. An example comes from Professor of Biology Lesley Hughes, who altered a well-known graph of rising global temperature over the next hundred years by adding three lines: 'me, my kids, my grandkids?' (Climate Commission 2013). This simple alteration, with its anxious question mark, puts the distance of decades into terms we can empathize with. This altered graph represents a new communication approach in which scientists recognize the value of extending quantitative data with qualitative information. Or, as science communicator Ketan Joshi (2017) puts it: 'it's time to build a bridge between data and emotion'. This example also highlights human inability to comprehend time (beyond our day to day terms of reference); an implied inability to understand the significance of the next hundred years signifies the almost impossible task of understanding deep time (the concept of geological time) and our entangled relationship with a planet billions of years old.

Three years after his call for ways to convert 'disasters that are slow moving and long in the making' into image and narrative, Rob Nixon was involved in a project which invited artists, scientists and scholars to pitch objects for inclusion in an 'Anthropocene Cabinet of Curiosities'. Shifting from image to object as carrier of narrative is significant:

> For in a world deluged with data, arresting stories and images matter immeasurably, playing a critical role in the making of environmental publics and the shaping of environmental policy. [...] What objects might jolt us into reimagining environmental time across diverse scales, from the recent past to deep history? How might certain kinds of objects make visible the

differential impacts – past, present, and future – that have come to shape the relationships among human and non-human beings, living in an era of extreme hydrocarbon extraction, extreme weather events, and extreme economic disparity?

(Mitman & Nixon, cited in Robin & Muir 2015)

The *Cabinet of Curiosities* project sought existing objects that offer allegories for the Anthropocene, such as the stories of the invention, use and consequences of an insecticide pump spray, batteries or a room thermostat.[1] However, the idea of objects as a narrative vehicle is also relevant for designing data visualizations in innovative forms. How could ecological data be communicated beyond the scientific chart, into objects and spaces that can be encountered, experienced, inhabited? How might such encounters affect our engagement with and reception of ecological issues and the data that describes them?

This chapter critiques a range of projects in which ecological datasets are communicated to non-expert audiences as 'uncanny encounters'; the data is materialized as an unsettling object or experience, rather than a visualization on page or screen.[2] Instead of foregrounding 'scientific truth' in the data set, the projects discussed below all use narrative to foster understanding of complex human and non-human entanglements, and instil a sense of agency (and urgency) in relation to the larger ecological issues at play. Narrative-based approaches to communicating ecological science can draw out conversations around the social, cultural and ethical impacts of scientific data, for non-expert audiences. This use of narrative goes beyond what has traditionally been referred to as data storytelling; the objects in question do not merely take on the role of illustrative story-teller imparting structured wisdom, but instead attempt to entangle our presence within the narrative, as encounter.

A sample of thirty-six projects were critiqued (not all are included in this chapter), considering how narrative is embedded in or generated within each project, and how this narrative points to, highlights, or even creates moments of uncanny encounter. Although every experience of the world could be read as an encounter, the encounters highlighted here intentionally allow audiences to think through human/non-human entanglement.

In this next section the idea of an encounter is elaborated, particularly in relation to the writing of anthropologist Anna Tsing, then projects which exemplify the use of 'uncanny encounters' to communicate ecological data are critiqued.

Encountering data

Data visualization's authority as a means of knowledge production and circulation is often underwritten by the assumption of representationalism: that data accurately and objectively mirrors the world (Drucker 2014, p. 125).

As a practice of knowledge production and communication, data visualization is generally conveyed and taught as a process of discovering a story or points of interest within a data set. However, treating the practice of data visualization as simple discovery fails to acknowledge the productive character of its work. Where drawing out 'things of interest' from data via selection and recombination alters the 'meaning and value of data' (Amoore & Piotukh 2015, p. 344). Disconnected from the time and place of its writing and now transpiring at extensive scales, data in numerical form can be intractable and difficult to comprehend. Therefore, graphical presentation is often used to make visible and perceptible the complex, invisible or large-scale phenomena being reported. Such visualizations tend to focus on the communication of a singular, coherent *story* through the combination and presentation of quantitative information in graphical form (Drucker 2012). Narrative has become a critical addition to data communication, according to N. Katherine Hayles (2012, p. 176), as it renders data structures meaningful; data structures alone are incapable of explaining the relational comparisons they perform. Hayles views narrative and data structures as *natural symbionts*; in turn data can bolster the authority and credibility of narratives.

In an account of big data analysis and its use in governance, Amoore and Piotukh (2015) detail how the heterogeneity and material contexts from which data emerges is pared back in data practice when data is shaped into calculable forms. Algorithmic techniques have become a key means through which to explore and comprehend data, especially when we are confronted by the sheer scales of contemporary data availability and production (Hayles 2012, p. 230). The immense quantities of data and the ability to scale it algorithmically, as Amoore and Piotukh (2015, p. 361) suggest, engenders a claim that data analytics and visualization represents the world, because 'it appears as though everything is calculable, everything about the uncertain future is nonetheless decidable'. This representationalism, we argue, is one of the key problems faced by data visualization.[3] Through its claim to show a certain and objective mirror of the world, its storytelling can render passive and deterministic the material realities and relations that it seeks to communicate.[4] This makes it difficult for us to grasp the messy and indeterminate entanglements of the world from which the data emerged, and to consider possible narratives or potential futures that worldly entanglements may engender, and moreover, our own human involvement and agency within the unfolding narrative. Donna Haraway (2016) asserts that in our time of ecological devastation we need to think *tentacularly*, or in other words, we need to think and build more liveable worlds through our entanglements with the rest of the world. For Haraway there is no 'arrow of time' or pre-determined story, rather in order to compose more liveable futures we need to be able to imagine ourselves as agential and collective participants in potential stories that are yet to occur.

At the heart of each of the following examples lies an *encounter* with data and the material realities and interrelations from which data emerge. Conceptually, the term 'encounter' is understood here through the work of anthropologist Anna Tsing. In Tsing's accounts of disturbance-based ecologies, different ways of living emerge through entangled ecologies of the human, non-human, living and non-living. For Tsing, ecology is not merely the interaction of stable pre-given entities; instead, ecologies – including the entities within them – become themselves through, and can be transformed by, encounter. This is exemplified in Tsing's (2015) account of the ruins of human-disturbed forests where pines, oaks and matsutake mushrooms assemble and form a fragmented ecology that fosters unexpected inter-relations and possibilities. For example, the specific conditions and symbiotic relations required for matsutake to grow, and the human livelihoods and global trade and commerce around sites where the mushroom crops up. In her narration of the collective actions of mushroom, oak and pine, Tsing demonstrates how encounters are indeterminate; the ways in which entities may or may not affect one another can never be settled or assumed prior to their interrelation. This extends to who we are as a human species and as individuals, as our ways of being also emerge out of encounter.

Therefore, we frame the examples below as 'encounters' because finding ourselves entangled within encounters means not only noticing the action that unfolds in the indeterminate histories of assemblages but can also lead to grasping human co-entanglement and how we are also 'unpredictably transformed' in encounters (Tsing 2015, p. 46). Encounters are less about 'coherence' or neatly pre-formatted depictions or stories, in the sense of how data visualization in its general form was described above, than noticing the 'potential histories in the making' that emerge in heterogeneous assemblages of human, non-human, living and non-living (Tsing 2015 p. 23).[5] This means that rather than being told a story after the event, we see and are potentially implicated in the action of the story as it is unfolding.

In encounter we experience things unfolding as part of ecological interconnections, we see relationships and can imagine how these might iteratively alter over (often very long) periods of time. Encounters are experienced as narrative structures by which we begin to understand and notice things outside of the usual scope and scale of our perception. They are perceived from within, we are directly implicated in the story being told, and unlike traditional scientific data visualization our own phenomenological positioning is vital; the encounter invites a subjective reading and writing of data to take place.

Uncanny encounters with ecological datasets

Zakpage is a collaboration between designer Alison Page, descendant of the Walbanga and Wadi Wadi people of the Yuin nation, and film-maker Nik

Lachajczak. Their three-part documentary *Clever Country*, co-produced by the National Museum of Australia, aims to communicate the science and technology embedded within Indigenous Australian cultural practices and knowledge sharing, to a broad audience. Western scientists are recognizing the potential for Indigenous knowledge to help solve urgent problems related to anthropogenic climate change – such as bushfires and floods – and finding alternative medicines.

Key to comprehending Indigenous Australian knowledge is the concept of 'songlines'[6] – an ancient mnemonic system of oral storytelling that produces a complex 'ancestral library of embedded knowledge' (Page 2020), a knowledge system which has allowed cultural and environmental data to be passed down for more than 60,000 years without written language.

In the documentary, Page demonstrates how songlines work by constructing a fishing-lure data visualization (Figure 6.1). She strings a network of fishing lines from the branches of a mangrove tree, and threads colourful lures along the lines to represent individual knowledge holders and markers on Country. Page talks through one line and set of lures at a time, explaining how one songline crosses another at certain lure-points. For example, a sequence of lures represent an Aunty who knows how to find and use hundreds of plants on her country and a grandfather who knows where to find sacred white ochre for Ceremony, who share the story-song of the River, which connects to a constellation that appears on the horizon pointing to where to find waterholes during the dry, what time of year fish are running and when a particular animal is good to eat. Page translates story into data; the fishing line/lure installation allows Page to perform storytelling in time and space, to communicate the way Indigenous Australians perform their own storytelling across time and Country. Although we are not invited 'into' this

Figure 6.1 Film still from *Clever Country* (Zakpage 2019).

encounter directly, Page's demonstration on Country invites us to see the world around us anew.

In the documentary, Page describes songlines as a multidimensional ancestral library made up of complex datasets, with people as 'key to activating this ancestral library, because as they moved around Country over time, they would upload and download knowledge at sites of learning, sharing it with each other and back into the land, until it became embedded knowledge'. Songlines work like a memory palace; spiritual and ecological knowledge is encoded into objects (such as constellations, distinct rock formations, bodies of water) and geographical locations on Country, which function as mnemonic devices to remember invisible forces (such as seasonal cues for harvesting or hunting), wayfinding, land and sea management, cultural stories and law. The oral storytelling of songlines by Elders is a living system; no single dialect group or tribe knows all the songlines, tribes come together in cross cultural exchange and Ceremony to share knowledge.

A different example of passing down ancestral knowledge is Erich Berger and Mari Keto's work *Inheritance* (2016). *Inheritance* is a set of precious yet radioactive jewellery pieces: a necklace, earrings and a brooch made using gold, thorianite, thoriate and uraninite. Uraninite, commonly referred to as pitchblende, is highly radioactive. The radioactive nature of the jewellery renders it harmful to human bodies. Although as 'heirlooms' they may be passed down generations, they are unwearable for deep time; the gradual process of radioactive decay would take many human generations for the jewellery to be safe to wear. The jewellery is encased, along with time and radiation measuring apparatuses, in a stackable concrete container. Concrete contains the emission of high-energy particles as the radioactive materials decay, and symbolically reference the concrete shielding in nuclear reactors, and a container for radioactive waste materials.

Humans cannot immediately or easily sense, see or smell radiation, although high doses of radiation poisoning can produce a metallic 'taste sensation' while it damages human cells. Jane Bennett (2010) argues that much of the earth's activity occurs beyond the threshold of human perception not only due to the limitations of our senses, but also because humans generally figure much of the non-human world as inanimate.[7] For Bennett, this view of matter obstructs humans from developing more ecological modes of understanding and engaging with the world, as we fail to recognize the affective power of the non-human and our entanglement with it. *Inheritance* asks us to consider that beyond providing energy for today, nuclear power produces millions of years of harmful radioactive waste that multiple future generations will be required to handle.[8]

It is only through measurement apparatus' that we are able to detect and measure radiation's invisible presence and *Inheritance* includes a gold-leaf electroscope for each generation to test if the jewellery is safe to wear yet.

Here data is not presented in a static chart or prediction of the objects' future radioactive decay but generated in the undertaking of a ritual, set out by Berger and Keto, by which each generation performs a measurement of the jewellery's radioactivity. When the ritual is performed, if the gold leaf of the electroscope falls faster when it is near the jewellery than when it is not, the items are still radioactive. The faster the leaf falls the more radioactive it is. Engaging with, or imagining engaging with, *Inheritance* creates an encounter with the invisible yet potentially harmful presence of radioactive material to our bodies, other bodies and future bodies, making apparent the affective capacity of radioactive materials as well as our ongoing entanglements with it.

Another encounter with the data of invisible forces comes from Ruth Jarman and Joe Gerhardt (aka Semiconductor)'s *Cosmos*, a two-metre wooden, spherical sculpture which represents a dataset of a forest's carbon uptake and loss. Commissioned by Jerwood Open Forest in 2014, the sculpture is situated in the Alice Holt Forest, a recreational site which attracts almost half a million visitors a year (Figure 6.2). The sculpture appears in the forest clearing like an alien relic, its charcoal-hue and large, spherical form an uncanny object within the pine glade. Closer inspection reveals a surface rippled in patterns similar to disturbed water, made by abstracting one year's worth of measurements of the uptake and loss of carbon dioxide from the forest trees, collected from a nearby research station. The complex interference pattern is created by wave forms and patterns in the data, digitally modelled, then rendered by a CNC wood router machine.[9]

Through this work, the artists explore the difference between how scientists represent the physical world, and how humans experience it. Re-contextualizing

Figure 6.2 Semiconductor's *Cosmos* in Alice Holt Forest, UK. Photograph by Laura Hodgson, 2014.

the carbon data from 'strings of numbers' into a tangible sculpture involved translating polar plot representations created by the scientists – a circular, 2D graph which plots a year's worth of carbon data from various instruments – into a 3D fabricated form which can be experienced in the environment it represents (the forest the data is drawn from).

However, through this translation the data is abstracted: 'These sculptural forms become unreadable within the context of science, yet become a physical form we can see, touch, experience and readable in a new way. Here, humanising the data offers a new perspective of the natural world it is documenting, introducing a new visual experience' (Jarman & Gerhardt 2014). In other words, the sculpture does not attempt to communicate the scientific data in a conventional way – which would be incomprehensible without a sophisticated understanding of carbon cycles – but to provide a surprising encounter through which to reflect upon the invisible ecological processes occurring around us.

Yet more than the invisible carbon cycles, an encounter with *Cosmos* invites us to reflect on the data collector, as well as data collected. Jarman explains (personal correspondence 2019):

> The digital nature of the work also suggests the presence of man in the forest; the collecting, observing and processing of scientific measurements. Semiconductor want people to consider the material nature of the forest in a new way; the hidden layers of matter, events and processes that occur beyond our sensory perceptions, whilst also appreciating the art works striking complex form.

Where the 'authorship' of the scientist is largely invisible in the conventional polar plot diagram – we are trained to see the data not the graphic form – the obviously human-made structure in the forest prevents us from ignoring the presence of the human in *Cosmos*. *Cosmos*' evocation of the work of the data collector in the forest draws attention to the human practices and material engagements from which data emerges. Rather than attempting to be a physical representation of the forest and its carbon cycle, *Cosmos* creates a nexus point, connecting the people experiencing the work, the forest, scientific practices and the forests ongoing invisible cycles of relinquishing and storing carbon.

Dillon Marsh takes a visually similar approach to communicating hidden layers of matter, events and processes in his project *For What It's Worth*, visualizing the quantities of copper extracted from seven defunct South African mines. Marsh photographs the mines, then digitally imposes large copper spheres into these ruined landscapes, accurately scaled by the quantity of copper extracted over the lifetime of the mine. One image captioned 'Jubilee Mine, Concordia (1971 to 1973) Over 100 m deep, 6,500 tonnes of copper extracted' shows a gaping hole filled with murky green water in the foreground, with steps of excavated rock rising to a mountainous horizon in the background. A shiny, copper sphere rests in the water – impossibly enormous to fabricate so perfectly, yet significantly smaller than the hole it was extracted from, pointing to the immense quantity of excavation needed to extract the precious metal. The narrative is drawn by connecting caption and image, relating the data to the source.

The description of the project on Marsh's (2020) website states:

> Whether they are active or long dormant, mines speak of a combination of sacrifice and gain. The intention is to create a kind of visualisation of the merits and shortfalls of mining in South Africa, an industry that has shaped the history and economy of the country so radically.

As with the *Cosmos* sculpture, although the data underpinning the work is accurate the primary aim is to communicate a sense of vast processes that are difficult to comprehend, by creating a surreal encounter with a landscape. Knowing that the work is based on scientifically accurate data, yet seeing the uncanny in the familiar is a powerful communication strategy.

An obvious difference between these projects is in how we encounter them. Where Jarman and Gerhardt's *Cosmos* sphere can be encountered in the forest, Marsh's CGI works can only be viewed on screen, separated from the environments they depict. The immersiveness of *Cosmos* affords an opportunity for quiet reflection, a space to consider the relationship between trees, invisible carbon, and ourselves as living actors entangled in nature. Experiences that may shift a visitor's sense of connectedness with the natural world.

Another difference is the 'authorial intervention'. Marsh's work is overtly political about the impact of human conquest of the earth. His image captions and the project rationale on his website point us towards an intended interpretation, in the same way the title and labels on an information graphic might. Conversely, although the location of *Cosmos* is included on the forest map and a 'making of' video is shown at the forest entrance hut, no signage or explanatory text is included on or around the work in situ. Where *Cosmos* communicates subtly, Marsh uses a combination of image and caption to spell out his intent.

In a subsequent series titled *Counting the Costs*, Marsh applies the same photographic manipulation technique to visualize the loss of glacial ice. From scientific reports, Marsh compiled data on the rate that particular glaciers in India and Nepal are losing mass, then digitally created accurately scaled balls of ice and imposed them on urban landscapes in these countries. Unlike his mining series, these landscapes feature people going about their everyday lives, captioned with statistics the ice balls are based on. An image of a young family walking hand in hand through a residential area, oblivious to the huge ball of ice on the road behind them, is captioned '92.58 cubic meters – the average volume of ice lost on Neh Nar glacier every hour'. In a ramshackle marketplace, three men talk over a cart of papayas, oblivious to the ball of melting ice metres away: '7.06 cubic meters – the average volume of ice lost on Naradu glacier every minute.' Bringing humans into the uncanny landscape adds an emotional hook. In particular, rather than depicting people reacting in shock, that Marsh's images depict people oblivious to the metaphorical problem as they move through daily life, strikes a powerful chord.

Olafur Eliasson's *Ice Watch* (2014–19) communicates glacial melting in a more tangible way, by placing twelve blocks of ice – cast offs from the Greenland ice sheet – in a clock formation in a prominent location. The work presents 'a tangible and immediate testimony of the dramatic effects of climate change'. Unlike Marsh's oblivious people, documentation of *Ice Watch* on Eliasson's website has multiple photographs of visitors, young and old, embracing the ice, eyes closed and faces pressed against the cold surface of the melting blocks. We see in them a sense of awe at these actual ice blocks, a distant crisis brought in view – the vastness, the speed of melt. Janet Brown (2015), Associate Director of Climate Generation, describes her experience:

> Pictures and words don't do justice to the visceral effect of standing in the middle of these massive pieces of ice while the bells tolled in the plaza. I openly wept. Not the teary-eyed, this-is-so-sad kind of cry, but a guttural, wrenching wail.

On Eliasson's site, translucent phrases scroll over the documentary images, including being with, looking up close, feeling present, community, connecting space, destabilization. These function as captions of Eliasson's communication aim. Eliasson's work is necessarily less permanent than *Cosmos* – the melting ice-clock being the material and the problem – so documentation is important. The first narrative was in the encounter, the secondary narrative is encountering the experience vicariously through the documentary images of others' encounters.

Eliasson's work also recalls a precedent to some of the projects under discussion here, that of the practice of Land and Environment art, which saw sculptural artists directly engaging with the landscape around them. Robert Smithson's *Spiral Jetty* (1970) is perhaps the most famous of this genre of work, representing what may have been seen as poetic and embedded engagements with the landscape at the time, but in hindsight appear as colonial intrusions upon it. Smithson does however create an environment for encounter to place, as does Mark Dion's *A Meter of Jungle* (1992), where by literally bringing a meter of Amazon Jungle into the gallery, and dissecting and classifying the contents of this (again in an ultimately Western and colonizing manner), Dion asks a viewer to begin to comprehend the immensity of scale of the natural elements that make up the Amazon, and how they may themselves be entangled in such a system.

Moving data installation to a more community-based setting, Pekka Niittyvirta and Timo Aho's (2018) installation *Lines (57° 59′ N, 7° 16′W)* is an eerie site-specific installation which communicates the impact of rising sea levels on the Scottish coastal town North Uist. Activated at high tide, sensors shine three beams of light which represent estimates of sea level rise based on current scientific modelling. A glowing line cuts across doors and windows of the towns' buildings – a luminous flood-mark from a speculative future – and across fields to illuminate the anticipated new shoreline. The town is already experiencing the adverse effects of climate change, with building development stunted due to storm surge threats. For this community, the installation is a nightly warning, making it impossible to ignore ecological and infrastructural problems ahead. The artists state: 'Art has the potential to convey scientific data, complex ideas and concepts, in a powerful way that words or graphs fall short of. Hopefully, through this work, people can better visualise and relate to [the] reality' (cited in Yalcinkaya 2019). It is difficult to ignore slow moving ecological threats when faced with a 'real time' visual reference to changes ahead. The narrative is community specific, but also generalizable when we empathize with North Uist by imagining those lines cutting across our own homes and shores.

Similarly, Natalie Jeremijenko and David Benjamin's site-specific installation *Amphibious Architecture* (2009) used a range of sensors in New York's East River and Bronx River to monitor water quality, presence of fish and 'human interest' in the river ecosystem, and represent this data through lights which illuminate the water's surface. Fish leave a trail of lights as they travel and another line of sensors track oxygen levels in the water. Via an SMS interface, people receive updates about the river's health and can text-message the fish or contribute to a display which shows 'collective interest in the environment'. Benjamin and Jeremijenko (2009) describe the work as a 'data-driven dialogue between humans, fish and their shared environment'.

In 2017, Jeremijenko installed an iteration of the project in Hobart's River Derwent. There, the lights bobbing on buoys in the river respond to sensors measuring oxygen levels – markers of water contamination and warming due to climate change. Rather than trying to communicate complex data, the lights simply illuminate red or green – with additional white lights indicating text messages received from the community. Reviewing this work, Jeff Malpas (2017) reports Jeremijenko's aim is to 'shift our conceptions of ourselves and of our environment so as to enable a shift in the kinds and possibilities of agency' and notes that beyond communicating information, the work is underpinned by playfulness which is 'surely also part of the freeing-up of thinking that is necessary if we are to enable a healthier environment'. Jeremijenko's playfulness opens new ways of thinking about kinship – of course the fish can't receive text messages, but the act of sending one anyway makes you a participant in this ludic encounter.

Jeremijenko's *Amphibious Architecture* and the *Lines (57° 59' N, 7° 16'W)* installations are examples of projects in which we see and are potentially implicated in the action of the story as it is unfolding, rather than being told a story after the event. Jodi Newcombe (n.d.) describes a new breed of environmental artists united by an aim to reconnect humans to the non-human world, to provide a counterpoint to the:

> often disempowering and disengaging stream of numbers and statistics presented to us about climate change, pollution, and species and habitat loss. By responding to the local environment, art as barometer can seek engagement at a community level and spur on grassroots activism and management efforts.

Conclusion

While the works explored here do not represent an exhaustive survey of narrative objects that give rise to encounter mediated via data, they do paint a picture of this emerging genre of visualization. The encounter at the centre of each project makes space for experiences which invite us to pause, feel, imagine and converse in order to bring scientific data into public discourse: Zakpage's performance of songlines demonstrates how indigenous Australian storytelling on Country is part of a long-standing mnemonic system of recording and sharing ecological data; Berger and Keto's tantalisingly impossible encounter with radioactive jewellery that can be inherited but not worn invites us to consider deep time and the consequences for future generation of the energy we are harnessing now; Jarman and Gerhardt's encounter invites us to consider the carbon cycles occurring imperceptibly in the surrounding forest, and conjures ghosts of the scientists who collect and graph such data; Marsh's surreal landscapes provoke us to comprehend the mass scarring of earth due to mining and other human interventions; Eliasson's melting ice-clocks, Niittyvirta and Aho's digital watermarks, Jeremijenko and Benjamin's river interventions which allow us to 'talk back' to nature, all bring climate disasters into the lives of people removed from the sites of actual destruction, but soon to be affected by the global consequences.

An encounter with these projects reveals entangled relationships between human and non-human, phenomenological time and deep time. Through realization of this state of entanglement, a narrative arises; for each viewer, the narrative is unique. An encounter with an object, or within a physical space, is fundamentally different to viewing a visualization on page or screen, because in the encounter, the viewer becomes a participant – a character among other characters within an unfolding narrative. An encounter invites a subjective reading and writing of data to take place.

We also see a familiar form of encounter emerging in each of the projects – one that can be described as 'uncanny'; a making-strange or de-familiarization as a result of rendering the unfamiliar in the familiar, or vice versa, to reveal human entanglement within the world. As Delphi Carstens and Mel Roberts (2017, p. 202) point out 'The uncanny describes troubled nature-culture relations, a ghostlike porosity of boundaries between fiction and fact celebrated by indigenous peoples but denied and reviled by post-Enlightenment Western ways of seeing.' This points to why we see these methods starting to appear as we begin to realize that these post-Enlightenment Western ways of seeing have not served us well, and have been devastating on multiple levels.

To move forward, we offer a provocation: how do we (those of us perpetuating a Western capitalist world view) represent, visualize, understand, exist within an entangled world without continuing to engage in ongoing colonial practices of collecting, labelling and boxing, and find alternatives to extending these practices into our approaches to fields such as big data? Indeed, if we think of one of the most celebrated historic symbols of this very thing, we may ask what a Wunder minus the Kammer may look like? The beginning of an answer is starting to appear in the projects outlined in this chapter, and while none of them may provide a solution, they do help to frame a way of looking for a solution in a new (yet ancient) way.

Notes

1. The project was documented in the 2017 book *Future remains: A cabinet of curiosities for the Anthropocene*, University of Chicago Press.
2. In *The Great Derangement*, Amitav Ghosh (2016) points to the increasing use of the term uncanny to describe both the freakish weather events associated with climate change, and the awareness of human entanglement in nature that is stirred by such events. See also 'Uncanny Objects in the Anthropocene', a special edition of *Australian Humanities Review* for a collection of essays exploring how 'the Anthropocene uncanny invites us to re-consider histories and objects in new and unexpected ways' (Stark, Schlunke & Edmonds 2018).
3. This is not to state that data practices are not useful and critical ways in which to investigate and communicate ideas about the world. However, they must be understood as 'material, contingent and fallible processes' that have specific ways of generating knowledge (Amoore & Pitoukh 2015, p. 361).
4. Engagement with charts, graphs and the like of climate data via representationalism also generates a public discourse focussed on which more 'truly' pictures the current status of the world or its future (see Latour 2010, 2014).
5. Monin, M. *Coding Materialities* (forthcoming doctoral dissertation), University of NSW, Sydney, uses Tsing's concept of encounter to describe artworks that enable

us to notice the material and epistemological actualities of recent machine learning assemblages and how they are reconfiguring knowing and seeing.

6. See www.commonground.org.au/learn/songlines for an overview of songlines, and the difficulty of explaining this knowledge system to non-Indigenous people, or Margo Neale's book *Songlines* for a more detailed account.

7. Long-living cultures with an ecological disposition must be noted here, such as the first nations people of the continent now known as Australia's enduring interdependent connection to Country. An example of this connection to an animate Country over deep time, is the Garuwanga calendar cycle of the D'harawal people of now-Sydney which encompasses four deep time seasons, taking into account ice-ages and massive sea level changes. As described by Frances Bodkin, D'harawal Woman of the Bidigal Clan, 'The Garuwanga Cycle is the longest cycle of all, lasting from 12,000 to 20,000 years. It has four seasons, and our position in this cycle is judged only by the sea levels.' (Bodkin cited in Malone, Truong & Gray 2017, p. xii)

8. An example of future impacts of radioactive waste as well as the indeterminacies of encounter is evident in the failing security of the concrete Runit Dome in the Marshall Islands. This site contains nuclear waste from atom bomb tests undertaken by the United States in the 1940s. Today, the containment site is threatened by the effects of climate change such as rising sea levels and more frequent storms. More immediately, the impacts of these tests have destroyed the livelihoods and health of the dri-Enewetak, people of Enewetak. See Jose, Wall and Hinzel (2016).

9. See Jarman and Gerhardt (2014) for a short film communicating the laborious design and production process.

References

Albrecht, G, Sartore, G-M, Connor, L, Higginbotham, N, Freeman, S, Kelly, B, Stain, H, Tonna, A & Pollard, G 2007, 'Solastalgia: The distress caused by environmental change', *Australasian psychiatry: Bulletin of Royal Australian and New Zealand College of Psychiatrists*, Vol. 15 Suppl 1, pp. S95–8, DOI:10.1080/10398560701701288.

Alderson, R 2014, 'Dillon Marsh visualises how much copper was produced in South African mines', *It'sNiceThat*, accessed 2 Oct 2019, https://www.itsnicethat.com/articles/dillon-marsh-for-what-its-worth.

Amoore, L & Piotukh, V 2015, 'Life beyond big data: Governing with little analytics', *Economy and Society*, vol. 44, no. 3, pp. 341–66.

Benjamin, D & Jeremijenko, N 2009, *Amphibious architecture: New York Harbour* Spontaneous Interventions, http://www.spontaneousinterventions.org/project/amphibious-architecture.

Bennett, J 2010, *Vibrant matter: A political ecology of things*, Duke University Press, Durham.

Berger, E & Keto, M 2016, *Inheritance*, Inheritance Project, http://inheritance-project.net/.

Brown, J 2015, 'The end of ice', blog post, *Climate Generation: A Will Steger legacy*, 8 December, accessed 31 October 2019, https://www.climategen.org/blog/the-end-of-ice/.

Carstens, D & Roberts, M 2017, 'The things that knowledge cannot eat', in T Reeves-Evison & JK Shaw (eds), *Fiction as method*, Sternberg Press, Berlin, pp. 193–234.
Climate Commission 2013, *Critical decade presentation*, video, Slideshare, https://www.slideshare.net/ClimateCommission/critical-decadepresentation-for-website-24639298.
Dion, M 1992, 'A meter of jungle. Rio Museum of Modern Art', in J Kastner & B Wallis (eds) 1998, *Land and environmental art*, Phaidon, London, pp. 22–3.
Drucker, J 2012, 'Diagrammatic writing', *New Formations*, vol. 78, pp. 83–101.
Drucker, J 2014, *Graphesis: Visual forms of knowledge production*, Harvard University Press, Cambridge.
Eliasson, O 2014-2019, *Ice Watch*, accessed 17 August 2019, https://olafureliasson.net/archive/artwork/WEK109190/ice-watch().
Ghosh, A 2016, *The great derangement: Climate change and the unthinkable*, Chicago University Press, Chicago.
Haraway, DJ 2016, *Staying with the trouble: Making kin in the Chthulucene*, Duke University Press, Durham and London.
Hayles, NK 2012, *How we think: Digital media and contemporary technogenesis*, University of Chicago Press, Chicago.
Jarman, R & Gerhardt, J 2014, *Cosmos*, https://semiconductorfilms.com/art/cosmos/.
Jose, C, Wall K & Hinzel JH 2016, 'This dome in the Pacific houses tons of radioactive waste - and it's leaking', *Guardian*, 3 July, https://www.theguardian.com/world/2015/jul/03/runit-dome-pacific-radioactive-waste.
Joshi, K 2017, 'Caring about climate change: It's time to build a bridge between data and emotion', *Guardian*, 7 June, https://www.theguardian.com/commentisfree/2017/jun/07/caring-about-climate-change-its-time-to-build-a-bridge-between-data-and-emotion.
Latour, B 2010, 'An Attempt at a "Compositionist Manifesto"', *New Literary History*, vol. 41, no. 3, pp. 471–90.
Latour, B 2014, 'War and peace in an age of ecological conflicts', http://www.bruno-latour.fr/sites/default/files/130-VANCOUVER-RJE-14pdf.pdf.
Malone, K, Truong, S & Gray, T (eds) 2017, 'Reimagining sustainability in precarious times', Springer, ProQuest Ebook Central, http://ebookcentral.proquest.com/lib/uts/detail.action?docID=4788929.
Malpas, J 2017, 'Amphibious architecture – what does the Derwent want?', *Landscape Australia: Design, Urbanism, Planning*, 9 January, https://landscapeaustralia.com/articles/Amphibious-Architecture/.
Marsh, D 2019, *Counting the costs*, Dillon Marsh, http://www.dillonmarsh.com/ctc.html.
Marsh, D 2020, *For what it's worth*, Dillon Marsh, http://www.dillonmarsh.com/fwiw.html.
Morton, T 2012, *The ecological thought*, Harvard University Press, Cambridge.
Newcombe, J n.d., 'Art as barometer: Uncovering a new breed of instrumental artist', *Carbon Arts*, accessed 17 October 2019, http://www.carbonarts.org/articles/art-as-barometer/.
Niittyvirta, P & Aho, T 2018, *Lines (57° 59' N, 7° 16'W)*, http://www.niittyvirta.com/lines-57-59-n-7-16w/.
Nixon, R 2011, *Slow violence and the environmentalism of the poor*, Harvard University Press, Cambridge.
Page, A 2020, personal communication, 8 Jan 2020.

Robin, L & Muir, C 2015, 'Slamming the Anthropocene: Performing climate change in museums', *reCollections*, vol. 10, no. 1, https://recollections.nma.gov.au/issues/volume_10_number_1/papers/slamming_the_anthropocene.

Stark, H, Schlunke, K & Edmonds, P 2018, 'Introduction: Uncanny objects in the Anthropocene', *Australian Humanities Review*, no. 63, pp. 22–30.

Stoknes, PE 2015, *What we think about when we try not to think about global warming*, Chelsea Green Publishing, Vermont.

Tsing, A 2015, *Mushroom at the end of the world*, Princeton University Press, New Jersey.

Tsing, A, Swanson, H, Gan, E & Bubandt, N 2017, *Arts of living on a damaged planet*, University of Minnesota Press, Minneapolis.

Yalcinkaya, G 2019, 'Lines light installation demonstrates the "catastrophic impact" of rising sea-levels', *Dezeen*, 18 March, https://www.dezeen.com/2019/03/18/lines-pekka-niittyvirta-timo-aha-light-installation/.

List of works

Benjamin, D & Jeremijenko, N 2009, Amphibious Architecture: New York Harbour. Available Online: http://www.spontaneousinterventions.org/project/amphibious-architecture

Berger, E & Keto, M 2016, Inheritance. Available Online: http://inheritance-project.net/

Dion, M 1992, A Meter of Jungle. Rio Museum of Modern Art Eliasson, O. (2014–2019), Ice Watch. Available Online: https://olafureliasson.net/archive/artwork/WEK109190/ice-watch (accessed 17 August 2019).

Jarman, R & Gerhardt, J 2014, Cosmos. Semiconductor Films, online: https://semiconductorfilms.com/art/cosmos/

Marsh, D 2020, For What It's Worth, Dillon Marsh. Available Online: http://www.dillonmarsh.com/fwiw.html

Marsh, D 2019, Counting the Costs. Available Online: http://www.dillonmarsh.com/ctc.html

Niittyvirta, P and Aho, T 2018, Lines (57° 59' N, 7° 16'W). Available Online: http://www.niittyvirta.com/lines-57-59-n-7-16w/

Smithson, R 1970, Spiral Jetty. Available Online: https://www.diaart.org/visit/visit-our-locations-sites/robert-smithson-spiral-jetty

Zakpage 2019, 'Songlines', Clever Country. Available Online: https://vimeo.com/383041274

7
EXPLORING DIGITAL-MATERIAL HYBRIDITY IN THE POST-DIGITAL MUSEUM

Daniela Petrelli and Nick Dulake

Introduction

Museums are, by their nature, the expression of the world's material culture: their acknowledged role is to collect and preserve artefacts for future generations and to communicate their meaning. The early museums were places where touching, holding and smelling were an integral part of the visit, a courtesy paid by the curator or the collection owner to their visitors or guests (Classen 2007). By the mid-nineteenth-century the personal, physical relation with the object was gone, mostly because the widening of the audience (and the consequent increase in visitors number) made the display behind glass inevitable (Classen 2007). In the twentieth century the object-information package became the norm (Dudley 2010). Today, much of the communication is performed by words rather than by the objects themselves and digital is the preferred way to deliver information. As digital media does not require space beyond the means of display, museums have a tendency to over package content that is often missed or underused by visitors. Indeed, since the multimedia PC arrived on the exhibition floor in the early 1990s (Serrell & Raphling 1992), through to mobile devices (Szymanski et al. 2007) and interactive tables (Hornecker 2008), field studies have repeatedly shown that only a fraction of visitors engage with a fraction of the digital content available on the interactive devices. There may be several reasons for this observed behaviour, such as a disinterest for the technology, usability issues or time available, but a repeated mistake made in the interaction design is to focus on how the information is *delivered* rather than how the information is *received* (Serrell & Raphling 1992): visitors to museums do not have the time or patience to seek if a digital communication device holds anything of interest (Hornecker 2008; Serrell & Raphling 1992) and enjoy much more looking, touching, smelling and listening (Falk & Dierking 2012).

The emerging Internet of Things (IoT) promises to bridge the gap between physical and digital: where objects are active and connected with other objects and people; they sense the environment and act in the world; they collect and communicate data that can be processed and used locally or remotely. IoT opens up new opportunities to designing museum-visiting experiences centred on tangible and embodied interaction: digitally augmented objects become interactive, they can control the delivery of digital media and collect usage data that, in turn, enable personalization and data analytics. Through IoT, it is then possible to bind together digital content with material collections, to provide visitors with radically different ways to engage with an exhibition and to museums new opportunities to monitor and stay connected with their audience.

This chapter discusses the way in which digital materiality has been explored within the EU project meSch – Material Encounters with Digital Cultural Heritage (2013–17). MeSch aimed to bring back the value of materiality in museums through the power of embedded digital technology and, in doing so, to close the gap currently existing between the material and the digital museum collections. From the many experiments and interventions within the meSch project, three interactive installations co-designed with museum curators that explore these issues of digital-material hybridity are shared here.

Making the digital and the material talk to each other

Through IoT, digital-material hybrids enter the toolbox of designer. The challenge in a museum context lies in weaving the digital and the material to create immersive and novel visitors' experiences that seamlessly cross the boundary between the physical collection and digital or online content. There is a fine balance to strike as the digital could detract from the physical experience rather than augment it. As we know digital media captures attention and can easily distract visitors from their surroundings, the museum and its heritage (Szymanski et al. 2007; vom Lehn and Heath 2003).

A first materialization occurs in making digital content located in place, integrated within the exhibition, rather than being an add-on, files uploaded on a separate device. When made material through the incorporation into tangible interactive objects, digital content, including data, can become more visible to visitors and more straightforward to access. Digital content materialization enables curators to make evident that any museum exhibition is an interpretation and that alternative interpretations are also possible. Through IoT technologies, multiple stories can be lined up in the physical space for visitors to choose from (see case studies 1 and 3). Museums can clearly put on display multiple stories or different opinions that surround a cultural artefact; multiple and contrasting voices can question a visitors' preconceptions and challenge them to make up their own minds and engage in an exercise of meaning-making.[1] Furthermore, offering options and asking visitors to consider and to choose changes the pace of the visit; it can make people slow down, think and look more carefully. Objects on display become means for discussion and exchange often across cultural divides created by geography, life experience, or by the passing of time. These multifaceted, connected, digital-material interfaces support museums in becoming more relevant to contemporary society, shifting their role from guardians of collections to ambassadors of cultural values and significance via an endless reframing of the past in contemporary culture (Thomas 2016).

In all this, the museum designer must play a collaborating role with the museum curators to create the network of content – through the collection or the exhibition – and the way to interact with it. Visitors can be invited to choose their own experience and can create their own storytelling out of the many possible paths lied down by the multidisciplinary team. To effectively capitalize on the potential of digital-material hybridities, the design of an interactive museum exhibition has to be both holistic and bespoke: it has to simultaneously consider the content, the objects and the technological platform for the specific visiting experience. Content must be designed and crafted (Not & Petrelli 2019). To design content is to create an evocative experience by intertwining the narratives with the sense of being in place and the bodily interaction with the collection. Indeed the ability to deeply engage visitors at both cognitive and emotional levels depends on the stories and the values communicated, as well as the way they are presented (crafted). Thus, although it is imperative that content remains rooted in the museum's archive and curators' knowledge, the way content is presented through fully utilizing the potential of digital media forms and is key to how this content is consumed: historical diaries performed by actors, archive videos and photos, songs and poetry are all media types that engage the visitor both emotionally and cognitively (see case study 1 and 3). Equally effective is to use humour and playfulness for example to ask visitors to step back in time to make choices that could change their lives (see case study 2). In essence, digital-material content can be designed to stimulate the senses, curiosity and reflection, and to amplify the emotion of being in a particular place or in the presence of a particular artefact.

In digital-material hybrid museum experiences, physical objects containing IoT technologies are often created to facilitate the interaction with multimedia content as visitors move around an exhibition; it is also a way for museum curators to collect data on visitor's movements and their choices. The design of the *objects* that the visitors can manipulate is important. While the museum content might question a visitors' beliefs and asks them to reflect on different perspectives, the objects visitors manipulate to access the content is a means of physical and emotional engagement. Touch is an interactive sense, when we touch we are touched in return. The action of touch is intentional and active. Moreover, the physical interaction with the world is not limited to the hand, it extends to the body and the physical experience of the body is the foundation of self-awareness (Sonneveld & Schifferstein 2008). Tangible and embodied interaction, then, is the bases of feeling in contact, a bodily involvement of the self: while hearing and seeing are distant senses that create a distance between the self and the other, touch brings us closer both physically and emotionally (Sonneveld & Schifferstein 2008). This phenomenon of embodied feeling is particularly important within the context of storytelling in digital-material hybrid museums when interactive tactile objects are the means to experience different ways of reading objects, places and lives. The design of such interactive, transitional objects can transform the museum visit into an active experience as these objects can hold the engagement, and trigger emotions (Dulake, Hornecker & Petrelli 2019). Through the product design of interactive objects, IoT in museums has the potential to bring to the fore the crucial role of materiality and embodiment to complement cognition with emotion, which is essential for our understanding, appreciation, imagination and creativity (Dudley 2010; Naumova 2015). Examples of hybrid objects are presented in the next section in this chapter together with a discussion on their evocative power and engagement potential.

Crucially, the design of the *technical platform* that complements the design of content and objects is of equal importance. An IoT platform is essential to operationalize the interaction across the physical-digital divide, and to create experiences that go beyond the here-and-now of the museum visit. By collecting data of use, IoT-enabled objects facilitate personalization, where extra content can be selected and packaged for a specific visitor on the bases of their own individual visit. Museums are rich cultural environments that invite exploration and stimulate curiosity wherein visitors can pursue their interests and discovery new ones they did not know they had (Thomas 2016). How each visitor experiences the same museum settings and the same stories is highly personal and embedded in the individual's interests, knowledge and experiences. Some visitors arrive with a specific learning intent, others just to pass the time, others from a sense of obligation (Falk 2009). Somewhat idealistically, what museums wish for is to meet all those different expectations. They want the visitor to leave with a lasting memory of the experience, and preferably for the memory to become the starting point for a long-term connection.

Three case studies

To illustrate how hybrid digital-material experiences emerge from the simultaneous design of content, object, interaction and data usage, we describe three case studies that shared the same IoT technology but implement very different museum experiences. Each installation used a combination of NFC (Near Field Communication) tags and readers (stickers with small microchips to store minimal information that can be read by in-range mobile devices), data logging of visitor interaction, and the generation of a personalized feedback and recommendations. What makes the experiences substantially different is that they were designed to provoke different emotive experiences: empathy and emotions, in the first case study centred on personal experiences of the First World War; playfulness and humour, in the second that introduced visitors to the ancient Roman belief system; and an understanding of the city past and present, in the third case study revealing the contrasting voices of occupied The Hague during the Second World War.

The three case studies also have in common the use of physical interactive objects that could be carried by the visitor through their museum experience. The interactive objects, all different and bespoke, log the visit when used: at the exit log data it transformed into a data driven souvenir that reminds the visitor of their experience while also providing a link to additional online resources as in case study 1, or to provide access to personalized content as in case study 3, and to conclude the visit in case study 2. These individually tailored souvenirs are not only the materialization of data drawn from the personal experience of the museum but are also a bridge to future online explorations which can keep visitors connected with the museum long term.

Case study 1: Touching and being touched

The installation 'Fort Pozzacchio: Voices from the Past' (Figure 7.1) comprises interactive stations to complement the displays of artillery and ammunition from the First World War in the Artillery Gallery at the Museo Storico Italiano della Guerra, the national museum of war in Italy.[2] Fort Pozzacchio is representative of the First World War conflict fought in this area, the northeast of Italy, between the Italian and Austro-Hungarian armies. Located on a mountain about 30-minute drive from the museum, Fort Pozzacchio is a masterpiece of Austro-Hungarian engineering: a three-story fortress of galleries and caverns dug into the mountain where soldiers lived, observed the movement of the enemies and fought them. The Artillery Gallery is situated in a very similar environment to Fort Pozzacchio: a Second World War bomb shelter dug into the rock under the museum's castle. In this evocative space the challenge was to create an immersive and expressive experience of the actual Fort Pozzacchio, a site with a strong physical and historical identity. Curators were keen to tell the story of how the fort affected the life of many before, during and after the war. Letters, diaries and oral history records from the museum's archives provided the exhibition content. This included the testimony of the engineer who designed the fort, officers and soldiers of both armies, and many civilians from the village nearby. The aim of the interactive installation in the museum was to make the visitors look with different eyes at the display of artillery and ammunition collected at the end of the conflict along the trenches in the Alps. Indeed, before the redesign of the gallery, only weaponry enthusiasts with a specific interest in munitions typically spent time in the gallery. According to the museum curators, most visits were very short (about 15 min), in part because of the cold and hostile environment and in part because the exhibits were difficult to interpret despite several panels presented the human dimension of the war, including statistical data on the human cost of a war that killed and displaced many.

For the exhibition redesign the content was selected and prepared by the museum curators in the form of first-person testimonies – as if voices from the past were speaking directly to the visitors. The stories were clustered in three themes around: the fort itself, the experience of the civilians and the memories of a single battle. These testimonies were labelled alongside a series of small bowls set into a physical interactive bench, which worked as a timeline: each bowl had the name and date of a testimony. At the entrance to the gallery the visitor received a 'pebble' which plays a story when placed on a testimony bowl (Figure 7.1). The pebble was designed to fit the hand comfortably, to invite the hand to play with it. Being made of polyurethane it retained some body heat; the size and shape made it feel friendly and familiar (Dulake, Hornecker & Petrelli 2019). The pebble, the content organization in themes and in a timeline, and the overall setting for the interactive components of the exhibition were the outcome of a co-design process. Through this process the metaphor of the pebble was chosen as a means of interaction and the media and the settings were chosen to enliven the cave-like environment and to create an emotional connection between the visitors and the testimonies. In the first station a hand-drawn white-on-black animation underpins the stories of the fort: the engineer who sank the fort within the mountain, the civilians who built the road and the fort itself, the commander and his soldiers' living in it and its dismantling after the war was over. Projected onto a black curtain hanging

DIGITAL-MATERIAL HYBRIDITY IN THE POST-DIGITAL MUSEUM

on the cavern wall, the drawings slowly emerged from the blackness of the cavern like memories resurfacing to the present.

The second station holds the testimonies from the village nearby: the happiness with the new road to the fort; the desperation when forced to flee their homes or join the army; and the slow return to normal life after the war. Their stories were made more vivid by the use of soundscapes: the whistle of the train taking the conscripts away; or the school bell signalling the return to normal life.

The third station, positioned at the end of the gallery deep within the mountain, held the memories of soldiers from enemy armies and that of the Austro-Hungarian chaplain, all recounting the same battle, a defeated night attack by the Italians. Excerpts from the protagonists' diaries were recited by actors in video portraits that talked directly to the visitor. These were projected on

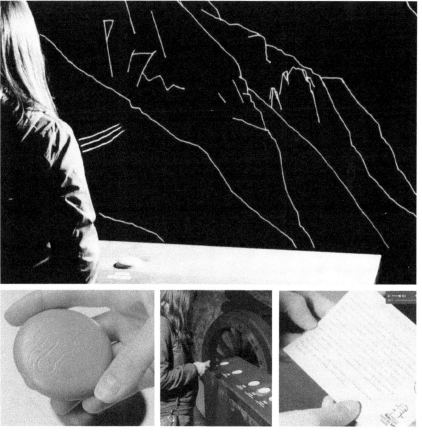

Figure 7.1 The elements of Fort Pozzacchio installation (from bottom left to right): the pebble; the interactive bench with the testimonies slots; the printed postcard; the animation in station 1 being played (top). Images: Daniela Petrelli/Nick Dulake.

a canvas hanging in the cavern to create a sense of intimacy, as in a confession – a theatrical setting.

In terms of technology, the 'pebbles' concealed a read-write NFC tag that recorded the usage data from the visit: what was listened to and the order of play. When leaving the exhibition, the visitor returned the pebble and received a printed personalized postcard, a keepsake composed on the bases of the log of their visit. The postcard had an historical photo of the Forte on one side and a 'handwritten' summary of the stories the visitor has listened to on the other, with the post stamp of the day. A URL printed on the postcard pointed to the museum archives for those visitors who want to know more.

Museum staff monitoring the new installation reported that visitors' tended to stay longer than before (30 minutes) despite it being a cold and damp place. The new interactive exhibition was described as immersive and evocative, the stories touching. Visitors commented that the experience gave meaning to the pieces on display: 'To my eyes, this is not a cannon anymore. I now see a means of destruction, not of the enemy, but of the lives of normal people'. The data-object, the interactive pebble, empowered visitors giving them the choice of which testimony to play, and a reason to listen. The pebble connected visitors with the people from the past, to stories that provoked a sense of personal empathy and affective responses, as another visitor said, 'With the pebble you take those stories with you … ' ' … I feel like I am entering the lives of others.'

Case study 2: Choose your future

The second case study is an intervention for Chesters Roman Fort and the Clyton Museum, one of the English Heritage properties along Hadrian's Wall in the north of England. The small one-room museum hosts John Clayton's collection of Roman archaeological finds from along Hadrian's Wall, mostly altars and religious relives displayed over several rows as at the time of its opening in 1896. This very dense display (Figure 7.2) was overwhelming for most visitors who consequently only spent a few minutes looking around and often left without appreciating the richness and relevance of a collection that holds several unique pieces. The purpose of the intervention was to slow down the visitors and engage them with the collection in a meaningful and enriching way; the curators wanted visitors to see the stones as objects of great significance for the Romans and to understand them as objects that were once interacted with, rather than just looked at as is the case today. The design process initially considered concepts that focused on the work of early archaeologists, such as John Clyton, but the final installation was designed as a means to challenge visitors assumptions (or knowledge) about Roman belief systems and the Roman Empire more widely. Roman religion was indeed very different from contemporary ones. It was transactional in nature meaning that, after an offering, one would expect favours from that deity. Moreover, the group of Roman deities was ever increasing in size as new gods were added every time a new land was conquered: the local gods became Roman gods and travelled with the Roman Empire. As such, along Hadrian's Wall, altars to the traditional Roman gods Minerva and Mercury were found, but also references to the cult of Mithras from modern-day Iran, local (British) deities and gods of war that arrived with German and Spanish troops.

On entering the redesigned museum vestibule, enhanced through the addition of interactive media, visitors are invited by Juno, the queen of the Roman gods, to collect a votive lamp with three offerings.[3] Inside the museum the visitors have the opportunity to gift the lights to three deities which will determine their future on Hadrian's Wall. There are thirteen deities ready to accept the offering so visitors have to make a choice based on if they prefer to secure health or wealth, success in war or in business, and if they prefer local or foreign deities. What choices they make in the museum determines 'the oracle' they will receive on their way out, when the extinguished lamp is returned to Juno. Data collected during the visit on the three deities that received the offerings informs what is said by the oracle, the conclusion of the ritual. The visitor's oracle is printed on a postcard and the message changes depending on the choices made in the museum (Figure 7.2). Besides a description of each of the three chosen deities, the card prints the date of the day and a humorous phrase hinting at the personal future of the visitor based on the offerings they made.

In this case study the strongly embodied experiential element is enacted through the theatrical performance that the visitor is invited to play when embarking on a journey of discovery of the Roman religion and culture. The lamp acts as both a token and a mechanism for engaging in a bespoke experience and the postcard is the resolution of the riddle that lets the visitor into part of the now obscure Roman culture, religion and customs.

From a technical perspective the IoT setting of the exhibition consisted of a set of NFC tags – one for each deity, an NFC reader within the lamp and the initiating/printing station for Juno's shrine. The design of the object, a beautifully crafted lamp in walnut, embodies the ritual of the offering (it fits the hand, is warm, and shows the lights still to gift) (Dulake, Hornecker & Petrelli 2019). Textual content is minimal and limited to the curatorial labels and the text on the postcard. While many visitors enjoyed the experience, others commented there was not enough information to understand to which deities they were offering until the experience is concluded. For some visitors not knowing the meaning of their choices until the end of the experience resulted in frustration, some visitors would rather have chosen more informed offerings based on a definite goal, for example, health versus wealth. A few visitors, probably very religious themselves, said they did not like to take part in a pagan ritual. We set out to design an experience to transform a quick and superficial visit into a deeper engagement

Figure 7.2 The interaction with *My Roman Pantheon* (from top left): collecting the lamp from Juno's shrine; in the museum offering a light; back at the shrine returning the lamp and collecting the 'oracle'; four different personalised postcards. Images: Daniela Petrelli/ Nick Dulake.

with the stones that would give visitors a better understanding of their meanings in the ancient Roman culture. Instead of telling a story, we invited visitors to act, to choose their gods: these adverse reactions may signal we were successful in engaging visitors with the intangible, the spiritual, others' believes.

Case study 3: A matter of perspective

'The Hague and the Atlantic Wall: War in the City of Peace' was a temporary exhibition at MUSEON in The Hague (the Netherlands) visited by about 40,000 people over a period of 6 months.[4] The exhibition explored the impact of the Atlantic Wall structure on the city of The Hague and the people living there, and what it meant for the identity of the city after the war. The Atlantic Wall was a defensive system built by the Nazis in the Second World War along the north coast of continental Europe to defend it against possible attacks by the Allies. During the German occupation, a third of the city of The Hague was demolished to make space for the Wall and the Nazi headquarters. Civilians were evacuated and displaced, their houses demolished; deep trenches, walls and checkpoints were built. After the war the defensive structure was dismantled and in its place was built the Peace Quarter with UN institutions and the International Court of Justice.

The exhibition had eleven stations representing the quarters of the city affected by the Wall, for example, how the beach became a mined field and why the Peace Quarter was built. Objects on display, labels and panels provided specific content while an eight-min introductory film gave an overview; a few multimedia stations had a quiz game and videos-on-demand. Finally, a wall-sized carousel of historical photos in the background set the atmosphere.

The curatorial team wanted to also include an optional interactive experience so that visitors not wishing to interact could still understand the main points and appreciate the exhibition by simply reading the panels and looking at the exhibits. The interactive experience had to offer something unique, that is to say, not a rephrasing of the content in the panels on a different medium, but a special, richer and personal experience mediated by tangible yet digital interaction. To complement the curatorial tone of the exhibition, the interactive elements were designed to reveal three personal perspectives of those involved in the events during the Second World War: how the German soldiers believed they were defending the Dutch population from the Allays; how the civilians were displaced, resisted and resented the occupation; and how the civil servants dealt with doing the bid of the German occupiers.

While the physical exhibition recounted the historical facts, the digital interaction offered three personal points of view as themes running through. At each station/city-quarter, visitors could listen to one or all of the three perspectives presented as personal stories (e.g. excerpts from diaries), newspaper and radio material (e.g. German propaganda), satirical songs or video archival material. Each point of view was represented by a replica of an object used in everyday life in the Second World War. There were six replicas, one for each perspective for Dutch and English (respectively): a beer mug and a Dutch-German dictionary for the soldier; a surrogate tea bag and sugar box for the civilian; an armband and a pass for the civil servant (Figure 7.3).

The crafted replicas, augmented with an NFC tag, were manufactured at a high quality, to the point of recreating a Nazi stamp to validate the passes: the intent was that of increasing the aesthetic value of the replicas as a way of engaging the visitors with the stories (Dulake, Hornecker & Petrelli 2019). The installation recorded the interaction: which stations had been visited, which perspective was played, in which language and for how long. As in the previous case studies, this data collected during the visit was used to print a personalized souvenir at the end of the visit: the replica triggered the printing of a postcard with the stamps of the three stations where the visitor spent the most of their time assuming those were the three topics the visitor was most interested in. The postcard had a unique code that could be used to access an extended experience online in the form of more content related to their visit preferences. The code corresponded to the full data set of the visiting log; the log was used to personalize online content: the code unlocked a personalized website where the visitor was able to look back to what they have seen in the exhibition or, more important, to listen to the stories they missed. The content of the exhibition was displayed online on the city map and visitors were invited to upload personal

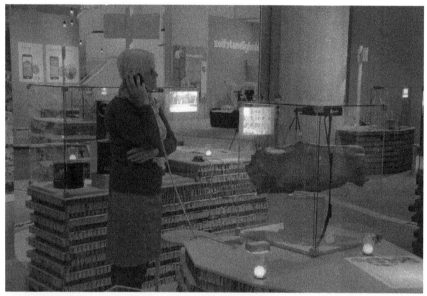

 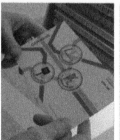 

Figure 7.3 The Interaction at the Atlantic Wall exhibition (from bottom left – clockwise): the replicas representing the different perspectives; a visitor using the sugar box to listen to the stories of the Dutch civilians; the personalized website; and the postcard. Images: Daniela Petrelli/Nick Dulake.

and family memories of the events, thus making the online experience richer in content than the exhibition itself.

Overall about 15,000 visitors used the replicas, but only a fraction continued online (see Petrelli et al. (2016) for a thorough analysis). Taken together, the visiting logs showed the curators that the audience had used the replicas representing the German perspective as much as they used the one for the Dutch, while the civil servant's point of view interested only a minority. This important finding helped to justify the extra effort of creating the three contrasting narratives that ran through the exhibition. Indeed, observations showed many visitors listened to more than one perspective at a time, for example, couples visiting together choose two different perspectives and joined in the listening. It showed that, given the opportunity, visitors were interested in contrasting perspectives of the war; the German propaganda or the collaborationism of some government officers, challenged the citizens of The Hague to reconsider what they thought about a critical period in the recent history of their city.

Designing across the digital-material divide

The pace of change brought about by digital technology has often changed and intensified our cultural experiences in recent years, a sign that

> we are in this postdigital phase where it is much more mixed. Design has changed, all of these things [exhibition and digital media] are now one ... the opportunities being in the links between physical and the digital rather than having them as distinct realms.
>
> (Romeo, cited in Parry 2013, p. 32)

Museum asset currently divided into a material collection and digital media become one as the material and the digital become porous and permeable to each other features. IoT enables new hybridity facilitating a continuous interplay between the digital and the material and vice versa. There is an opportunity to rethink the way museums offer content and engage visitors across multiple media channels.

The three museum case study interventions explore how the digital and the material can be combined to bring places and stories from the past into the present, creating immersive experiences where technology complements heritage (as opposed to competing with it for the visitors' attention). Taken together, the case studies illustrate this process of continuous shift and exchange between the visitors and the museum and between the material and the digital. Some key reflections on designing across the physical-digital divide in a museum context are outlined below:

By making digital content tangible via smart objects, the digital becomes physical, evident and available for the visitors to consume. Seeing alternatives makes the visitor active: materialization allows the visitors to choose and empowers them to create their own interactive storytelling.
Tangible and embodied interaction makes the visit personal: touching, holding, carrying and using an interactive object supports a sense of embodiment and presence that an app does not.
Augmented objects can challenge the visitor to make choices; when they choose, they leave a digital trace (log); in this way the physical (exhibition) becomes digital via the logs. The logs, in turn, can be used to further engage the visitor online or onsite.
When used to print personalized souvenirs (for example, the visitor postcards), the digital (logs) becomes physical (postcard) to embody the personal experience. Interestingly, these tangible data souvenirs enable personalization without collecting personal data as the algorithms do not need to know who you are, but what you have done.
By using the postcard to go online, the physical experience is reshaped digitally. Many options are possible, all powered by personalization via the logs, for example, a personalized ezine can be automatically composed from the museum digital archives selecting content that is of potential interest or a personalized comic with the visitor as character can continue the storytelling started with the visit. Other forms of online participation could be envisaged, for example, to display the avatars of visitors as a way to let them compare to what others have done and possibly recommend things to discover.
A continuous engagement of the visitor online enriches the personal profile held by the museum that can propose a new itinerary and gently push the visitor to come back to discover another part of the collection or to visit a related site, for example, a garrison along Hadrian's Wall.

This continuous shift between the digital and the physical is kept coherent and meaningful by the IoT infrastructure that supports a seamless long-term engagement with the museum. It is a perpetual cycle that transforms the audience from passive recipient of information into active agents that make choices and take decisions, that can be reached with personalized offers online as well as onsite, that can be invited to try new things, for example, evenings talks, or to engage even more, for example, to become a volunteer.

Conclusions

Museums are rich cultural environments that invite exploration and stimulate curiosity. Visitors enter the museum with their own agenda and pursue their own goals. What is key for a fulfilling experience is to be able to follow one's interest. Indeed it is the arousal of interest that feeds attention that is at the basis of the aesthetic experience defined as 'exceptional state of mind which is qualitatively different from 'normal' everyday mental states' (Markovic 2012,

p. 12). The aesthetic experience is not the experience of beauty – for it can be pleasant or unpleasant; it is characterized by intense attention, extended cognitive engagement and affective responses (Markovic 2012). In the heritage context, the aesthetic experience is multisensorial and can provoke a visceral response (i.e. to paintings (Joy & Sherry 2003) or to living history (Naumova 2015)) that results in a feeling of connection at a deep, personal level (Markovic 2012; Naumova 2015). It is in creating such connection that interactive exhibition design has a role to play. The process of making an exhibition can be reformulated in terms of creating an aesthetic experience where design facilitates museums to shift from being object-centred to being experience-centred by means of the physical engagement with hybrid digital-physical objects.

It is in this context of designing bespoke multisensory aesthetic experiences that engage the audience of museums beyond the objects on display that we see the contribution of this chapter. The case studies show how a personally meaningful, sensorily rich and socially expanded visiting experience with digital content can bridge the gap between digital content and the specific social and material contexts in which heritage comes to matter. Here, the interactive objects have multiple roles: they are hybrids that materialize digital stories connected to exhibits; they are means for the visitors to choose within an interactive storytelling setting; when used, these smart objects capture the visiting experience as personal and unique. These data-objects can be symbolic, interactive and transitional; they augment the exhibition, engage the audience (both physically and emotionally) and extend the visitor-museum connection beyond the here and now.

Acknowledgements

meSch, Material Encounters with Digital Cultural Heritage (2013–17) was funded by the European Community's Seventh Framework Programme, 'ICT for access to cultural resources' (ICT Call 9: FP7-ICT-2011-9) under the Grant Agreement 600851. We are grateful to all meSch partners for the inspiring collaboration and the cultural organizations for their expertise, knowledge and enthusiasms in co-designing the installations described: Anna Pisetti at the Museo Storico Italiano della Guerra, Italy; Andrew Roberts, Joe Savage and Frances McIntosh at English Heritage, UK; Gert-Jan van Rijn and Hub Kockelkorn at MUSEON, The Netherlands.

Notes

1. The museum of immigration on Ellis Island in New York has a physical bar-chart showing immigration by countries through the centuries. It makes evident how

different nationalities arrived in the USA through time. It is an excellent example of how 'dry' statistics can become an interesting exhibit that triggers discussion and meaning making.
2. A video of the interactive installation 'Fort Pozzacchio: Voices from the Past' at the Museo Storico Italiano della Guerra, the national museum of war in Italy can be seen at the following URL: https://www.youtube.com/watch?v=QuIFrWmJMOw (accessed 21 March 2020).
3. A video of the 'My Roman Pantheon' interactive installation at the Chesters Roman Fort and the Clayton Museum, an English Heritage property in the UK, can be seen at the following URL: https://www.youtube.com/watch?v=68yRPP2PXfA (accessed 21 March 2020).
4. A video of the interaction at 'The Hague and the Atlantic Wall: War in the City of Peace' exhibition at MUSEON, The Hague, The Netherlands, can be seen at the following URL: https://www.youtube.com/watch?v=sK3AdQU9kkc&t=62s (accessed 21 March 2020).

References

Classen, C 2007, 'Museum manners: The sensory life of the early museum', *Journal of Social History*, vol. 40, no. 4, pp. 895–914.

Dudley, S (ed.) 2010, 'Museum materialities: Objects, sense and feeling' in *Museum materialities: objects, engagements, interpretations*, Routledge, UK, pp. 1–18.

Dulake, N, Hornecker, E & Petrelli, D 2019, 'A conversation around the design and the experience of artifacts', *Interactions*, vol. 26, no. 5, pp. 52–7.

Falk, JH 2009, *Identity and the museum visitor experience*, Left Coast Press, Walnut Creek.

Falk, JH & Dierking, LD 2012, *The museum experience revisited*, Left Coast Press, Walnut Creek.

Hornecker, E 2008, '"I don't understand it either but it's cool" – Visitor interactions with a multi-touch table in a museum', *Proceedings of TABLETOP 2008*, pp. 113–20.

Joy, A & Sherry, JF 2003, 'Speaking of art as embodied imagination: A multisensory approach to understanding aesthetic experience', *Journal of Consumer Research*, vol. 30, no. 2, pp. 259–82.

Markovic, S 2012, 'Components of aesthetic experience: Aesthetic fascination, aesthetic appraisal, and aesthetic emotion', *i-Perception*, vol. 3, no. 1, pp. 1–17.

Naumova, A 2015, '"Touching" the past: Investigating lived experiences of heritage in living history museums', *The International Journal of the Inclusive Museum*, vol. 7, pp. 1–8.

Not, E & Daniela, P 2019, 'Crafting content across the physical-digital divide', *Interactions*, vol. 26, no. 5, pp. 46–51.

Parry, R 2013, 'The end of the beginning – normativity in the postdigital museum', *Museum Worlds: Advances in Research*, vol. 1, pp. 24–39.

Petrelli, D, Marshall, MT, O'Brien, S, McEntaggart P & Gwilt I 2016, 'Tangible data souvenirs as a bridge between a physical museum visit and online digital experience', *Personal Ubiquitous Computing*, vol. 21, no. 2, pp. 281–95.

Serrell, B & Raphling, B 1992, 'Computers on the exhibit floor', *Curator: The Museum Journal*, vol. 35, no. 3, pp. 181–9.
Sonneveld, MH & Schifferstein, HNJ (eds) 2008, 'The tactual experience of objects', in *Product experience*, Elsevier, pp. 41–67, https://doi.org/10.1016/B978-008045089-6.50005-8.
Szymanski, MH, Aoki, PM, Grinter, RE, Hurst, A, Thornton, J & Woodruff, A 2007, 'Sotto voce: Facilitating social learning in a historic house', *Computer Supported Cooperative Work*, vol. 17, pp. 5–34.
Thomas, N 2016, *The return of curiosity: What museums are good for in the 21st century*, Reaktion Books, London.
Vom Lehn, D & Heath, C 2003, Displacing the object: Mobile technology and interpretive resources. Proc. of Cultural Institution and Digital Technology.http://www.archimuse.com/publishing/ichim03/088C.pdf.

8
SOCIO-MATERIAL TRANSLATIONS OF DATA AND VALUE(S)

Bettina Nissen

Introduction

This chapter focuses on the value of tangible translations for education, pedagogy and knowledge transfer. The aim is to discuss and highlight concepts of technologies that can be translated into tangible and interactive experiences for general public audiences to gain a deeper understanding of digital technologies, while facilitating creative and critical discussion of the value and impact such technologies may have on their own or the lives of others in the near future. In this review, aspects of data physicalization are utilized to make data processes and user behaviours of technology more accessible and playful. The work presented was designed to allow non-specialists to investigate new and complex technologies experientially and speculatively to provoke discussion and raise critical awareness. With data gradually becoming the new currency of big business in the digital economy, the general public need to increasingly adapt to and understand how digital technologies and processes generate, handle and share their data. This field of interaction with data – be it through visual or tangible means – is increasingly being referred to as 'Human Data Interaction' (Mortier et al. 2014) and debate in this area is already moving beyond how to visualize data towards a more socio-political conversation around how we might 'explore social, legal and ethical aspects of personal data processing' (Oberlander & Speed 2016, p. 3). Despite the potential for misuse, data collection continues to increasingly pervade people's daily lives and routine activities across 'social interactions, shopping, work practices, banking, healthcare and transportation' (Prendiville, Gwilt & Mitchell 2017, p. 226). However, the focus in this chapter is not predominantly on data itself but on understanding the underlying processes and technologies involved in data generation and exchange, to further data literacy of non-tech specialist publics. Today's data collection mechanisms often occur 'out of sight of the people involved in the data flows, and so it is quite understandable that they [the general public] distinguish the material, visible things from the immaterial, and sometimes invisible data flows' (Oberlander & Speed 2016, p. 4). To open up these often complex, sometimes abstract mechanisms of technology, this work explores design research approaches that attempt to make technologies more tangible, within different social contexts, in an attempt to allow non-specialist audiences to question and critically engage with these immaterial 'black box' technologies. And ultimately, 'to turn the abstract and intangible nature of Big Data into human-centred services with social and economic value' (Prendiville, Gwilt & Mitchell 2017, p. 226).

The work presented here broadly follows a *material-oriented ontology* foregrounding that 'things or materials are central to an understanding of the world' (Woodward 2020, p. 7) and utilizes a range of different material methods for public engagement, knowledge exchange and education. The chapter showcases a series of accessible, playful and provocative activities with complex new technologies and unpacks their social implications beyond static tangible representations, understanding the performative and social nature of material engagements as entangled and complex relations. And revealing the differing experiences need to be viewed within their social contexts of their making and interactions. This performative approach of translating technologies into socio-material experiences acknowledges a complex, subjective and entangled understanding of technology. Rather than knowledge being produced as a process of articulation and communication, meaning emerges from within our actions, and design research in data physicalization is uniquely placed to re-configure 'the role "we" play in the intertwined practices of knowing and becoming' (Barad 2003, p. 812). By conveying the concepts of data processes in tangible and interactive experiences, the research here aims to highlight the embeddedness of technologies and data processes in the everyday, to offer a wide range of stakeholders opportunities for experiential learning and understanding. As the American feminist theorist Karen Barad suggests 'knowing does not come from standing at a distance and representing but rather from a direct material engagement with the world' (Barad 2007, p. 49). Following this more performative approach the research here is not to be understood as solution-focused design but rather as the design of infrastructures for experiential, socio-material engagement, a concept formulated by Bjögvinsson and colleagues as the 'infrastructuring' of design activities, 'performatively staged' for participation and involving collectives in processes of meaning making (Bjögvinsson, Ehn & Hellgren 2012, p. 102). Art-based methods, Speculative Design and Research through Design approaches have long highlighted the value of creative practices to open up new spaces for dialogue, debate and critical reflection. Such creative practice-based enquiries privileges 'play, intuition, serendipity, imagination and the unexpected as resource for making sense' (Kara 2015, p. 22) over more representational or factual representations of data and technological processes.

Blockchain, cryptocurrency and distributed ledger technologies

Specifically, the work described in this chapter focuses on exploring experiences of blockchain, cryptocurrency and distributed ledger technologies to offer non-specialist audiences a space for education and investigation. Introducing several related translations of technologies into material and interactive forms, the focus of the projects here is not intended for technical learning but to stimulate open-ended considerations of socio-economic imaginaries (Speed et al. 2019) addressing possible futures of currency, value and value(s) in an increasingly digital and data-driven economy. A number of the projects presented here emerged from a research project entitled *After Money*, while others arose from a collaboration with artist Ailie Rutherford[1] whose work on feminist economics includes setting up alternative economic projects such as the long-running *People's Bank of Govanhill*[2] collective in Govanhill, Glasgow exploring how feminist economic theory can be put into practice and *Swap Market*[3], a local feminist exchange space for sharing resources, skills, knowledge and cultures without the need for money. These projects spurred on community discussions on current developments in blockchain and distributed ledger technologies and inspired a collaborative project entitled *Crypto-Knitting Circles* to investigate how these new technologies could be utilized in the space of alternative currencies and value exchange practices from a feminist economic perspective and to empower communities and grassroots movements. The resulting workshop activities offered a social space for discussion and learning, similar to knitting circles, and were consciously based on craft practices often associated more with women's work, to engage women and broader audiences with blockchain and cryptocurrency concepts. Thus, challenging the predominantly male nature of the programming environment of cryptocurrencies (Meiklejohn et al. 2013). Through material qualities and tangible processes, ideas of gender norms and stereotypes that are still very present in the development of blockchain technology were problematized to challenge ideas of social practice, value and care in alternative economic futures (de Vries et al. 2019).

Feminist economic approaches aim to understand and challenge the future of labour and value in an increasingly digital and automated society perpetuating capitalist and neo-liberal practices (Fischer et al. 2018; Trebeck & Williams 2019). While challenging existing power structures and societal norms, feminist economists are revisiting the value of labour, and in particular labour practices, which often remain undervalued and hidden in the current economic model. To view the Economy as an Iceberg (Gibson-Graham 2002) highlights the invisible labour and value practices of care, knowledge and skillshare which actually prop up our current economic system and the idea of *economic value*. And a range of scholars, economists and artists are increasingly exploring new ways to heal society[4], build distributed cooperative networks of care[5], arts and culture[6] through feminist economic practices in an increasingly digital economy where data has become currency.

As part of this conversation, the projects discussed here aimed to challenge and question labour practices as well as the highly engrained understanding of fiat currency[7] for a future where human actions, behaviours and activities may increasingly become data points sold, valued and shared by big business and third-party companies. In a digital economy which is increasingly leaving the more vulnerable or less privileged behind, what it means to translate technologies of currency and value(s) into socio-material experiences for discussion, education and knowledge exchange and what considerations should be taken into account when translating technology into material practices, is not often discussed.

Material translations of value(s)

This section introduces a series of workshop activities predominantly focusing on material translations of technological concepts to open up a dialogue focusing on potential use and issues of blockchain or distributed ledger technologies for communities and grassroot organizations. Throughout these workshops themes of tokenization, power structures, governance and consent in distributed networks were debated through the material engagement with technological concepts.

The *Block Exchange* workshop by Maxwell, Speed and Campbell (2015) was designed to make complex technology more tangible and accessible. With its physical translation of technological concepts of blockchain technology and value exchanges into simple toy bricks (Figure 8.1a), this workshop was adapted into the context of the Swap Market allowing participants to understand the novel and complex blockchain technology in tangible ways. By using preexisting and well-known toy bricks, the activity allowed participants to easily and playfully understand how the technology works by enacting the technology and acts of exchanges themselves. By walking, trading and adding their transactions to a ledger, participants learnt through embodied interaction (Figure 8.1b). In the context of the Swap Market community, existing community resources, such as skillsharing, language lessons or clothing (rather than abstract concepts), were exchanged to consider what the implications for meaningful exchange would be. The participants in this workshop ranged from local members of the community

SOCIO-MATERIAL TRANSLATIONS OF DATA AND VALUE(S)

Figure 8.1 (a, b) *Block Exchange* workshop. Photo: Bettina Nissen; (c, d) *Weaving Crypto-Ledgers* workshop. Photo: Bob Moyler; (e, f) *Strings of Distributed Value* workshop. Photo: Bob Moyler.

with no prior blockchain knowledge to academics and technologists with more knowledge of the concepts and technical aspects. The Block Exchange activity offered a common ground for discussion, for learning what this technology may offer to a local community exchange project and what issues may emerge. While some of the more blockchain savvy participants pointed out where and how the metaphor of using toy bricks in this translation falls short of the actual technology, non-expert participants came out of the workshop with a new understanding of not just the technology but the broader question around fiat currency and the socially constructed nature of money. By trading resources for toy bricks in different scenarios, participants experienced the tokenization of value and the agreed nature of currency and exchange rates. This experiential learning of economic exchange practices and blockchain technologies opened up a discussion and debate about the technological implications, control and power of setting up such a digitally focused system in communities that are less technologically advanced.

The *Weaving Crypto-Ledgers* workshop activity was based on a similar approach to Block Exchange in its aim to translate the concept of value exchanges, mining and cryptography into a physically accessible format for an audience with a diverse background and knowledge of the subject. While Block Exchange specifically focuses on understanding tokenization, acts of exchange and a distributed ledger, *Weaving Crypto-Ledgers* aimed at understanding issues of consent and verification in a distributed community network. During the workshop, participants would engage in trade and exchange activities which would be recorded simultaneously on everyone's individual blocks by weaving an agreed pattern of the transaction into the pre-made templates (Figure 8.1c). After a set of transactions were woven into patterns, all ledger blocks were compared to find consensus on the final and correct block to be verified (Figure 8.1d). Any patterns that were incorrectly woven or unfinished were discarded and the majority pattern was agreed upon. Each colour weave represented an exchange or transaction in the workshop and participants could keep their block as record of this set of exchanges during the workshop. Similar to blockchain technology, the resources themselves that were exchanged remained anonymous and only the fact of a transaction and its value (size/shape) remained as record. In addition, the top and bottom notches of the woven ledger were intentionally made to interlock with a previous or future workshop template. So, in any given workshop, participant ledger templates were identical so a new verified ledger or block could be placed on top of the previous workshop and the order of workshops that took place could not be altered by swapping ledgers. While these workshops opened up discussion and debate about the issues of consensus and agreement in a community setting, it was also felt that a combination of conceptual exchange of value with the technical processes of encryption seemed to overcomplicate the matter. The conflation of these two aspects resulted in discussions and debates about both technological aspects and community driven issues rather than disentangling the conceptual exchanges from a technical limitations perspective. As a result, further clarification was required that by weaving the ledger, the participants were ultimately acting as 'verification nodes in a distributed network'.

The *Strings of Distributed Value* activity built on the previous workshops, exploring and designing for distributed networks through tangible means (Nissen, Tallyn & Symons 2019). Adapting this approach to a grassroots community and the context of a sharing economy, string was used to map and create a distributed network of potential blockchain applications, allowing participants to collectively discuss and design shared concepts. As a metaphor for the complex entanglements in such distributed networks of people, things and value, each spool of string in this workshop represented a resource a participant was either offering or looking to exchange, for example, knowledge share, practices and labour they could offer or other items of exchange beyond a one-off sale of one item (Figure 8.1f). Upon labelling a spool with their intended resource (Figure 8.1e), participants would read out their resource and place the spool in the centre of the room. All participants were then asked to choose a resource and discuss why they made this choice. Used as an icebreaker, this activity opened up debates and discussion about governance, power and control in a more conceptual or speculative sense than previous more technically focused activities. In subsequent iterations, this standing/walking workshop activity was altered to include figures around which string could be wrapped to record what resources a person or organization may want to exchange. As a whole, when done with individuals on a more personal perspective this string-based workshop opened up interesting conversations but was less targeted than when exploring specific community organizations and their resources of exchange in a distributed community network.

Interactive translations of value(s)

This section focuses on interaction design driven explorations around currency and value. While these are again predominantly based around socio-material interactions, the format and different model of interaction go beyond workshop activities described in the last section and take a more experiential and dynamic form of public installations and provocations. These explorations range from specific cryptocurrencies and smart contracts to alternative forms of currency in the digital economy and socially constructed systems of exchange.

The *GeoCoin* activity was developed as an '*unfinished*'[8] software allowing non-specialist audiences to understand potential implications of smart contracting technologies and location-based currencies in the city (Nissen et al. 2018). The focus of this app was to allow participants to collect coins in different ways based on their location data: debit or credit coins as one-off deductions or collections, and debit or credit zones where one's wallet would continuously gain or lose coins (Figure 8.2a). *GeoCoin* was not designed to visualize data but to make location-based smart contracts experiential for general public audiences and allow them to critically think through the implications of this technology while ideating and conceptualizing how this technology may be utilized in potential future scenarios. As such, this digital representation of possible value creation or

Figure 8.2 (a, b) *GeoCoin* experience. Photo: Bettina Nissen; (c, d) *Currency After Money* installation. Photo: Yuxi Liu; (e, f) *Alternative Rates of Exchange* installation. Photo: Bob Moyler.

transactions in physical and embodied spaces allowed participants to experience the city in different ways and reimagine smart contracts in the city (Cila 2017). The open-ended or *unfinished* software could be used to further influence the actual activity and experience people had during a given workshop. At times, the workshop activity was random and people were collecting coins that were dropped in the city without specific narrative. In other instances, participants were guided through a precise scenario of how the coins were laid out in a specific space for a more focused exploration. The open-endedness of this software offered both the workshop facilitators and participants the opportunity to create their own scenarios for location-based currencies and smart contracts (Figure 8.2b). By translating conceptual ideas and models into physically experiential activities, participants developed a different sense of the impact and issues resulting in an approach or design. They could judiciously engage with the actuality of such a technology and critically question socio-technical implications inherent in such systems through their own experiences.

Currency after Money is an experiential installation allowing visitors to an exhibition to consider the monetization of data as it is commonly represented in online systems, apps and devices. Most users (you and me) trade data for access or use of a software or device. Although many users do so knowingly or unconsciously, data is being recorded and sent to businesses around the world. It is often difficult to understand from a general public's perspective how to stay informed about such processes and how data is being used. This installation (Figure 8.2c) was aiming to bring such processes to the fore. A specially created app and shopping system allowed visitors to pay for sweets by either paying with regular fiat currency, by sweeping the exhibition with a broom for a set period of time or by paying with a selfie (Figure 8.2d). In addition, participants were offered choices to pay with alternative forms of currencies (cryptocurrencies or virtual in-game tokens), alternative data streams (steps, biometrics, GPS data or sharing information about friends) or alternative time-based activities. This model of offering participants the choice between money, time and data acted as a representation of our current existing economic models and structures and allowed participants to bring up and question their understanding and perceptions of value. While monetary exchanges are often clearly defined, other forms of exchange are more hidden or implicit. This installation allowed participants to question their own perceptions of what they understood as cost of specific value exchanges. When 'paying' with a selfie many participants seemed to consider the exchange for sweets as free or cheaper than a monetary exchange, despite the increase in use of facial recognition software. While industry and big business are making money from people's data and sharing of data, participants were negotiating their thinking and decision-making throughout and after the interaction, for example, participants were considering the temptation and convenience of the sweets in relation to trade-offs such as effort, loss of privacy or perceived value of different data they felt comfortable sharing. These interactions allowed participants and visitors to reconsider the value of their own data, their own daily habits and what can be seen as currency in today's or a future economy. The design aimed to offer a playful educational experience of complex technological matters to raise awareness, provoke questions and critique current practices rather than directly translating data or technology in specific form.

Returning to the Swap Market in Glasgow, an interactive installation *Alternative Rates of Exchange* was developed to offer participants and staff of the Swap Market a space to explore more dynamic and responsive models of exchange based on feminist economic practices. The interactive visualization of alternative economic models and exchange rates of skill share knowledge as well as objects allowed visitors to the shop to investigate and understand connections or relationships between values and what can be considered currency. The installation consisted of a counter-top board of value dials where participants could decide what they value most to 'set the values of the system' or what should be valued most in an alternative economic system (Figure 8.2e). Once the visitor had set their value system, the interactive exchange rate installation on the wall would then adjust accordingly to show what could be exchanged for which value (Figure 8.2f). Oftentimes, the translation of value system to exchange rate was intentionally programmed to be surprising to the visitor as it was not based on our engrained economic understanding of supply and demand. But instead, turned on its head to highlight that a different economic system may be possible that emphasizes and values environmental and social aspects beyond monetary gain. This dynamic data physicalization of a pricing structure not only gave people something to think about but also captured data about how people engaged with the device and how they might game the system (or not). Responses were unsurprisingly varied, from visitors intentionally trying to game the system for the 'cheapest' transactions in their favour, while others did not attempt to intentionally influence the price of an item for their own benefit. Overall, participants were playfully provoked to rethink their mental models of the economy and how a system could potentially be set up to benefit the majority of people more (or not). While the Swap Market staff were involved in the design and decision of the complex mapping of values to exchange rate in the development phase, this translation was intentionally left opaque or hidden from visitor's view to create these provocative moments of surprise and critical thought. Only in conversation with staff or each other could they investigate and explain why the exchange rate may have changed a certain unexpected way. This opaque nature facilitated debate and provoked thinking that would have otherwise not taken place if the translation of values to exchange rates were made more transparent or expected.

Conclusion

Valuing socio-material translations

Drawing on the variety of work presented here, there are key issues that have come to the fore that might be considered when attempting to translate financial technologies into provocative socio-material experiences for non-specialist communities. Some of these considerations and themes emerging from this work apply more broadly while others more specifically to the context described. Aiming to engage a general public with critically reflecting upon and questioning not just technological systems and their own behaviours but the broader economic system is challenging. Many aspects relating to perceptions and understanding of currency and value are engrained in one's understanding of society and often the sense of self within the existing system. To challenge these conventional and pervasive structures in people's minds, provocative and imaginative activities offering public audiences first-hand experiences of new or alternative socio-economic systems or ideas of value(s) was crucial. Further considerations for the exploration of data translations that can be applied more broadly by design researchers are described in the following three sections.

Accessibility for audience versus accuracy of technology

The participants' background knowledge is essential in considering the translation of technology for education and knowledge exchange as it directly guides the level of simplicity or complexity of a workshop activity. If aimed at experts of a technology a more complex understanding of the technology can be expected. But with the experience of the above projects, a mixed level of expertise and background knowledge is often more common. When it comes to designing data translations it is important to consider the expertise of the audience for whom the activity is meant for. For example, Block Exchange for experts would need more nuanced and technical details while for a more general public a less accurate and more experiential translation was essential. While there may always be flaws in a tangible translation or a metaphor of a technology (e.g. weaving or building blocks), the key aspect to consider is what the material or tangible experience can add to someone's thinking. While perhaps not being 'technically' accurate, a playful experience can sometimes offer a more accessible point of entry to a complex subject for a broad audience and facilitate a more common ground for discussion that does not fall into technical jargon and debates. There is always a challenge when trying to translate complex technological processes into different, potentially more accessible formats without the loss of accuracy.

However, the key aim when designing tangible experiences for and with different audiences should not be focused on the accuracy or detail of the technological description but in considering what 'infrastructuring' is required in either making a technology more easily understandable or offering space for more critical debate (Bjögvinsson, Ehn & Hellgren 2012, p. 102). While accuracy and accessibility are not mutually exclusive, it is essential to consider the main focus when translating technologies into a workshop activity or public experience. Is the main aim educational, shared knowledge, facilitating dialogue or to provoke critical reflection, reimagining or ideation of new systems? It is important to consider what or how much of a designed activity is open for participants to engage with, change or alter, while maintaining a clear scaffold for the socio-material experience.

Interpretation over representation of technology

Often data physicalization approaches are focusing on the representation of data and with the focus on representation rather than interpretation come concerns around legibility, accuracy and rigor. In most of the work discussed here, the focus is on interpretation and provocation. Similar to any translation work (be it data science, interaction design or writing), it is never free of subjective interpretation and should be approached as such. More specifically design research such as this is always based on a more personal experience-based approach and includes the researcher's own creative practice, interpretations and style to imagine novel engagements and translations. However, there are two aspects to consider in this translation process in regard to the main purpose of the designed activity and what direction of translation to take. If the predominant aim is educational or to foster understanding of new technology, then a more accurate, descriptive or representative approach may offer a better learning experience for the audience. However, from an experiential participatory perspective one has to question if the most accurate or rigorous translation of a technology also offers the most accessible or playful engagement. Often it requires striking a balance or compromise between accurate representation and engaging activity. While there is always a drive to stay close to the actual technology or data, one may have to compromise on accuracy, fidelity or even legibility in favour of a more provocative or engaging experience. In some instances, the compromise may actually add new dimensionality to an often predominantly technological focus. It should also be remembered that 100 percent fidelity can never be achieved when translating data or technology from one medium into another. From a data science or data visualization perspective alone, whenever data is collected and analysed there are always processes of translation, filtering or mapping that may compromise data in favour of a clearer and more meaningful narrative being brought to the fore. Equally, the process of translation into physical materials and experiences offers opportunities of three dimensionality, material affordances and playful interactions but may in turn be limited in terms of resolution, state and scale. For facilitating a space for playful learning, new imagination or critical thinking, accuracy of representation may not always be the guiding principle.

Hidden or transparent translations

Beyond concerns around fidelity of data or technology as representations, an additional and important aspect for translating such technologies into socio-material experiences is the legibility not just of the data or technology but of the translation work itself. Much of the work in Design and HCI translates data or meaning through or across different media and platforms to critique, challenge and provoke new thinking. With the work described here, the transparency of the translation exercise is an interesting aspect to consider. For example, in *Alternative Rates of Exchange*, the translation of how the value dials influenced the different exchange categories was purposefully obscured so that visitors had to experiment with the values to explore how exchange rates responded. This obfuscation challenged the user's understanding of current systems and started conversations about the reasons behind the affected changes in the interaction. Often the interaction was counter-intuitive to how the users perceived economic value, which resulted in new understanding and reconsidering of economic system norms. In other cases, like *Block Exchange* or *Crypto-Weaving Ledgers,* the transparency of the physical translation was key to the engagement as the material activity acted as a tangible metaphor and direct representation of different aspects of blockchain technologies. In order to meaningfully engage novel and expert audiences with such technologies a very clear translation of the technology was important in supporting new learning and understanding. For an educational and knowledge exchange intentioned activity, a more transparent approach to translating technologies or data is beneficial for facilitating and scaffolding participant's understanding and thinking. However, if the intent of the activity is of a provocative nature to raise awareness or instigate debate then a transparent approach may not always be the most appropriate direction to offer challenging and critically engaged activities. The level of opaqueness or transparency however will need to be individually and consciously designed into any experience.

In summary, this chapter has introduced and discussed a variety of related projects on topics of currency, value(s) and new digital technologies such as blockchain and distributed ledgers. Having drawn out broader considerations for socio-material translations the key focus remains on the overall experience created for non-specialist audiences. Often utilizing tangible metaphors, the socio-material translations of value have opened up conversations, facilitated new learning and reimaging of new economic models or systems. Overall, the entangled contexts of making data and technologies tangible do not only focus on existing data sets but on the gaps, the not yet existent and the potentially newly imagined as critical reflections on current practices and systems. This is where creative practice and socio-material translations can thrive in designing imaginative, playful and provocative experiences for education, pedagogy and knowledge exchange that critically engages a general public with new technologies to reconsider our socio-economic futures.

Acknowledgements

Thanks to my collaborators Ailie Rutherford, Libby Odai and the community at the Swap Market in Govanhill for their co-creation and creative engagement with the Crypto-Knitting-Circles project. This work was funded by Creative Scotland, Vibrancy Fund and Edinburgh College of Art. The GeoCoin and Currency after Money work were funded by the UK ESRC grant After Money (ES/N007018/1). Thanks to all the participants and to colleagues in Design Informatics who contributed to the design and development of the work, specifically Shaune Oosthuizen, Hadi Mehrpouya, Yuxi Liu and Chris Speed.

Notes

1. Ailie Rutherford https://ailierutherford.com/
2. The People's Bank of Govanhill https://thepeoplesbankofgovanhill.wordpress.com/
3. Swap Market https://swapmarket.info/
4. Cassie Thornton, The Feminist Economics Department (FED) http://feministeconomicsdepartment.com/
5. Distributed Cooperative Organisation (DisCO) https://disco.coop/manifesto/
6. Furtherfield https://www.furtherfield.org/culturestake-2/ and http://www.daowo.org/
7. Fiat currency is a medium of exchange established and issued by a centralized, often governmental organization. Fiat money has no intrinsic value in itself (paper notes) nor is it tied to the value of a natural resource such as gold or silver. The value of fiat money is largely based on a general understanding of trust and maintenance of the currency and its value by a country's government or central bank. The term is rooted in the Latin word *fiat* which stands for 'let it be done' as a form of proclamation, demand, decree or order.
8. By 'unfinished' or open-ended software I refer here to a term described as 'open, experiential platform [that] offers basic technical functionality without prescribing goals' (Nissen et al. 2018, p. 4) which can trigger participants imagination to apply the experienced technology to their own ideas and concepts. Instead

of understanding GeoCoin as a solution-based prototype focusing on specific practices, behaviours or contexts, this unfinished software 'invites appropriation and translation of complex technologies into participants' own ideations' (Nissen et al. 2018, p. 7).

References

Barad, K 2003, 'Posthumanist performativity: Toward an understanding of how matter comes to matter', *Journal of Women in Culture and Society*, vol. 28, no. 3, pp. 801–31.

Barad, K 2007, *Meeting the universe halfway: Quantum physics and the entanglement of matter and meaning*, Duke University Press, Durham, NC.

Bjögvinsson, E, Ehn, P & Hellgren, PA 2012, 'Design things and design thinking: Contemporary participatory design challenges', *DesignIssues*, vol. 28, pp. 101–16.

Cila, N 2017, 'Blockchain city – centre for design informatics', in G Ferri & M De Waal (eds), *A lab of labs. Methods and approaches for a human-centered design*, Amsterdam Creative Industries Publishing, Amsterdam, pp. 59–68.

De Vries, P, Gloerich, I, Lovink, G, Eckenhaussen, S, Imamovic, M, Koelemij, F, De Koning, A, Braun, AF, Beckenbauer, L & Sokoloff, N 2019, 'Outside of finance: On feminist economics, social payments, corporate crime and the "blokechain"', in *MoneyLab #7*, Hogeschool van Amsterdam, Lectoraat Netwerkcultuur, Amsterdam.

Fischer, L, Hasell, J, Proctor, J, Uwakwe, D, Perkins, Z & Watson, C (eds) 2018, *Rethinking economics*, Routledge, London.

Gibson-Graham, JK 2002, *A diverse economy: Rethinking economy and economic representation*, accessed May 2020, http://avery.wellesley.edu/Economics/jmatthaei/ transformationcentral/solidarity/solidaritydocuments/diverseeconomies.pdf.

Kara, H 2015, *Creative research methods in the social sciences: A practical guide*, Policy Press, Bristol, UK.

Maxwell, D, Speed, C & Campbell, D 2015, '"Effing" the ineffable: Opening up understandings of the blockchain', in *Proceedings of the 2015 British HCI Conference (British HCI '15). Association for Computing Machinery*, New York, NY, USA, pp. 208–9, https://doi.org/10.1145/2783446.2783593.

Meiklejohn, S, Pomarole, M, Jordan, G, Levchenko, K, McCoy, D, Voelker, GM & Savage, S 2013, 'A fistful of bitcoins: Characterizing payments among men with no names', in *Proceedings of the 2013 conference on Internet measurement conference (IMC '13). Association for Computing Machinery*, New York, NY, USA, pp. 127–40, https://doi.org/10.1145/2504730.2504747.

Mortier, R, Haddadi, H, Henderson, T, McAuley, D & Crowcroft, J 2014, 'Human-data interaction: The human face of the data-driven society', http://dx.doi.org/10.2139/ ssrn.2508051.

Nissen, B, Pschetz, L, Murray-Rust, D, Mehrpouya, H, Oosthuizen, S & Speed, C 2018, 'GeoCoin: Supporting ideation and collaborative design with smart contracts', in *Proceedings of the 2018 CHI Conference on Human Factors in Computing Systems (CHI '18)*, New York, pp. 1–10, https://doi.org/10.1145/3173574.3173737.

Nissen, B, Tallyn, E & Symons, K 2019, 'Tangibly understanding intangible complexities: Designing for distributed autonomous organizations', in M Phillips & C Speed (eds),

Ubiquity: The Journal of Pervasive Media, vol. 6, no. 1, pp. 47–63, DOI:10.1386/ubiq_00007_1.

Oberlander, J & Speed, C 2016, 'Designing from, with and by data: Introducing the ablative framework', in *Proceedings of DRS2016*, Brighton, UK, http://www.drs2016.org/433/.

Prendiville, A, Gwilt, I & Mitchell, V 2017, 'Making sense of data through service design – opportunities and reflections', in D Sangiorgi & A Prendiville (eds), *Designing for service: Key issues and new directions*, Bloomsbury Academic, London, pp. 225–36, http://dx.doi.org/10.5040/9781474250160.ch-016.

Speed, C, Nissen, B, Pschetz, L, Murray-Rust, D, Mehrpouya, H & Oosthuizen, S 2019, 'Designing new socio-economic imaginaries', *The Design Journal*, vol. 22, pp. 2257–61, DOI:10.1080/14606925.2019.1595023.

Trebeck, K & Williams, J 2019, *The economics of arrival: Ideas for a grown-up economy*, Policy Press, Bristol, UK.

Woodward, S 2020, *Material methods: Researching and thinking with things*, SAGE Publications Limited, London.

9
PERSONAL DATA MANIFESTATION: A TANGIBLE POETICS OF DATA

Giles Lane and George Roussos

Introduction

We live now in a world where almost every action and interaction has been datafied in some way – sensed, measured, aggregated, synthesized, analysed and transacted. Much of this is our personal data, captured not only through our own devices and the platforms and services to which we are signed up, but also through our interactions with others – friends and families – as well as our interactions with other systems – transport, banking, retail and the ever present surveillance cameras that have proliferated into every public and private space imaginable.

But how are we to make sense of this ocean of data? To ride its swells and plumb its depths? How can we feel our way around it? How can we hold onto meaning when its ephemerality means it is constantly slipping through our grasp, like trying to pluck a handful of water? How might we enliven relations between humans and machines so that they can be mutually influential rather than unbalanced in favour of one side or the other?

The point of departure in this chapter is to question the use of information visualization as typically exemplified in the variety of user dashboard designs commonly provided as a means to make sense of activity and performance measurements captured by wearables and other mobile technologies. Despite their promise, there is accumulating evidence to suggest that people only briefly engage with the self-monitoring and sense-making opportunities offered by these technologies, leading to very high abandonment rates for such visualization services (Arthur 2014; Farago 2012; Rapp & Cena 2016).

Can our relationship to data be enhanced by bridging the biological and digital and if so, can we can design ways to utilize the whole human sensorium (rather than not just vision and hearing only) for sense-making and interpretation, by making complex information tangible and appreciable in richer and more nuanced ways. This approach implies departing fundamentally from normative data representations on computer screens. It means embodying information in reciprocally interactive engagements that afford us greater use of our highly developed senses – what we have been calling *'data manifestation'*. Moreover, this approach allows users the opportunity to experience data in more engaging ways that can reveal things we have hitherto not considered possible. It reveals contingencies and limitations in what kinds of data are being collected – and can lead us to collect different kinds of data that have perhaps been overlooked, with the potential to improved sense-making, insights and potentially, sustainable behaviour changes.

However, cognition is more than simply seeing how humans perceive and create meaning, it is an associative, complex and not fully understood process. Yet, it is widely accepted that human meaning-making is substantially different to processes of algorithmic inference which can be drawn from digital data. One could also argue that human and machine meaning-making systems also differ fundamentally in purpose as well as function (Sloman 2011). It is an expression of the difference between consciousness and a structured system, and, more than what is offered by systems that mimic 'neural nets'. Aesthetics and how we make meaning from artworks offer a concrete example of how this operates in practice. Aesthetics are acquired subjectively and flow from a dynamic interweaving or perhaps an entanglement of our memories and experiences with our physical senses (Kant 1790). At each moment of experiencing something in an encounter with an artwork – writing, painting, sculpture, music or performance – we are existing in an entangled moment blending the now with the summation of our conscious sense of self. We are not inferring meaning (as a structured data-driven system might), but actually actively making meaning from the experience itself (Dewey 1934).

The inspiration for our approach towards establishing data manifestation as a practical methodology is grounded in the conceptualization of works of art as tools for investigating ourselves, so-called Strange Tools, by philosopher Alva Noë (2016). For Noë, art is not a practice in need of an explanation but a method of investigating what makes us human. Strange Tools philosophy challenges us to make sense of what it is all about: they aim not for satisfaction but for confrontation, intervention, and subversion and through this process make sense of how the world around us is organized and how we fit within it. Following this way of thinking, the role of painting for example is revealed to go beyond depiction and representation and to call into question the role of pictures in our lives. Accordingly, art cannot be reduced to some natural aesthetic sense or trigger and for this reason recent efforts to frame questions of art in terms of neurobiology and evolutionary theory alone do not and cannot work. The point of engaging with Strange Tools thinking is therefore to be able to study ourselves in profoundly novel ways and we adopt this as a guiding principle in developing artefacts through data materialization (de Jaegher & di Paolo 2007).

Lifestreams: Realizing uncommon insights through data manifestation

The Lifestreams project explores new ways to engage nominally healthy people in monitoring their health and lifestyle as a preventative measure, rather than waiting for a medical condition to arise and then find themselves having to adopt biosensor monitoring as part of a recuperative regime. The artist-led creative studio Proboscis were invited to collaborate on the idea with scientists from the Philips Research Laboratory in Cambridge.[1] The aim of the project was to think of emerging biosensor systems as part of a continual, holistic process of healthy living and well-being, rather than as technological aids for post hoc medical intervention. In particular, the project addressed a practical problem: that the statistics concerning the use of commercial biosensor products and related smartphone apps indicated that the vast majority of users tended to abandon the devices and ignore the data visualizations within weeks of first using them, undermining any potential beneficial impact they could have in the medium to long term.

Through a series of intense monthly meetings, rapid conceptual development and iterative prototyping the Lifestreams project was developed as an experimental response and novel way of thinking about the nature of biosensor data and its relationship to how we live our lives. The concept sought to move beyond the simple graphs and number counting that pervades so much of the 'quantified self' meme and move more towards the poetic and numinous; to capture something of the epic in everyday life. The aim was to transform people's relationships to digital data from the ephemeral of screens and interfaces into something that encompassed the tactile and material, in the hope of producing a more subconsciously emotive and emotional experience – an artefact or 'Lifecharm'. Having developed the basic concept we grappled with the form that such an artefact should take, asking the question: What physical form could be mathematically driven by data to create dynamic and interesting shapes that could also communicate some sense of the whole person? Revisit nature for archetypal forms and generative principles, a list of the attributes that an artefact generated from information pointed to a description of the growth patterns and expressiveness of shells. Patterns in shell growth (such as a mollusc or snail) are determined by the health of the creature and are dependent on what the creature consumes, as well as stress factors and the environmental conditions that they exist within. Shells have a near universal fascination and are prized in many cultures across the world – using contemporary technologies to artificially allow a human to 'grow' their own shells from data generated by monitoring their own health and lifestyle patterns was explored.

Shell-like Lifecharms were created by capturing a range of personal biosensor data types (heart rate, body temperature, blood pressure, step count, sleep pattern, exposure to air pollution) and applying the data to a workflow using algorithms to extend the principles of the helico-spiral with time-based rules. Shells were 'grown' in a 3D modelling environment to produce the initial 3D model surface, then post-processed and exported as a stereolithographic file. The files could then be sent to a 3D printer to generate a physical artefact in a variety of different materials such as plastic, metals, glass, resin and ceramic (Figure 9.1). What makes the Lifecharms unique is that they are not just parametric or formulaic transmogrifications of the raw data but *generative* – because time as a key element informs the variations in the growth grammar that evolves the shells. Each of the biosensors' time-series data drives one of the parameters governing the shell's growth form. The data points are iterated through time intervals and become parameters altering the shell's growth rules as more data is fed into the model. This gives each shell a non-deterministic morphology inspired by the way a shell would be grown by a living creature – the chances of ever generating two shells exactly the same are almost nil, as the arrays of data are unlikely to repeat exactly. Like Heraclitus's adage, 'Ever-newer waters flow on those who step into the same rivers', the Lifestreams process seeks to observe the fluid, experiential nature of our lives, linking them together in a sequence of reflective objects that comprise a 'flux of things' (Whitehead 1977).

Unlike screen-based data visualizations the Lifecharms are generated through a process of non-deterministic spatial data *transformation*. Not confined to the instrumental purpose of relaying original data back to us as information, in a simplified and easy to comprehend manner, instead, the Lifecharms are *embodiments* of the data, a *concrescence* transformed from the abstract and ephemeral into the concrete and present. They establish the potential for uncommon insights to be perceived into the health conditions and lifestyle patterns in which the data was collected. Such insights are prompted by tactile, sensorial engagement and intuitive reflection. They are indeed Strange Tools.

A TANGIBLE POETICS OF DATA 145

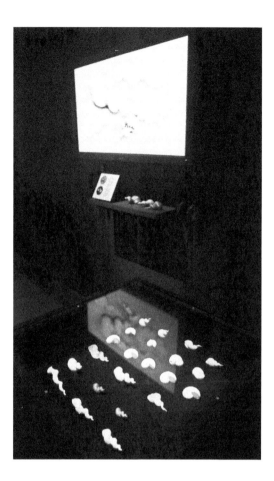

Figure 9.1 *Lifestreams* by Proboscis (2012) installed in the group show, *The New Observatory*. FACT, Liverpool (2017). Image: Gareth Jones.

Lifecharms as Strange Tools

Proboscis first began exploring tactile interfaces and tangible souvenirs in 2004 as a key part research into the way people create and share knowledge, stories and experiences – a form of 'public authoring' (Angus, Lane & Roussos 2014). An element of the handmade often features in the outputs we design, but here the imprint of the person about whom the data being shared is directly embodied in the object itself. A Lifecharm shell synthesizes the intrinsic qualities of the data within its morphology; conventional 2D visualizations, on the other hand, make extrinsic interpretations of such data. The Lifecharm is, at one and the same time, both an informational object – representing a state gleaned from sensor data – and also a philosophical thing triggering intuitive reflection. It unites different traditions of investigation and meaning making: the scientific and the mythic, or magical, both being and becoming. However, a Lifecharm is neither an icon nor iconic, nor yet an implement or tool – it embodies a state without merely, banally, representing it. What it exemplifies is not knowledge in the form of a 'transactable' commodity or product but a path to knowing that arises from an ongoing process of continuous interaction with and intervention within everyday habits. The Lifecharms are not rational, functional objects, instead they are magical, irrational, indeed talismanic things by which, through tactile familiarity, people may come into knowledge or understanding by way of revelation. Like poetry, which is much more than the sum of words and their arrangement on a page, they are *more than* the sum of the data that drives their growth parameters.

Carrying a Lifecharm and touching it every day, both consciously and even as a displacement activity, causes a person to develop a relationship with it over time. Over time the person becomes familiar with its materiality – the feel of the shape in your hand; the weight of the material it is made of, the textures of its surface. Like poetry, the Lifecharms are also *diachronic* – meaning that we can experience and relate to them across time, whilst the meaning or data they embody is fixed in time (i.e. the shape of the shell or the words of the poem do not change). Dynamic data visualizations may often be synchronous – that is driven by live or recent data streams – but the way we experience and relate to them is likely to be mediated (through devices such as smartphones, tablets or computers) and determined by our behaviours and patterns of using those devices they are mediated through. This makes the Lifecharms intrinsically different to screen-based visualizations of data. The information that we may glean from them is less to do with an instrumental replay in visual form and much more to do with how we begin to learn about the patterns they embody through a growing tactile familiarity with their physical form. This difference becomes an opportunity to augment our means of understanding the phenomena recorded in the biosensor data – an opportunity to explore meaning making through a relationship to complexity and intersubjectivity, a kind of sublime reciprocity.

Lifestreams for Parkinson's Disease

The ideas developed while working on the *Lifestreams* were further explored in the digital healthcare domain with a view to adapt and extend the data manifestation concepts in the specific context set by Parkinson's Disease (PD). PD is a degenerative neurological condition associated with a wide spectrum of motor and cognitive symptoms including tremor, slowness of movement and freezing, muscular stiffness, poor postural stability, sleep-related difficulties, depression and psychosis (Jankovic 2008). Care for patients with PD involves the management of both motor and cognitive symptoms and palliative care. Since there is no cure, symptom management is a life-long process that affects not only the patients but also their families and carers (Clarke, Zobkiw & Gullaksen 1995).

To address this challenge a smartphone app cloudUPDRS was developed to offer clinician and patient dashboards mapping the wide variation of symptoms that people experience with Parkinson's (Stamate et al. 2018). The Lifestreams concepts was also used to find ways to express the unique characteristics of an individual's actual experience of PD. In an investigation by Stefan Kueppers (Stamate et al. 2018) a series of Lifecharm shells generated by extracting features from raw measurements of tremor and slowness of movement which were demonstrated to have predictive value in conducting digital assessments (Figure 9.2).

These Lifecharms were offered to participants who were involved in the developmental study of the cloudUPDRS app as *tangible souvenirs*. The motivation for the use of the Lifecharms was the fact that progressive cognitive impairment and changing symptoms often result in people with PD questioning their recollections of disease experience: the cloudUPDRS Lifecharms were used as *aide de memoirs* to help people with their memories and take some measure of control over the disease by making sense of their condition. Moreover, they

Figure 9.2 *Lifestreams*, Parkinson's Disease Lifecharms by Proboscis (2016). Photo: Alice Angus.

were used to investigate how the different attributes of the Lifecharms such as size, form and texture, and the mapping of features extracted from PD symptoms affected the readability of the artefacts for clinicians. In particular, the question of whether clinicians can develop a richer understanding of specific patient profiles and their evolution, a process often referred to as patient stratification, by employing non-verbal, non-symbolic, instinctive insights through the involvement of touch, vestibular and proprioception senses.

Data veiling

The Lifecharms developed for PD were presented at the Alan Turing Institute in March 2016 to demonstrate qualitative differences in the *experiences* of particular individuals. The presentation provoked a number of interesting conversations with participants about the applicability of data manifestation as a means of communicating information on different levels. Issues of privacy and cybersecurity within the field of medical ethics and patient data were raised in respect to the potential of data-object. A proposal emerged that encoding patient data in physical forms could be a useful means of allowing data to be safely transported and 'shared' with different people – such as a patient discussing their conditions with a physician. In such a situation both parties might interpret the data-object and use it to have an informed conversation because they already understand the context in which the patient's data was collected and from which the data-object has been created. However, any third party intercepting the data-object would simply be unable to access the source data from which the object was generated (e.g. via reverse engineering) or be able to ascertain its context from the object itself. Hence the term 'data veiling' – or hiding in plain sight.

Healthcare often necessitates treatment at different hospitals and clinics and illustrates how often patient data needs to be shared between multiple parties. Often this means patients having to carry paper records of their data with them to every meeting; sending paper copies by post or emailing unencrypted attachments across the internet. The opportunities for private and extremely personal data to leak out into the wider world are manyfold and a real problem for individual privacy given the interest in acquiring private medical data now being shown by the companies at the heart of digital technology and AI/machine learning.

By encoding sensitive data into physical abstractions it might be possible to conduct informed discussions about the real world *meaning* of datasets within specific contexts – without having to access or share the data itself all the time. Data veiling could offer a form of signposting or symbolically representing data without having to reveal its full detail. Shifting our focus from data to the patterns and meanings we can interpret from it.

Reciprocal entanglement: Towards a theory of data manifestation

The category of the sublime in literary theory and aesthetics refers to encounters with phenomena that are excessive – too much to handle – and which inspire awe or dread in the subject. What renders the experience sublime is our ability to, nevertheless, address this vastness or dreadfulness and to incorporate it into a perceptual register for meaning or sense-making. It has been a hugely important and influential category of perception in the Humanities for almost three centuries – as well as having roots in Roman-era Greek philosophy (Longinus' *On the Sublime*, first century AD). Edmund Burke was one of the earliest English philosophers to write about it (in *A Philosophical Enquiry into the Origin of Our Ideas of the Sublime and Beautiful*, 1756), followed by the German philosopher Immanuel Kant (in *Observations on the Feeling of the Beautiful and Sublime*, 1764), then Arthur Schopenhauer, Georg Hegel, Rudolf Otto and others since (notably Jean-François Lyotard).

What the sublime offers us is a conceptual mechanism by which we can recuperate an almost overwhelming encounter with things which are too massive or complex to calculate, measure or fully comprehend. It allows us to make sense, to make meaning of an encounter with the ungraspable. It describes an ontological encounter that transforms something from being *numinous* (or unknowable) into something phenomenological – which we can incorporate into a narrative experience and a type of knowledge. Joseph Addison's description in 1704, 'The Alps fill the mind with an agreeable kind of horror' (Addison 1703, p. 350), captures the internal ambiguities of the sublime – that horror can be at all agreeable – which make it such a powerful perceptual register of recuperating the excessive. Such a rupture and intertwining of perceptual and critical abilities within a person's consciousness could, perhaps, be figured as a form of entanglement between oppositional states and phenomena – the sublime being the moment of awareness of the entanglement itself. It is, of course, always relational between the person and the thing they are encountering.

Coming back to the challenge of making sense of data too big to understand, algorithms too complex to represent and the decision-making processes too opaque to be grasped by mere humans, we could reframe our experience of interacting with information as a *monumental* encounter. Such an encounter could then be approached as moment of the 'data sublime'; an encounter where artistic practice may offer us alternative opportunities to assimilate and make meaning from it. Art and aesthetics offer different ways to conceive of what happens in complex encounters than those utilized by the sciences. When you encounter a work of art, it is the experience itself which determines your aesthetic reaction to the piece. It could be one of awe, delight, revulsion or indifference – whatever it is, it is driven by similar complex factors. Each person's own aesthetic experience is affected by the use of materials, colour, scale, lighting, sense of space and proportion as well as by their own memory, critical thought and emotion. There can be no right or wrong aesthetic experience: each person experiences a work of art in relation to the summation of their own existence.

The methodologies and critical analyses from the arts and humanities, such as aesthetics and categories like the sublime, offer alternative ways to develop new ways of realizing knowledge from data and computational systems through encounters that work on multiple senses, not just via sight and sound as most contemporary technologies currently deliver it. We don't just have to simplify and summarize data in linear ways to make it easier to represent visually on a screen (e.g. in a chart or diagram), we can also use our other senses – touch, sense of scale and balance, taste, smell, hearing, time and temperature. The data sublime in artistic encounters allows for multiple sensorial engagements, where we are *reciprocally entangled* in the possibility for meaning making with the work itself, through our own consciousness. It is a route away from the reductive reasoning of standardization, quantification and calculation that lead to probabilistic and statistical interpretations. Instead it is a route to knowledge that reinserts key human qualities of judgement and imagination that can encompass the kinds of ambiguity, diversity and the unknowable that would be routinely excised from analytical systems based on quantification alone.

Evolving technologies of extraordinary complexity and subtlety run counter to mundane understandings of the phenomenal world and stretch the limits of human perception. The intangible, counter-intuitive nature or sheer vastness of the science makes it hard for people to grasp, and yet so exciting in its implications for the future. The complexity and interdependence of life, and natural systems (such as climate), is another sphere that often seems overwhelming in terms of the scales involved.

Conclusion

In this chapter we have attempted to describe ways in which personal data can be encoded in the form of objects that we can establish a physical, sensorial relationship to. Suggesting that to do so creates the potential for modes of meaning making to expand from just the quantifiable to encompass the qualitative – and that in the traditions of art and literature there are sophisticated analytical perspectives for comprehending such poetic and sublime experiences.

What we gain from a poetics of data in addition to its more common articulations is a weaving together of harmony and dissonance, rhythm and inconsistency – a way of encompassing adaptation and irregularity within a transcendent whole.

This approach offers a way to enhance our cognitive abilities by challenging us to flex other senses in meaning-making, to enhance our capacities by widening the frames in which we encounter and engage with data. A poetics of data is about engaging with its *qualities*, not just its quantities.

Note

1. In January 2012 Stefan Kueppers and Giles Lane, from the artist-led creative studio Proboscis, were invited to collaborate in a critical and creative dialogue with scientists from the Philips Research Laboratory in Cambridge. The collaboration was commissioned by Andy Robinson of Futurecity with Dipak Mistry of Arts & Business Cambridge as part of Anglia Ruskin University's Visualise public art programme, one of several initiated between artists and industry in Cambridge that were intended to communicate the benefits that could come from such partnerships.

References

Addison, J 1703, *Remarks on several parts of Italy etc. in the years 1701, 1702, 1703: Addison, Joseph, 1672–1719*. London: printed for J. Tonson, 1718.

Angus, A, Lane, G & Roussos, G 2014, 'Public goods: Using pervasive computing to inspire grassroots activism', *IEEE Pervasive Computing*, vol. 13, no. 2, pp. 44–51, DOI:10.1109/MPRV.2014.33.

Arthur, C 2014, 'Wearables: One-third of consumers abandoning devices', *Guardian*, 1 April, website https://www.theguardian.com/technology/2014/apr/01/wearables-consumers-abandoning-devices-galaxy-gear

Clarke CE, Zobkiw RM & Gullaksen E 1995, 'Quality of life and care in Parkinson's disease', *The British Journal of Clinical Practice*, vol. 49, no. 6, pp. 288–93.

De Jaegher, H & Di Paolo, E 2007, 'Participatory sense-making', *Phenomenology and the Cognitive Sciences*, vol. 6, no. 4, pp. 485–507.

Dewey, J 1934, *Art as experience*, London: Allen & Unwin.

Farago, P 2012, 'App engagement: The Matrix Reloaded', blog post, *Flurry Analytics*, 22 October, https://www.flurry.com/blog/app-engagement-the-matrix-reloaded/.

Jankovic, J 2008, 'Parkinson's disease: Clinical features and diagnosis', *Journal of Neurology, Neurosurgery & Psychiatry*, vol. 79, no. 4, pp. 368–76.

Kant, I 1790, *Critique of Judgement*, Translated by James Creed Meredith, Oxford: Oxford University Press, 2007 (original publication date 1952), Oxford World's Classics. ISBN 978-0-19-280617-8.

Leach, J 2012, 'Leaving the magic out: Knowledge and effect in different places', *Anthropological Forum: A Journal of Social Anthropology and Comparative Sociology*, vol. 22, no. 3, pp. 251–70, http://dx.doi.org/10.1080/00664677.2012.723611.

Moore, A 2003, 'MAGIC IS AFOOT: A conversation with ALAN MOORE about the arts and the occult', interviewed by Jay Babcock, *Arthur*, no. 4, https://arthurmag.com/2007/05/10/1815/.

Noë, A 2016, *Strange tools: Art and human nature*, Hill and Wang, New York.

Proboscis, 'Lifestreams', *Proboscis*, http://proboscis.org.uk/projects/2011-2015/visualise-lifestreams/.

Rapp, A & Cena, F 2016, 'Personal informatics for everyday life', *International Journal of Human-Computer Studies*, vol. 94, pp. 1–17.

Sloman, A 2011, 'Varieties of meta-cognition in natural and artificial systems', in MT Cox & A Raja (eds), *Metareasoning: Thinking about thinking*, MIT Press, Cambridge, MA, pp. 307–23.

Stamate, C, Magoulas, GD, Kueppers, S, Nomikou, E, Daskalopoulos, I, Jha, A, Pons, JS, Rothwell, J, Luchini, MU, Moussouri, T, Iannone, M & Roussos, G 2018, 'The cloudUPDRS app: A medical device for the clinical assessment of Parkinson's Disease', *Pervasive and Mobile Computing*, vol. 43, pp. 146–66, https://doi.org/10.1016/j.pmcj.2017.12.005.

Thelen, E, Schöner, G, Scheier, C & Smith, LB 2001, 'The dynamics of embodiment: A field theory of infant preservative reaching', *Behavioural and Brain Sciences*, vol. 24, no. 1, pp. 1–34, DOI:10.1017/S0140525X01003910.

Walker, D 2013, 'Lifestreams', in B Ferren (ed), *Visualise: Making art in context*, Anglia Ruskin University, Cambridge.

Whitehead, AN 1977, *Process & reality: Corrected edition*, Free Press, New York.

10
DATA AND EMOTION: THE CLIMATE CHANGE OBJECT

Karin von Ompteda

Introduction

Objects can play intimate roles in our lives. Objects can be beautiful. Objects can be meaningful. Objects can be the focus for quiet contemplation. We can touch, move and hold objects. Objects can tell a story.

How can the potential of objects be utilized to create meaningful connections between people and climate change? While many people intellectually understand the issues, it can be difficult to truly connect with the data that lies at the foundation of our knowledge. How can we help people to relate a global process to their everyday lives? How can we help people comprehend the significance of *only* a one degree Celsius increase in temperature? And how can we help people to connect with environmental effects of climate change that may be occurring in geographically distant places?

This chapter presents three responses to these questions in the form of data-objects created by graphic design students Ka Leng Kong, Paz Pereira-Vega and Kathleen Stever at OCAD University in Toronto, Canada. They are the outcomes of climate change briefs that have been running since 2017, which focus on creating meaningful connections between people and scientific data. The challenge is undertaken through the practice of data manifestation; defined as the communication of quantitative information through objects, installations and sensory experiences (von Ompteda 2019a). This work on the physical manifestation of data began in 2010 at the Royal College of Art (London, United Kingdom) and has continued at OCAD University since 2014. The climate change briefs have resulted in dozens of student projects ranging from precious objects to large installations and explore everything from tactile engagement to sonification (von Ompteda 2019b).

When we map data to an object, we fundamentally change the way that we engage with that information. The object itself creates a new context for interpretation. The three data-objects presented here serve as exemplars of a data product, data sculpture and a tactile data-object. Possibilities for the data communication inherent in these types of objects are discussed and the techniques that are unique to each of the projects explored, including making connections through analogy, metaphor and indexical methods.[1]

While data manifestation can help people to connect with complex information, it is important to also remember that this practice plays a role for the students themselves. This form of creative practice offers a rich opportunity for design authorship and research, as information is sourced and communicated about issues they are truly passionate about. Climate change is a (if not *the*) critical issue of this generation. In this way, these projects are personal, and through these works the designers are speaking. The following sections showcase three of these reflexive design responses.

The Climate Clock (data product)

The *Climate Clock* (2019) by Ka Leng Kong brings climate change directly into our homes and everyday lives. This data product replaces the 12 hours of the clock with almost twelve decades of global temperature data (Figure 10.1). Everyday objects offer interesting possibilities for data communication due to their immediate closeness and emotional connotations (Vande Moere 2008). By mapping data onto a domestic product that we already have a personal relationship with, Kong has created an immediate connection with this information. In her words:

> The clock is the first thing that I look at when I wake up. It is an object that we frequently look at throughout the day, reminding us of what we have to do.

What we have to do in this case refers to the many choices we make which affect our carbon footprint.

The *Climate Clock* communicates global surface temperature anomaly data sourced from NASA's *Global Climate Change* website (NASA 2020). This data refers to how much warmer or colder any one year is, compared to the long-term (1951–80) average temperature. Kong has communicated the data through a typical bar graph, which she has modified and bent into the shape of a circle (Figure 10.1). Temperature anomaly has been graphed as a function of time, with each bar representing averages over ten-year periods. The bars are then flanked on both sides with temperature averages written in degrees Celsius and the relevant year ranges. Using data spanning from the beginning of the twentieth

DATA AND EMOTION: THE CLIMATE CHANGE OBJECT

century to 2018, Kong was able to create twelve bars representing almost twelve decades.

The twelve decades of climate change data were seamlessly integrated into the design of a clock, replacing the usual demarcations for each of the 12 hours. Kong purchased the clock from a dollar store and then removed its face and replaced it with her own. She created the face of the clock by laser engraving the bar graph, alongside temperature averages and years, into a 1/8-inch piece of Baltic birch plywood. In this way, temperature data is literally burned into a natural material, referencing the increased temperature of the Earth's surface. Kong also painted each bar, mixing the paint herself, resulting in colours that are vibrant, yet still reveal the wood grain beneath. She described the process of hand painting as requiring deep concentration, just like how much attention she feels that she should be giving the issue of climate change.

Mapping the data onto a very practical object, Kong has created a way for herself – and others – to pay attention. Essentially, the data is piggybacking on top of a useful object, in order that it will be communicated and paid attention to. Yet this object does not only receive attention through its utility, it also does this through its beauty. In many homes, clocks are prized design objects; objects that we look at not only to tell the time, but to derive aesthetic pleasure. The *Climate Clock* is communicating threatening information through a visually pleasant façade; the wood is warm, the colours are attractive. The clock offers a welcoming invitation into climate change data.

Figure 10.1 *Climate Clock* (2019). Designer: Ka Leng Kong. Photography: Ka Leng Kong.

In keeping with the original function of the clock, the *Climate Clock* is designed to be read clockwise. Temperature data from the first decade of the twentieth century is located at one o'clock, and the most recent data is located at twelve o'clock. The engraved inner circle represents a temperature anomaly of zero degrees Celsius, meaning that the temperature is neither colder nor warmer than the long-term average. Bars that are pointing into the centre of the clock (i.e. 'below' this line), represent decades where the average temperature is colder than the long-term average. Bars that are pointing outward (i.e. 'above' this line) represent decades where the average temperature is warmer than the long-term average.

We can see that since the beginning of the twentieth century, the Earth's surface temperature has been increasing, as the bars change from pointing inward to pointing outward. This is emphasized by Kong's use of colour. She has used dark blues to represent the coolest years, and lighter blues to represent decades that were less cold. Similarly she has used orange to represent warmer years, and reds to represent the most recent and warmest years on record. While blues are often used to represent cold (e.g. sink taps), they are also often used to represent health (e.g. World Health Organization logo). Similarly, we associate oranges and reds with heat and the sun, but they are also colours used as signs of warning or danger (e.g. lights at intersections). According to NASA (2020), nineteen of the twenty warmest years have occurred since 2001. We can see this information represented by the longest bars, the deepest red colours, and the location on the clock: eleven and twelve.

By mapping temperature data onto a clock, Kong has given it new meaning. Analogy is a powerful device employed in the design of data-objects (Klanten et al. 2010), helping people relate complex information to their own experiences (von Ompteda 2019a). Here, Kong is creating an analogy between the Earth's temperature over almost 120 years, and the 12 hours within our day. In so doing, she has collapsed time to a human scale. We are now able to engage with this information in the way that we engage with the hours of our day. In this way, we ascribe values and emotions to these decades in history as they relate to our own daily experience with time.

One o'clock is early; we have many more hours in the day. Similarly, in the early twentieth century, temperatures are colder than the long-term average and we do not have to worry yet. As the day progresses, the hour hand moves closer to recent temperature data, carrying with it a certain feeling of dread. As with any clock, the *Climate Clock* causes an ebb and flow of anxiety. We are more hopeful in the early hours, and experience more stress as we approach whatever time aligns with the deadlines of the day. The *Climate Clock* has a deadline: twelve o'clock. At twelve, the bar graph reaches to the edge of the clock's face, as if to say that this is the maximum temperature that we can allow. In the words of Kong, 'we need to change before it's too late.' This sense of urgency is accentuated by the 'tick' 'tock' sounding at every second. Interestingly, Kong chose to photograph the *Climate Clock* at approximately 12 minutes before twelve (Figure 10.1), capturing the object at a time of heightened anxiety for the viewer. Between twelve and one o'clock the graph then breaks; a representation of our unknown future. What will you do with your time, to make any sort of difference? And then we start all over again, seemingly getting another chance. However this is recorded history, and there is no other way around it. We will have to experience this temperature increase, this threatening trajectory, twice a day.

Disruption: The Materiality of Global Temperature (data sculpture)

Disruption: The Materiality of Global Temperature (2018) created by Paz Pereira-Vega offers an engagement with global temperature increase – at a safe distance. In contrast to Kong's data product, which brings climate change data into our homes and lives, Pereira-Vega's sculpture is meant to be experienced in a gallery. Figure 10.2a shows the sculpture photographed in OCAD University's Great Hall. For most people, the gallery exists outside of everyday experience; it offers the opportunity for an external engagement, in this case with threatening information, detached from our lives. This experience is further engineered through the sculpture's method of data mapping, which does not employ a graph; a recognizable representation of numbers. Pereira-Vega's sculpture instead communicates through a more abstract manner, manifesting the data through metaphor and materials. Data sculptures are often not immediately understandable and are meant to be discovered (Vande Moere 2008).

Disruption communicates global surface temperature anomaly data through a complex intertwining of natural and human-made materials (Figure 10.2). Pereira-Vega chose wood to represent the surface upon which temperature acts, and red-coloured resin mixed with gold leaf to represent the disruption created by increased temperatures, and how this in Pereira-Vega's words 'can overpower and change the Earth's surface'. Wood, resin and gold each speak to industrial processes, chosen intentionally to create a context for people to question our responsibility regarding the changes that we make to our environment.

The *Disruption* installation consists of a series of three objects which represent temperature anomaly recorded for three years: 0.4°C (2000), 0.7°C (2010) and 0.99°C (2016).[2] Pereira-Vega purchased framing lumber from a building supply store (2 inch x 7 inch x 5.5 feet) and cut into the surface of each piece with a chisel. Resin was then poured into these cutout areas, with gold leaf mixed in with the resin. The width of the cutout area, and therefore the resin, represents temperature anomaly data for each of the three years. This was measured by creating a scale from 0.0°C to 1.0°C stretching across the width of each piece of wood, framed by a narrow border. The border can be seen in Figure 10.2b on the right side of the resin. The border serves an aesthetic and practical function, framing the resin and keeping it from spilling over the edges, respectively. The year and temperature anomaly data were also marked on the side of each object with a wood burning pen (see Figure 10.2a). The three objects are presented leaning against a gallery wall, ten inches apart. At five and a half feet tall, they are unmistakably anthropomorphic in scale. One does feel a certain personal relationship with the piece, as it stands there before us.

Pereira-Vega was challenged to communicate the significance of what may appear to be a small increase in temperature, as small changes in temperature correspond to very large changes in the environment (NASA 2020). The years 2000 and 2010 were chosen to capture the first decade of the twenty-first century, which has seen significant increases in temperature. The year 2016 was chosen as it is the warmest year on record (NASA 2020), with temperature anomaly reaching almost one degree Celsius (0.99°C). It should be noted that NASA's (2020) updated data for 2016 shows a temperature anomaly of 1.02°C. Therefore global temperature in 2016 met and surpassed a one degree Celsius increase in temperature, compared to the long-term average.

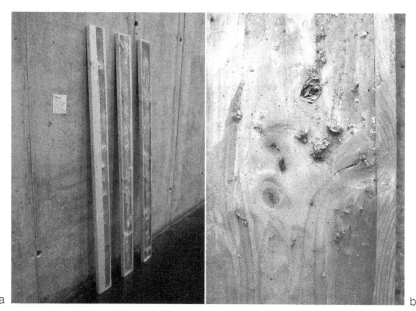

Figure 10.2 *Disruption: The Materiality of Global Temperature* (2018); (a) sculpture in OCAD University's Great Hall; (b) detail of object representing the year 2016. Designer: Paz Pereira-Vega. Photography: Paz Pereira-Vega.

Reading the sculpture from left to right (see Figure 10.2a), we begin with the object representing the year 2000 (0.4°C), which has resin stretching across almost half of its width. In the middle we have the object representing the year 2010 (0.7°C), which has resin stretching across most of its width. Finally, on the very right is the object representing the year 2016 (0.99°C), which has resin covering almost its entire width. A close up of the 2016 object is pictured in Figure 10.2b, showing the resin framed by a small border on the right. Pereira-Vega made a subjective choice that one degree Celsius would be the maximum temperature that the objects – and the artist – would allow, with each object representing fractions of one degree Celsius, according to the year's temperature anomaly data. Similar to Kong's clock which cannot show higher temperatures, the object representing 2016's temperature anomaly reaches what is effectively a maximum, designed into the object's dimensions.

While the object representing 2016's temperature anomaly communicates the most extreme and troublesome information, it is also the most beautiful of the three objects (Figure 10.2b). Pereira-Vega employs the power of aesthetics to engage the viewer. The piece is mesmerizing in its beauty, and one can lose themselves in the aesthetic pleasures of the work. The red-coloured resin glazes over the wood, thin and thick, producing light oranges and deep reds. The resin reveals, and even accentuates, the textures of the wood; its grain, knots and cracks. Gold leaf of various sizes and shapes are speckled over the resin, immersed and floating, reflecting the brilliant yellow light that gold affords. It is through these pleasures that one's eye and mind can rest here, immersed in the most distressing information.

Disruption connects with the viewer not only through aesthetics, but also through the handcrafted quality of the piece. The hand carving of the wood, the pouring of the resin – both imperfect – carry the marks of the artist. Pereira-Vega spoke of the difficulty and frustration in controlling the precision of the data mapping. This can be seen in the upper right area of Figure 10.2b, which shows an accidental slip of the chisel on the border's inner edge. While handcrafted methods may lack precision, they can serve to communicate abstract data in a way that feels human. This can serve to make the data more relatable, while also honouring the nature of data as human-made (von Ompteda 2019a), and imperfect. One only needs to consider the differing values for temperature anomaly recorded for 2016 to be reminded of the inherent uncertainty of data.

The handmade qualities of *Disruption* embody the journey of the artist; her relationship with the materials, and therefore with the data. In Pereira-Vega's words:

> I remember realizing that as I was carving, I became physically aware of the rise in temperature. The wood was so hard to carve; the transition from 0.04°C

to 0.99°C was quite a difference. I remember thinking that it was through this tangible interaction, that I was able to truly grasp the meaning of a one degree Celsius rise in temperature. It was sheer exhaustion that translated that to me.

The marks of the artist's hand embedded within *Disruption* do not convey an objective mapping of the data, but instead the brutality of humanity's impact on the Earth. Artistic communication of data is subjective, resulting in works which embody a point of view (Viégas & Wattenberg 2007). There is a certain violence imparted through the craft, particularly the way in which the wood has been carved. There is a roughness in it, evidenced by scratches and uneven surfaces. This piece becomes increasingly grotesque as the viewer considers the gauging of the wood and an artificial material in its place. The longer one looks, the more the piece appears raw, flesh-like and bloodied. *Disruption* conveys a deep sadness; it tells the story of our broken Earth, and our role in it. Through a complex relationship between craft methods and materials, we are seduced by this beguiling sculpture, captured at once by its beauty and brutality.

Burning Acres (tactile data-object)

Kathleen Stever's tactile data-object (*Burning Acres* (2018)) offers an opportunity to engage with climate change information in a direct and physical way (Figure 10.3). Instead of communicating through analogy and metaphor, as we have seen previously, Stever employs indexical methods. She created a series of burnt wood objects to tell the story of wildland fires, connecting us directly to the subject of the data. The objects are designed to be touched and explored. In this way, environmental effects attributed to climate change occurring in geographically distant places are literally placed into our hands. We might expect to see an object like this in a science museum or educational institution, as a hands-on learning tool. While the previous two projects were focused on visual communication, Stever exploits an important opportunity in the physical manifestation of data, enhancing meaning through communication with the other senses (Jansen et al. 2015).

Burning Acres communicates the number of acres of land burned in wildfires in the United States within each of three years: 1985, 2000 and 2015. Stever wanted to capture the increases over fifteen-year intervals, dating from approximately the time of reliable record keeping (1983) to the present. The data was sourced from the National Interagency Fire Centre's (NIFC) (2020) website, which publishes annual wildland fire statistics compiled by the National Interagency Coordination Centre. The number of acres burned in wildfires was 2.9 million acres (1985), 7.4 million acres (2000) and 10.1 million acres (2015). While there is variability

DATA AND EMOTION: THE CLIMATE CHANGE OBJECT

Figure 10.3 *Burning Acres* (2018). Designer: Kathleen Stever. Photography: Nicole Torres and Karin von Ompteda.

from year to year, a graph of wildland acres burned as a function of time (based on the same NIFC data) was published in a Carbon Brief article,[3] showing 'a clear trend in increased area burned by wildfires in the US since the 1980s' (Hausfather 2018). In presenting regional effects of climate change in the United States, NASA (2020) note increasing wildfires in the Northwest and Southwest. In the Southwest, increased heat, drought and insect outbreaks, all linked to climate change, have contributed to this increase (NASA 2020).

Burning Acres presents a series of three wooden objects, stacked directly on top of one another. Each object is made of 1/4-inch Baltic birch plywood, laser cut into a circular, irregular shape to resemble a cross section of a tree stump (Figure 10.3). Laser engraving was utilized to remove the surface layer of the plywood around a 1/2-inch perimeter of each object, creating a dark border resembling bark, framing each of the pieces. Stever also laser engraved the year and acres burned in wildfires into the framed area of each piece. Laser engraving was further utilized to create ten concentric circles resembling tree rings, through a shallower cut of the laser, resulting in slightly lighter lines than the dark perimeter. The laser engraved areas contrast strongly with the pristine top layer of wood, a light-coloured birch. Similar to the *Climate Clock*, laser engraving is thoughtfully employed here, as the burning of wood aligns with the subject matter. Students who work with laser cutting and engraving usually sand their wood projects to remove the appearance of burnt edges. Too subtle to be seen in the photograph here, Stever left evidence of the process, with burnt edges adding to the visual interest of the piece.

The data was mapped to the objects by assigning each tree ring to represent one million acres of wildland. Starting from the inside circles and moving outward, Stever burned the wood within each tree ring using a lighter, according to the number of acres burned that year in wildfires. While in nature, tree rings represent growth, here they are used to represent loss. Through her material choice (i.e. wood) and craft methods (i.e. burning), Stever has physically related the information to its context.

The three wood objects stack neatly on top of one another, revealing only the data for the top object initially. We must interact with this series of objects in order to discover the underlying information. Through this tactile engagement, the data becomes something that we can explore, in our own way. Pictured in Figure 10.3, the data-objects are ordered chronologically, with each subsequent layer corresponding to a later year. The top object shows almost three entire tree rings burned at its centre, representing the 2.9 million acres burned in wildfires in 1985. Beneath the top object, we find another one with more than double the tree rings burned, representing the 7.4 million acres burned in wildfires in 2000. Finally, the object at the bottom has all of its rings burned, with the burning extending into the border, representing the 10.1 million acres burned in wildfires in 2015.

Subjective choices are again being made, as we have seen in the previous works. A maximum value has been designed into the objects, in this case ten million acres of wildland. Similar to the other pieces, *Burning Acres* says 'no more'. Stever makes a further subjective choice, which serves to increase the dramatic impact of NIFC's (2020) wildfire data. Burning within the central tree ring and moving outward, each additional tree ring adds a disproportionate increase in the area burned on the object. This is because the tree rings are concentric, with outer tree rings having larger radii than inner tree rings, therefore enclosing a larger area.[4] In this way, Stever is disproportionately increasing the impacts of wildfires over time. Each acre burned in wildfires is not the same as the acre before it; this project says 'it is worse'. The emphasis that Stever has placed on larger numbers of acres burned speaks to the urgency surrounding this issue which is increasingly in the news (e.g. Hausfather 2018).

While data is mapped precisely in the *Climate Clock* through a laser engraved bar graph, *Burning Acres* is less precise, both by design and due to challenges posed by the handcraft methods. First, the tree rings are not perfectly circular or equally spaced and instead reflect the organic forms found in nature. Considering the disproportionate increases discussed above, this choice does not interfere with the reading of the objects, with each ring representing 'more'. Second, Stever struggled with the mapping itself, similar to the experience of Pereira-Vega. In speaking about the creation of the work, she found it 'difficult to control the flame and contain the burning according to the tree rings, as it tended to always go slightly outside of the boundaries'. Stever also spoke of the fatigue resulting from holding the wood pieces directly parallel to the flame in order to achieve the marks that she had intended. This was especially difficult for the object representing 2015, which required burning all of the tree rings. Again, like Pereira-Vega, Stever physically experienced this information through the handcraft elements of the project.

The handcraft method here, like Pereira-Vega's piece, speaks violence against the natural world perpetrated by human beings. *Burning Acres* shows us destruction and desecration. Where there is a beauty in the data sculpture, here we see marring and ugliness. Where the data sculpture metaphorically destroys the natural world, Stever does this literally; a human being holds the lighter, and the wood burns.

Like a map, we can look down and witness the burning move across the acres. The burning itself is inconsistent, with areas of light and dark resembling the appearance of smoke. This adds a dimensional quality to the piece, with the 'smoke' seeming to exist above the wood base. The burning looks like it is spreading from the inside outward, as the burnt areas are darker in each object's centre, and less easily controlled towards the periphery. This can be seen in the object representing the year 2000 (Figure 10.3, middle object), where the burned areas look lighter as they 'spill' over the seven-acre tree ring. These inconsistencies in appearance give *Burning Acres* a dynamic quality, a life, as if it is in progress, moving along the surface from one acre to the next. In this way, the tree tells its own story, each object a microcosm.

We can also trace the story of these wildfires with our hands. Running one fingertip along the object's surface, we can feel it dip gently into each engraved tree ring as we move from the darkest burned epicentre of each object outward. Engaging with this piece, the burn becomes a part of us, leaving a dark soot circle on the tip of our finger. This accentuates our fingerprint and invites a comparison with the appearance of tree rings. Like fire, the piece itself is not easily contained. *Burning Acres* is messy, with soot rubbing onto whatever surface the objects are on, including each other. Unlike the *Climate Clock* and *Disruption*, *Burning Acres* does not have a precious quality. Created as a learning tool, it is designed for unhindered interaction, to be picked up, moved and explored, leaving messy surfaces and hands behind. Enhancing this experience, *Burning Acres* also invites olfactory engagement. Through the laser cutting and engraving, and the burning done by hand, Stever's piece has the distinct smell of burnt wood. What is quite a pleasant smell is juxtaposed with the dark subject matter, intensifying the emotional response to the piece.

Burning Acres tells a story of loss. As we explore one object to the next, we learn of environmental destruction, increasingly dramatic in scale. We experience not only sadness, but a certain shame regarding our failings to protect this wildland. These empathetic objects connect us to the lives of trees. Macabre in nature, objects resembling tree stumps tell this story of life lost. They offer before us, a slice of a tree, a dissection for our examination. These stories from distant places are transported into our hands, where we can see, touch and smell the burning.

Conclusion

The *Climate Clock*, *Disruption* and *Burning Acres* offer insight into the vast opportunities for communication afforded through data-objects, even when based on the same dataset (in this case, global temperature anomaly). *Data products* can bring climate change into our homes, integrating this information into our daily lives. *Data sculptures* offer an engagement that is detached from our everyday experiences, keeping threatening information at a safe distance but also providing the space for meaningful contemplation. *Tactile data-objects* offer to communicate information physically and viscerally, placing climate change data into our hands.

While these object types create a context for engagement, further techniques are needed to elicit an emotional connection with climate change data. The *Climate Clock* uses analogy to help us relate global processes to our own lives and experiences. *Disruption* employs metaphor and materials to create a new lens through which to comprehend our impact on the Earth. *Burning Acres* utilizes indexical methods to connect us to the reality of environmental destruction.

Each student's perspective is embodied within their work. Through subjective choices in data mapping, each project says 'no more'. Kong places recent global temperatures at twelve o'clock midnight, communicating a sense of urgency. Pereira-Vega conveys the disruption created by these temperatures through emotive craft methods. Stever emphasizes environmental destruction through her disproportionate mapping of the data. The students' personal experiences are also embedded in these objects, Kong's painting, Pereira-Vega's carving and Stever's burning; their attention, physicality and fatigue. These data-objects are personal. They ask for our emotional engagement, and for us to understand this information as the students have come to through this process. They ask us to feel anxiety, sadness and a sense of responsibility. They ask us to take it personally.

Acknowledgements

I gratefully acknowledge the ingenuity and passion of my students who inspire me every day, with special thanks to Ka Leng Kong, Paz Pereira-Vega and Kathleen Stever. Thank you to Ian Gwilt for his invitation to contribute to this exciting book and invaluable comments on the manuscript. I am grateful to Elizabeth Harvey for insightful feedback and rich discussions regarding this work. Thanks to Nicole Torres who has photographed many of my students' projects with me. I thank Saadia Kardar for her careful formatting, proofreading and photo editing. Lastly, my profound thanks to John Obercian for his support.

Notes

1. See Vande Moere and Patel's (2009) classification of data sculptures based on a semiotic taxonomy (symbolic, iconic or indexical). An indexical representation is one in which the signifier bears a direct relationship (either physically or causally) with the signified. It is through this direct relationship on which an understanding is formulated (Vande Moere & Patel 2009, p. 7).
2. Pereira-Vega created her project in 2018, based on data available at that time. At the time of writing this chapter (7 March 2020), temperature anomaly data downloaded from NASA's website was 0.4°C (2000), 0.73°C (2010) and 1.02°C (2016) (NASA 2020). The latter two years are slightly higher than the data presented in the text.
3. Carbon Brief is a UK-based website covering the latest developments in climate science, climate policy and energy policy (https://www.carbonbrief.org/).
4. The area (A) of a circle is calculated based on its radius (r) as follows: $A = \pi r^2$.

References

Hausfather, Z 2018, 'Factcheck: How global warming has increased US wildfires', *Carbon Brief*, 9 August, accessed 9 March 2020, https://www.carbonbrief.org/factcheck-how-global-warming-has-increased-us-wildfires.

Jansen, Y, Dragicevic, P, Isenberg, P, Alexander, J, Karnik, A, Kildal, J, Subramanian, S & Hornbæk, K 2015, 'Opportunities and challenges for data physicalization', in *CHI'15: Conference on Human Factors in Computing Systems*, Seoul, Korea, pp. 3227–36.

Klanten, R, Ehmann, S, Bourquin, N & Tissot, T (eds) 2010, *Data flow 2: Visualizing information in graphic design*, Gestalten, Berlin.

NASA 2020, *Global climate change: Vital signs of the planet*, NASA, accessed 7 March 2020, https://climate.nasa.gov/.

National Interagency Fire Centre 2020, *Total wildland fires and acres (1926–2019)*, National Interagency Fire Centre, accessed 9 March 2020, https://www.nifc.gov/fireInfo/fireInfo_stats_totalFires.html.

Vande Moere, A 2008, 'Beyond the tyranny of the pixel: Exploring the physicality of information visualization', in *IEEE Conference on Information Visualisation (IV'08)*, pp. 469–74, DOI:10.1109/IV.2008.84.

Vande Moere, A & Patel, S 2009, 'The physical visualization of information: Designing data sculptures in an educational context', in M Huang, Q Nguyen & K Zhang (eds), *Visual information communication*, pp. 1–23, Springer, Boston, MA, https://doi.org/10.1007/978-1-4419-0312-9_1.

Viégas, FB & Wattenberg, M 2007, 'Artistic data visualization: Beyond visual analytics', in D Schuler (ed.), *Online communities and social computing* (Lecture Notes in Computer Science), vol. 4564, pp. 182–91, Springer, Berlin, https://doi.org/10.1007/978-3-540-73257-0_21.

von Ompteda, K 2019a, 'Data manifestation: A case study', in T Triggs & L Atzmon (eds), *The graphic design reader*, Bloomsbury Press, London, pp. 763–71.

von Ompteda, K 2019b, 'Data manifestation: Merging the human world and global climate change', in *IEEE VIS Arts Program (VISAP'19)*, Vancouver, Canada, pp. 1–8.

SECTION THREE
MAKING DATA: TECHNIQUES

Section 3 showcases how digital technologies and fabrication processes are enabling new kinds of data-objects. For example, to take advantage of AI computational models to drive new visualization techniques or to explore the potential of networked communities to contribute to, evolve and iterate data-objects. The potential of utilizing smart surfaces, augmented reality and even data sonification to create new interfaces that blend physical and digital elements in creative ways of interacting with and comprehending the data saturated world we increasingly inhabit are revealed.

11
HYBRID DATA CONSTRUCTS: INTERACTING WITH BIOMEDICAL DATA IN AUGMENTED SPACES

Daniel F. Keefe, Bridger Herman, Jung Who Nam, Daniel Orban and Seth Johnson

Introduction

The preceding chapters have made the case for making data physical. Historical and contemporary examples of data physicalization together with design theory and evidence from cognitive science all back the strong potential to provide people (architects, artists, doctors, engineers, scientists, museum visitors and the public) who use or experience data physicalizations with some powerful advantages when compared to our more common digital representations of data. These include improved data legibility, engagement and emotional connection.

In this chapter, we highlight a new application area: biomedical data. Here, the 'users' of our physical data constructs are medical practitioners, engineers and scientists. In the biomedical field, digital data visualizations are already common practice and provide valuable aids for research and clinical practice alike. However, biomedical researchers and practitioners still struggle to make sense of many important datasets. Consider, for example, the challenge of analysing how disease impacts the wiring of neural fibre tracts in the brain or how several alternative designs for an implantable medical device might impact cardiac blood flow for a particular patient. Both examples come from interdisciplinary collaborative research projects with a computer science data visualization lab. Computational simulation techniques and experimental data collection have advanced to the point that data with potential to transform the science of healthcare are finally available, but, unfortunately, the ability to collect and generate these data has far outpaced our ability to understand them. Often these datasets are challenging or impossible to interpret with even our most advanced digital data displays.

In theory, physical data constructs may provide an urgently needed solution that makes it possible to *more readily and accurately perceive* complex biomedical data. These data are typically spatial, with critically important but difficult-to-see spatial relationships. So, the first place to start when designing any data representation is to understand that the data require viewing from many angles. Consider just this requirement for a moment. When the data are made physical, there is no need to reach for a mouse or keyboard to digitally rotate the data to a new view; instead we just pick up the object and rotate it in our hands or walk around it. To get a close look, there is no need to use a zooming tool or data filtering widget, just move your head closer. Compared to typical digital representations, this style of interpreting data engages the human visual sense with the same perceptual cues (e.g. light, shadow, texture) that our visual system has evolved to recognize, and the same physical interactions for exploration (e.g. simply moving one's head) that we have learned to use since birth. These are critical advantages for interpreting Biomedical Data. They not only mean that we are likely to more accurately understand the spatial relationships when represented physically but also that we are likely to do this quite naturally, without thinking about the 'user interface'. Physicalizations that engage additional senses (e.g. via sound, scent, haptics) might in the same way make it possible for us to leverage our built-in human perceptual abilities to understand ever more complex biomedical data. Based on work in this area, the table below indicates the arguments for physicalizing data that have the most potential and resonate with biomedical researchers and practitioners.

1	More accurate perception of data by leveraging real-world perceptual cues as opposed to the approximate cues (e.g. approximated lighting, limited resolution displays) that are available with digital representations.
2	A new ability to convey increasingly complex data by engaging multiple physical senses, increasing the bandwidth into the human brain that can be used to understand data beyond the typical use of the visual sense only.
3	Lowering the cognitive effort required to interact with and explore data by leveraging physical interactions that come naturally and, thereby, freeing more cognitive resources for data analysis.

But despite these advantages, there can also be shortcomings. Beyond the ability to naturally view a physicalization from different angles, most data physicalizations do not provide an ability to interact with the data. Most are static in terms of the data they represent. So, the interactive tools that are used so successfully in digital biomedical visualizations to explore data (e.g. selecting sub-volumes for deeper analysis, filtering the data, inserting widgets to view flow lines or particles) do not translate to physicalizations. What's more, most biomedical datasets are time-varying. So, static, physical representations that do not support animation are limiting. These limitations have motivated our search for some form of hybrid data construct that might provide a 'best of both worlds' solution.

This search led us to exploring immersive virtual reality and, especially, augmented reality techniques, where digital data are displayed superimposed in a real-world physical context, either through the use of projectors or head-worn displays. Immersive data visualization using these technologies is not new, and, remarkably, the case for immersive digital data visualization has historically followed much of the same reasoning as the case for physicalization. In the seminal article, *Immersive VR for Scientific Visualization: A Progress Report* (van Dam et al. 2000, p. 32), the authors provide a rationale for immersive visualization that includes statements such as,

> IVR allows much more use of peripheral vision to provide global context. It permits more natural and thus quicker exploration of three- and higher-dimensional data (Leigh et al. 1994). Additionally, body-centric judgments about 3D spatial relations come more easily (Pausch et al. 1997), as can recognition and understanding of 3D structures (Bryson 1996). It's easier to do such tasks when 3D depth perception is enhanced by stereo and motion parallax (via head tracking).

This adds to our confidence that immersive digital visualizations and data physicalization can fit together naturally, and that integrating data physicalization and immersive digital data visualization may lead to a powerful hybrid data construct.

The remainder of this chapter presents the experiences of developing such a hybrid visualization technology and applying it to specific biomedical data understanding problems. It begins with some background on the biomedical applications that motivate the work, then proceeds to present a series of three successive design studies to explore immersive digital representations, physical representations, and how they might be integrated to produce a new hybrid data construct.

Background on biomedical applications

Biomedical engineers creating a new implantable cardiac device need to understand trade-offs in the design space so that they can optimize the performance of the device, but this is a major challenge when the metrics for success are all based on how the device interacts with blood flow inside a specific patient's heart. Recently, computer models and supercomputer simulations have completely redefined the data engineers can work with to understand these phenomena. For example, when designing an improved cardiac lead passing through the right atrium of the heart, engineers have the option to choose an optimal stiffness and length for the lead wire. In the past, these design decisions would be made based on time-consuming bench tests and, perhaps, working with animals. Now, the intent is to shift this type of design testing to computer simulation as much as possible. Using a supercomputer, tens or hundreds of alternatives for the lead stiffness and length parameters can be tested relatively quickly. In a sense, these data are a goldmine. They provide a 4D volumetric model for the heart that allows engineers to ask 'what if' questions as they proceed through the design process. However, these benefits are only possible if the engineers can make sense of the data coming out of the simulations, and this is the current roadblock.

In this case, to understand data like these, engineers need to analyse vortices that form within the right atrium. The time at which these vortices form during the heartbeat cycle is important, as is their shape. For example, the tilt of each vortex needs to be understood spatially relative to the shape of the interior walls of the heart. The speed of the blood flow and how it varies throughout the volume is also important. Finally, the stress and pressure on the heart walls is critical, especially near the attachment point for the lead, which is an area where calcification will occur. These data features are not the type for which one can easily develop a statistical test. To understand what is happening in such complex physical phenomena requires human intuition and seeing the data in context. The design studies described, which took place over several years, can be thought of as a form of multivariate volumetric data visualization for science, a search for more effective strategies for depicting complex vortices, pressure on heart walls, and more in order to make these data more readily understandable and actionable for teams of engineers, surgeons and other stakeholders.

Toward hybrid data constructs: A series of design studies

This section presents a series of three design studies, working toward a new understanding of hybrid data constructs that co-locate digital and physical data representations.

Study 1: Immersive digital visualization

The vast majority of digital data visualizations are viewed through a flat display screen, even for 3D data. Computer graphics engines use perspective projection, lighting models with varying levels of realism and other computational techniques to make data appear 3D, but they are always fundamentally a picture on a surface. In contrast, immersive data visualization as supported by perspective-tracked stereoscopic displays is fundamentally different. The sense of presence that is possible to create in these environments can transport participants to another place, time or even body in ways that can be concretely measured by physiological and emotional responses (Sanchez-Vives & Slater 2005). This property has enabled applications to phobia therapies (Parsons & Rizzo 2008), physical rehabilitation (Schultheis & Rizzo 2001), non-opioid treatments for acute (Hoffman et al. 2000) and chronic pain (Schroeder et al. 2013), and promoting empathy for people of a different race, age, gender or ability (Peck et al. 2013). In a way, this sense of presence mimics the benefits of physicalization. Thus, our first design study focused on creating a digital immersive data visualization experience that provides users with a sense of being present with the data, immersed inside the blood flow of the heart so as to enable body-centric judgements of flow patterns, pressure on the heart walls etc.

Figure 11.1 *Bento Box*. Top-left: Digital visualizations of blood flow in the right atrium use animation to make it possible to see the flow develop over time and interactive techniques to select and filter the data. Bottom-left: Physical representations provide the most solid understanding of the 3D form, where it is possible to encode additional data variables 'on top of' the form using a pattern of data glyphs, but these physical printouts are inherently static. Right: Optimal understandings of the data may come from a hybrid construct that combines the best of both strategies. Image credit: Interactive Visualization Lab, University of Minnesota-Twin Cities.

Figure 11.1 (top-left) shows the result. This is part of an immersive data visualization application we call Bento Box (Johnson et al. 2019) because it addresses not just the challenge of how to immerse the viewer inside a single cardiac simulation but also how to divide 3D space into a logical grid to support simultaneous analysis of multiple simulations, specifically to compare different lead length and stiffness parameters. In the simulation, the 'lead length' parameter defines the length of wire that is present in the atrium, an important consideration because if it is too short the wire might pull at the heart walls as the heart beats, and if it is too long the wire might disturb the blood flow or bump the heart wall during the heartbeat. The 'stiffness' parameter is closely related. It defines the flexibility of the wire, that is, how much it will bend when blood flows past it and the heart walls contract. So the overall movement of the device and its impact on blood flow in the heart is closely tied to both parameters. To help the engineers to understand this design space, the visualization combines an intelligent layout and effective use of interactive techniques for exploring the data. Each grid cell contains an interactive 3D volume of the simulation data that appears to hang in space just within reach of the user. These data-driven graphics portray heart walls and device surfaces coloured by the user's choice of stress or pressure variables, and streaks of light arc and twist along the paths taken by the simulated fluid. With a gestural bimanual user interface (one designed to accept pointing, sweeping, and other inputs from the hands and to treat the dominant hand as the primary input and the non-dominant hand as a secondary input), new internal views are carved out using 3D click-and-drag interactions with a six degree-of-freedom tracking device (similar to Figure 11.1 right), the orientation of each example is adjusted to tweak the view for the best analysis, and the timepoint is adjusted with an interactive timeline widget to inspect critical moments in the regular beat of the heart.

This design study illustrates important benefits of immersive digital visualization (sense of presence, interactivity, animation), but at the same time, there are some significant weaknesses that motivated the next studies. The presentation of rich immersive virtual experiences like Bento Box requires expensive, specialized head-tracked stereoscopic displays. And due to technical limitations, such head-tracked systems are generally limited to a single participant at a time, requiring collaborators to take turns immersing themselves in their data. For as 'real' as these interactive images appear to the eye, upon manual inspection they are found to be truly illusory, lacking any substance with which the human hand might make a familiar physical connection. Thus, despite the profound experience that immersive digital visualization can provide visually, such methods only begin to take advantage of the senses used daily for discerning information in our physical world.

Study 2: Multivariate data physicalization on 3D printed surfaces

The second design study centres data physicalization. Reinforcing the arguments established in the introduction, the early experience with the 3D printed atrium data was compelling. It seemed that despite best efforts with high-resolution, low-latency, perspective-tracked, stereoscopic displays there is still something special and intuitive about holding a 3D printout of the data (similar to those in Figure 11.1 bottom left). There is no longer much of a technical barrier to accomplishing this; 3D printers are now easy to use and relatively cheap (at least for most engineers, scientists and surgeons working with these data). So, physicalization in this way makes a lot of sense. On the other hand, there are clear tradeoffs. Moving from working with the data-rich digital visualizations described in study 1 to a simple printout of the 3D surface of the atrium, illuminated the obvious limitation that with the typical 3D printer, the only 'data' that one can display is the surface itself. Whereas with digital representations it is trivial to apply a colour map to this surface to depict pressure on the heart walls, even this seemingly basic data encoding is not possible with a typical 3D printout.

To better understand this limitation and how the way we encode data on the heart walls might be adapted to better suit the potential of data physicalization, a series of prototypes that physicalize both surface data *and* scalar data fields (e.g. pressure) on the surface were designed (Herman & Keefe 2018). These prototypes methodically explored the visual channels seen in current visualization research, such as colour, length, angle and curvature (Munzner & Maguire 2015). Since some of these visual channels are not well adapted for use with current consumer-grade digital fabrication techniques, the prototypes primarily focus on those that translate well into the physical medium. As a preliminary step in enabling a single scalar variable to be physicalized on top of a physical surface, a glyph-based visualization strategy is used (see Figure 11.1 bottom left).

Where physical glyphs representing that variable are distributed over the physical surface four primary considerations need to be accounted for when designing a glyph-based physicalization.

1.	For the purposes of visualizing a single variable, it is best to stick to primitive glyphs like spheres and boxes (Lie, Kehrer & Hauser 2009).
2.	For spherical glyphs, one might think that using radius to encode a variable is an obvious first step, but it turns out that, especially in a physical medium, radius of objects is not perceived linearly (Jansen & Hornbæk 2015). It is better to use a less ambiguous channel, such as the length of box-shaped glyphs.

3.	Since glyphs are discrete, we must sample into the continuous data. Three sampling types explored during the course of these physical prototypes are Cartesian grid-based sampling, Poisson-disc sampling and Metropolis-Hastings sampling (Chib & Greenburg 1995).
4.	For boxes and irregular glyph shapes, not all orientations are created equal. For example, on a 3D surface, axis-aligned glyphs look jagged and disorienting. This problem can be partially fixed by aligning the upward normal of the glyph with the surface normal where it is placed. However, in order to avoid arbitrary secondary orientation of the glyph, we must also consider the direction of steepest descent on the surface at the location of each glyph.

While these physical glyphs are a remarkable step forward for physicalizing both a surface and data together, there are still some important limitations to mention. We've noticed that certain types of glyphs don't translate well into the physical realm, for instance using angle or curvature on physical glyphs to represent a scalar variable leads to a confusing visualization. Additionally, there are still limitations on the capabilities of consumer-level digital fabrication devices. Resolution is still limited for affordable 3D printers, and they lack features such as continuous, multi-colour printing; one must still resort to professional 3D printing services for these benefits. As digital fabrication technologies continue to improve and their prices continue to drop, the constraints placed on physicalization as a means for developing scientific understanding will continue to loosen, and more people will be able to benefit from the immediate comfortability that comes from picking up a physical object and examining it. While prior work (e.g. Thrun & Lerch 2016) has only physicalized surfaces for helping domain scientists develop new insights about their data, we have brought both surfaces and data together into a unified physical model where one can study the relationships between them. In the future, this approach of combining the surface and the data in a tangible medium can be expanded to include multivariate data, vector fields and stress tensors.

Study 3: Initial interactive hybrid data constructs

The two design studies presented thus far (1. immersive digital design and 2. multivariate data physicalization on printed surfaces) confirm hypotheses about the relative strengths and weaknesses of the approaches and advance the underlying technologies for hybrid methods. In this third study, we describe three specific interaction techniques for bringing the technologies together. Focusing specifically on enabling interaction techniques for exploratory data analysis, since that is so critical to biomedical applications. Drawing upon the

INTERACTING WITH BIOMEDICAL DATA IN AUGMENTED SPACES 177

Figure 11.2 Initial hybrid design studies focus on bringing the interactivity that works so well in digital spaces to physical data constructs. Image credit: Interactive Visualization Lab, University of Minnesota-Twin Cities.

results of design study 2, we assume a hybrid construct where the form of the heart is represented physically, and this serves as a consistent 'base' for the visualization, a solid form that can be held in the hands and where there is no question about the spatial orientation of data. To this base, we add digital representations that are capable of displaying animated fluid flow and interactive controls for adjusting the view of virtual data relative to the physical base and for interactively querying the data.

Figure 11.2 (left) shows the first interaction technique. By attaching a 6-degree-of-freedom tracker to the object (e.g. using reflective markers with a motion capture system), the physical construct, which provides a solid frame of reference, may be used to control the position and rotation of a corresponding digital visualization, like a physical world-in-miniature and building upon early work on tangible prop-based 3D user interfaces (Goble et al. 1995). The extension here is that the tangible interface is itself a multivariate data visualization. This first interaction technique establishes a definite interactive link between the two forms of visualization (physical and digital) and so might be considered a 'first attempt' at a hybrid technique. However, it is quite limited in the interaction relative to what we typically see in digital visualizations. Notably, for data like blood flow in the heart, much of the data we wish to explore are inside the surface. A typical exploratory data interaction in an immersive digital visualization, for example, would involve reaching into the blood flow with one's hand and then clicking a button to create a flow visualization widget (e.g. a virtual particle emitter) at that location. How would one accomplish an exploratory data visualization task like this with the new hybrid construct where the interaction is based on holding a solid surface?

Figure 11.2 (middle) illustrates one specific solution to this problem. Extending the collapsible pen prototype introduced by Lee and Ishii (2010) for interacting with virtual tabletops, a collapsible pen interface device was introduced, with passive elastic haptic feedback for interacting with visual elements beneath the surface of the data physicalization. The collapsible, tip-end of the pen consists of a rod that extends from a hollow tube and that can partially slide into the tube. The tip of the rod has a rubber pen tip attached and between the tip and the hollow tube are springs. Thus, the springs hold the rod at an extended length until the pen tip is pressed against a surface. As force is applied, the springs compress and the rod 'collapses' into the tube, shortening the overall length of the pen. This core design, adapted from Lee and Ishii, makes it possible to create the illusion of the pen getting shorter as it is pressured against surface. This was combined with a handheld physicalization and immersive digital visualization to create an interface that adds interactive pointing to physicalizations as shown in the pictured in Figure 11.2 (middle). This interaction can be utilized to control many interactions with volumetric data. In the example pictured the interface is used to place several 3D control points inside the volume of the right atrium. Together these control points define a 3D spline to mark the path that the cardiac lead would take through the tissue.

The final interaction technique moved outside of the heart context in order to provide an easier starting point for the design. This interaction moves beyond interaction with or within the space of the data physicalization to the harder problem of interactions that actually deform the data physicalization itself. This could be used in the biomedical context to adjust the shape and placement within the heart of a replacement heart valve, but in the first example reported the problem is simplified to visualizing a cross-section of 2D flow past two surfaces connected at a hinge, as in an airplane wing. The physicalizations depict the two surfaces, and these are placed directly on a projection screen surface where their positions are tracked by the computer. The digital data visualization is superimposed using a calibrated projection (Figure 11.2, right). The significant advance in this interface is the ability to interactively modify the visualization in real-time. As the physicalization, which takes the form of the two 3D modelled wing shapes, is adjusted using the hands to define the angle at the hinge, the fluid flow simulation responds in real time with an updated digital animation of particles flowing past the surfaces.

Discussion and future work

Design study 3 focuses specifically on interactive techniques, and the rationale for this is worth some more discussion. We believe interaction facilitated by both the digital technologies and physical forms is the most powerful approach to closely integrate the digital and physical spaces that make up hybrid data constructs. A co-located hybrid space enabled by today's latest augmented reality displays can support displaying animated data in the same spatial context as a physicalization without too much additional infrastructure. This is a very good start, but it does not quite live up to the potential for interactive data exploration that can be found in digital-only displays. Yet, if we can discover new techniques (in the style of those explored in design study 3) to support the interactive selection, filtering, slicing and probing operations that are so essential to today's digital visualizations in the new hybrid spaces, making them just as powerful for data exploration as their digital counterparts, then there will be a clear win. Thus, supporting interactivity seems to be the key aspect to continue to explore in future work.

It is worth noting that design study 3 also explores several paradigms for how the digital and physical spaces might be related. With the first two interfaces discussed (Figure 11.2, left and middle), the data physicalization and digital visualization are not co-located. This leads naturally to a focus plus context style of visualization, where the physicalization provides a strong spatial contextual reference and the digital visualization provides (typically zoomed-in) focused views. Naturally, because they are digital, these focused views support easy customization, this is a potentially useful metaphor. Further, the interface follows good practices for bimanual user interaction. The non-dominant hand holds the physicalization and is used, as is typical in bimanual user interfaces, to set the context, while the dominant hand holds an interaction device, like the collapsible pen, to perform fine interactions within the space. In the third interface (Figure 11.2, right), the digital and physical spaces are co-located. This approach feels more integrated, but there are practical concerns to continue to explore in future work. Precise registration and fast rendering with good augmented reality displays are needed to make this approach work well, and these are still expensive and challenging to calibrate and maintain. This approach also constrains the size of the digital display to the size of the physicalization. For biomedical data it may be useful for the physicalization to be real-life scale since this is what surgeons are most used to seeing. If the digital visualization superimposed in the same space, then this means it must also be life-size scale, but in many digital immersive data visualizations users find it useful to zoom far into the data to see details.

Conclusions

This body of work is an important step towards an emerging medium of hybrid data constructs that merge the benefits of physical and digital representations in the biomedical context. Theoretically, this aspiration makes sense. It is fascinating to reflect on the similarities in the theory the visualization research community has used over the years to argue for the utility, first, of immersive visualization and, more recently, of data physicalization. Both strategies are ideal for creating sensate data experiences, and there are strong perceptual benefits to this. Each strategy also has limitations, but, interestingly, the limitations of one tend to be strengths of the other. Design study 1 confirms the utility in the biomedical context of using interactive techniques to explore 4D data, exploring data changes both over time (i.e. as the heart beats) and across different biomedical simulation scenarios (i.e. different cardiac lead parameters). Analysing 4D blood flow in this context requires making complex spatial judgements of both 3D surfaces, such as the heart walls, and the dynamic fluid flow within them. Design study 2 suggests that, for surfaces like the heart walls, working with physical rather than virtual constructs can not only improve our understanding of the form, but we can also extend the physical printing methodology to print data glyphs directly on such a surface in order to encode scalar (1D) data fields. Since our understanding of the spatial relationships with physical displays like this is so strong, this approach can be even more effective than purely virtual ones when working with static data (i.e. a snapshot of a moment in time). However, since biomedical contexts are dynamic, often involving complex changes over time, design study 3 explores a hybrid approach that combines the key results of design study 1 (interactive techniques and animation for the best understanding of dynamic data) with the key results of design study 2 (a well-defined, touchable, physical printout for the best understanding of complex 3D surface data). The results are preliminary but promising and already demonstrate three complementary interaction techniques: (1) inspecting data from multiple vantage points, (2) selecting points of interest within a 3D physical printout and (3) manipulating the physical construct as a control interface for a virtual counterpart. In conclusion, the three studies provide a strong starting point, but it is recognized this is just the beginning for creating hybrid data constructs within a biomedical context. Much more is possible, and work will continue to focus on 'interaction', to help to intensify the link between digital and physical, this is the key to making hybrid data constructs a tool that is greater than the sum of its parts.

Acknowledgements

This work was supported in part by the National Science Foundation (1251069, 1704604, 1704904), the National Institutes of Health (1R01EB018205-01) and computational resources from the Minnesota Supercomputing Institute. Special thanks also to interdisciplinary partners who guided the medical device design applications, including Dr Arthur Erdman, Dr H. Birali Runesha, Bethany Juhnke and Lingyu Meng.

References

Bryson, S 1996, 'Virtual reality in scientific visualization,' *Communications of the ACM*, vol. 39, no. 5, pp. 62–71.
Chib, S & Greenberg, E 1995, 'Understanding the metropolis-hastings algorithm', *The American Statistician*, vol. 49, no. 4, pp. 327–35.

Goble, JC, Hinckley, K, Pausch, R, Snell, JW & Kassell, NF 1995, 'Two-handed spatial interface tools for neurosurgical planning', *Computer*, vol. 28, no. 7, pp. 20–6.

Herman, B & Keefe, DF 2018, 'Boxcars on potatoes: Exploring the design language for tangible visualizations of scalar data fields on 3D surfaces', in *International workshop toward a design language for data physicalization* http://ivlab.cs.umn.edu/generated/pub-Herman-2018-Boxcars.php.

Hoffman, HG, Doctor, JN, Patterson, DR, Carrougher, GJ & Furness, TA III 2000, 'Virtual reality as an adjunctive pain control during burn wound care in adolescent patients', *Pain*, vol. 85, no. 1–2, pp. 305–9.

Jansen, Y & Hornbæk, K 2015, 'A psychophysical investigation of size as a physical variable', *IEEE Transactions on Visualization and Computer Graphics*, vol. 22, no. 1, pp. 479–88.

Johnson, S, Orban, D, Runesha, HB, Meng, L, Juhnke, B, Erdman, A, Samsel, F & Keefe, DF 2019, 'Bento box: An interactive and zoomable small multiples technique for visualizing 4D simulation ensembles in virtual reality', *Frontiers in Robotics and AI*, vol. 6, DOI: 10.3389/frobt.2019.00061.

Lee, J & Ishii, H 2010, 'Beyond: Collapsible tools and gestures for computational design', in *CHI'10 Extended Abstracts on Human Factors in Computing Systems*, Atlanta, Georgia, pp. 3931–6.

Leigh, J, Vasilakis, CA & DeFanti, TA 1994, 'Virtual reality in computational neuroscience', in R Earnshaw (ed.), *Proc. Conf. on Applications of Virtual Reality*, British Computer Society, Wiltshire, UK.

Lie, AE, Kehrer, J & Hauser, H 2009, 'Critical design and realization aspects of glyph-based 3D data visualization', in *Proceedings of the 25th Spring Conference on Computer Graphics*, Budmerice, Slovakia, pp. 19–26.

Munzner, T & Maguire, E 2015, *Visualization analysis & design*, CRC Press/Taylor & Francis Group, Boca Raton.

Parsons, TD & Rizzo, AA 2008, 'Affective outcomes of virtual reality exposure therapy for anxiety and specific phobias: A meta-analysis', *Journal of Behavior Therapy and Experimental Psychiatry*, vol. 39, no. 3, pp. 250–61.

Pausch, R, Proffitt, DR & Williams, G 1997, 'Quantifying immersion in virtual reality' in *SIGGRAPH 97: The 24th International Conference on Computer and Interactive Techniques*, New York, pp. 13–18.

Peck, TC, Seinfeld, S, Aglioti, SM & Slater, M 2013, 'Putting yourself in the skin of a black avatar reduces implicit racial bias', *Consciousness and Cognition*, vol. 22, no. 3, pp. 779–87.

Sanchez-Vives, MV & Slater, M 2005, 'From presence to consciousness through virtual reality', *Nature Reviews Neuroscience*, vol. 6, no. 4, pp. 332–9.

Schroeder, D, Korsakov, F, Jolton, J, Keefe, FJ, Haley, A & Keefe, DF 2013, 'Creating widely accessible spatial interfaces: Mobile VR for managing persistent pain', *IEEE Computer Graphics and Applications*, vol. 33, no. 3, pp. 82–8.

Schultheis, MT & Rizzo, AA 2001, 'The application of virtual reality technology in rehabilitation', *Rehabilitation Psychology*, vol. 46, no. 3, pp. 296–311.

Thrun, MC & Lerch, F 2016, 'Visualization and 3D printing of multivariate data of biomarkers', in *WSCG '2016: Short Communications Proceedings: The 24th International Conference in Central Europe on Computer* Graphics, *Visualization and Computer Vision*, University of West Bohemia, Plzen, Czech Republic, May 30 - June 3 2016, p. 7–16.

van Dam, A, Forsberg, AS, Laidlaw, DH, LaViola, JJ & Simpson, RM 2000, 'Immersive VR for scientific visualization: A progress report', *IEEE Computer Graphics and Applications*, vol. 20, no. 6, pp. 26–52.

12
SONIC DATA PHYSICALIZATION

Stephen Barrass

Introduction

Data physicalisation involves representing numbers and relationships using physical, tangible displays. These displays provide tactile, as well as visual metaphors for expressing and experiencing data, and can unlock new analytical insights and emotional responses.

(Alexander et al. 2019)

This definition of data physicalization includes tactile and visual metaphors but is missing any mention of sound! In the physical world everything we touch and anything we do makes a sound. Tapping on a keyboard, walking around the room, opening a door, boiling a kettle, pouring tea, eating a biscuit. Sounds carry information about shape and material, as well as the energy and kind of activity. Sounds tell us how big things are, what they are made of, whether they are hollow, hard, rough and much more. Like any other object, a data physicalization will produce a sound if you tap it, or scrape it or drop it. Physicalizations with different shapes and made from different materials will naturally sound different. This made me wonder whether it might be possible to design a data physicalization so that tapping it provides sonic information about the dataset it is made from. Designing a data physicalization to also sonify the dataset requires the mapping from data to physical shape to also include a mapping from physical shape to sound.

3D printed musical instruments

Musical instruments have interactive interfaces that produce sounds by blowing, striking or plucking actions. Moreover, musical instruments have been designed with CAD software, and 3D printed musical instruments do make sounds. Since CAD and 3D printing are often used to create data physicalizations, these experiments point to the possibility to augment a data physicalization with sound using these technologies. The use of sound to convey emotions in music and movies suggests that sound could be a way to add emotional effects to data physicalizations too.

In 2009 a CAD model of a whistle was uploaded to the Thingiverse.com 3D printing community site (Zaggo 2009). The whistle generated considerable attention because it was designed to make a sound, something no 3D printed object had done before. But what generated even more attention was the difficulty of 3D printing a version that actually whistled. The variability in the results produced by different printers and different settings highlighted the sensitivity of the coupling between shape, material and acoustic vibrations.

The challenge of 3D printing musical instruments was investigated further by Arvid Jense (2012) who experimented with a series of percussive temple blocks, as well as whistles, blown tubes (e.g. pan pipes), Helmholz resonators (e.g. a blown bottle) and 'impossible' instruments of a complexity that is only possible with CAD/CAM processes.

Most of the experiments did not produce sounds at all, and Jense observed that the precision of edges, angles, holes and surfaces was critical. He also noted that instruments printed in plastic did not generally produce sounds of musical quality, with the exception of one particular temple block that had an infill pattern that produced a more wood like timbre.

In 2013 a workshop on 3D printing for Acoustics was organized to introduce product designers to 3D printing with 'music making in mind'. The participants modelled acoustic objects with parametric CAD/CAM tools, and 3D scans of pre-existing objects, to produce a slide flute, a pretzel shaped flute and a percussive washboard (CCRMA 2013).

In 2013 the Shapeways 3D printing service announced the dawning of a 'New Bronze Age' with the introduction of bronze and brass metals for jewellery making in particular (Shapeways 2013). Different metals have different acoustic properties, and brass is especially 'musical' as exemplified by its use in brass bands.

As well as musical instruments, there are other examples of 3D printed acoustic objects that include gramophone records (Ghassaei 2012), speakers (Wolter 2013), music boxes (Left Field Labs 2013) and noise mufflers (Miller 2013). The range of metals and other materials such as wood and rubber continues to expand, opening up a range of acoustic possibilities. High resolution printers can produce mechanisms with moving parts. The capability to print in multiple materials makes it possible to 3D print electro-acoustic objects such as a fully functioning loudspeaker with plastic, conductive metal and magnetic parts (Lipson 2013).

Data sonification

Data sonification is the mapping of information from a dataset or sensor into useful sounds.

Researchers at the first International Conference on Auditory Display in 1992 presented examples of sonification that included exploring multidimensional datasets, monitoring sensors on a medical patient, analysing seismic recordings, debugging parallel computer programs and designing computer interfaces for the blind. They also presented a range of techniques that included the mapping of data parameters to music synthesizer parameters (parameter mapping), physical models of sounding objects (auditory icons), direct playback of the data (audification), hierarchical glyphs modelled on Chinese characters (earcons), triggered samples such as the rate of coughing to represent CO_2 levels (opinionated sonifications) and perceptually weighted beacons for navigating multidimensional datasets (Kramer 1994). Since then there has been an ongoing development of techniques (Hermann, Hunt & Neuhoff 2011).

However, in the context of physicalization, Auditory Icons are of particular interest because the sound is computationally modelled on interactions with simple physical objects, such as striking a rectangular bar made of wood or metal. As an example, the type and size of a file on a computer desktop could be represented with an Auditory Icon that maps file size to the length of a bar, and file type to either wood or metal material (Gaver 1993). A software toolkit for creating interactive Sounding Objects for computer interfaces includes algorithms for synthesizing the sound of impacts, friction and rolling, crumpling, and walking on various materials (Rocchesso & Fontana 2003). Sounding Objects include physical-acoustic models for texture, shape, size, length, material, hardness, density, hollowness, fluid, gas or solid, force of breaking and bouncing events, and rate of pouring of liquid.

Tuning forks

The Fourier theory states that any continuous waveform (such as a sound) can be represented by a set of simple sine tones. This theory underlies the invention of the first electronic music synthesizers that used banks of oscillators to produce a range of instrument-like sounds by additive synthesis. However, long before the invention of electronic circuits, Hermann von Helmholz used the principle of additive synthesis to invent a sound synthesizer made from ten tuning forks. The Helmholz sound synthesizer had a keyboard that could activate different combinations of tuning forks to produce more complex sounds for experiments in speech and music perception.

The sonification technique of Auditory Icons that simulate physical acoustics could be implemented using the mathematical model of a tuning fork in Equation 1.

The tuning fork equation calculates the frequency of vibration of the prongs from the length, radius and shape, and the stiffness and density of the metal.

$$f = (1.875^2 / 2\pi l^2) * \sqrt{((I/A) * (E/\rho))}$$

l = length of the prongs in metres
r = radius of the prongs in metres
E = elasticity (Youngs modulus) in Pascals
p = density in kg/m²
I = the second moment of area of the cross-section in meters⁴.
A = the cross-sectional area of the prongs in meters².

From a CAD/CAM model we can 3D print a tuning fork to find the speed of sound in the 3D material it is printed from. A parametric model of a tuning fork was programmed using the OpenJSCAD software, by using Equation 1 to calculate the length required to produce a specified frequency, as shown in Figure 12.1a.

This software was used to produce a range of 3D printed tuning forks with different shapes shown in Figure 12.1b. The tuning forks with thin handles did

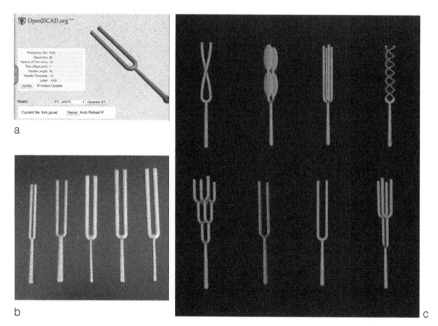

Figure 12.1 (a) Parametric tuning fork programmed in OpenJSCAD (Barrass 2015); (b) Parametric Tuning Forks (Barrass 2021); (c) Tuning Fork and Variations (Barrass 2014).

not ring very loudly. Forks with thicker prongs rang for longer periods. The frequency of the forks varies with the length of the prongs as expected. These initial experiments show that it is feasible to map a dataset onto the shapes of customized set of tuning forks. A set of tuning forks like this could be used in a Helmholz sonification synthesizer that would allow the player to interactively synthesize vowel-like sounds from different combinations of the data values.

The tuning fork has been specifically designed to produce a simple waveform at a specific frequency. However, if a pure tone is no longer the object, then varying the shape could allow more complex tones to be produced. I explored this idea by programming eight variations of the parametric tuning fork, with branches, twists and multiple prongs, shown in Figure 12.1c. These variations increase the number of shape parameters so that more than one data value, or a multidimensional data point, could be mapped onto a tuning fork. Some of these tuning forks do not vibrate very well, but several produce sounds with higher partials and more complex timbres.

Data bells

A bell rings with a frequency like a tuning fork, but the more complicated shape resonates with harmonic frequencies that make a richer timbre. Bells are traditionally cast in metal and shaped by lathing the interior to tune up to six harmonics of the fundamental frequency. The shape and characteristic sound of Western church bells is due to the tuning of the third harmonic to a minor third. Bells tuned to a major third have a more 'bulgy' shape and a different timbre. Eastern and Asian bells have shapes that are even more different in shape and sound (Fletcher & Rossing 1998). The kind of metal affects the speed of sound S and hence the fundamental frequency of the bell. A bell cast in iron is 30 per cent larger than bronze because the S value is 30 per cent higher, and it will ring more softly but for longer (Fletcher & Rossing 1998). Medieval church bells were cast in bronze, which is hard enough to prevent damage from the clapper.

To establish the acoustics of the bell shape a parametric bell was designed in Open JSCAD and 3D printed with a radius of 20 mm, in steel, brass and bronze (Figure 12.2a). This design was used to explore whether it is possible to hear the effects of mapping a dataset onto the basic shape.

On spatial hearing

The first dataset chosen for this experiment consists of measurements that characterize the effect of the outer ear (pinnae) on spatial hearing, known as a Head Related Transfer Function (HRTF). The HRTF data is measured by placing a microphone in the ear canal and measuring the acoustic waveform when a white noise is moved in small steps in a circle around the head. The HRTF is measured for both the left and right ear because human pinnae are not perfectly symmetrical and the different shape of the left and right have effects on binaural hearing. The dataset consists of a 1,024-point spectral filter profile at 90 increments around the head at ear height, which amounts to 180,000 data values in all. The spectral profile data was mapped onto the profile of the bell at 90 steps around the circumference. The left and right ear datasets were mapped onto left and right data bells, resulting in a pair of Binaural Data Bells, shown in Figure 12.2b. The basic bell (no data) rings at 3,000 Hz, the left bell at 3,094 Hz and the right bell at 3,188 Hz. The left bell sounds brighter and more dissonant in timbre than the right bell. Although it is difficult to distinguish the left and right bell by shape or feel, the difference in sound is immediate and clear, lending support to the hypothesis that acoustic data sonifications could allow analytical insights into datasets (Barrass 2012).

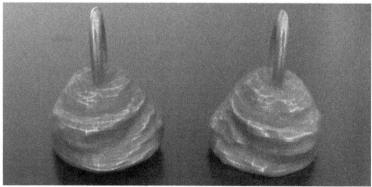

Figure 12.2 (a) 3D printed bells in Steel, Brass and Bronze (Barrass 2021); (b) Binaural Data Bells (Barrass 2021).

Blood pressure singing bowls

Hypertension, or high blood pressure, is a common disorder afflicting one in seven adult Australians. It is sometimes called 'the silent killer' because there are no symptoms, and many people are unaware that they have this potentially lethal condition. When I was diagnosed with hypertension I began measuring my blood pressure with a cuff that sends the data to an app on a mobile phone. The data consists of systolic pressure, which is the maximum pressure on the arteries when the heart beats, and diastolic pressure, which is the minimum pressure when the heart relaxes. The data measurements are usually graphed as a time series, the generic nature of the graph made me wonder if there could be a way to present health datasets in a more emotionally engaging and motivating way. Could the sound of your own blood pressure provide an antidote to the silent killer?

In the previous experiment the choice of a bell set up an expectation of how the acoustic sonification would sound. However, other 3D printed instruments, such as the pan-pipe, whistle, flute, percussion block, rattle or gramophone record could also be used. For this particular health dataset I chose the Tibetan Singing Bowl due to its association with meditation and other wellness and relaxation therapies. Antique singing bowls are sought by collectors for their unique and individual sounds which are the result of hand crafting from alloys that include combinations of gold, silver, mercury, copper, iron, tin, lead, zinc, nickel and other trace elements. Modern singing bowls, such as the one shown in Figure 12.3a, are mass manufactured by casting in bronze which makes them much more uniform in material, shape and the sounds they produce. I wondered if customizing a 3D printed singing bowl by modifying the shape with my blood pressure dataset might be a way to give it a personal and unique sound.

The simple shape of a singing bowl makes it straight forward to model in a CAD/CAM programming environment. The next stage was to map blood pressure data onto the shape in some way so that it would have an acoustic effect. The dataset consists of pairs of systolic/diastolic measurements recorded twice a week over the period of a year, resulting in ninety pairs of points. I began by mapping the timeline onto the shape profile of the bowl in a manner similar to the Binaural Data Bells. The systolic data value was mapped to the inner wall profile, and the diastolic data to the outer wall. The resulting 3D printed Blood Pressure Singing Bowl, shown in Figure 12.3b, rings with a dominant frequency of 3,609 Hz for 3 seconds. However it does not 'sing' when it was rubbed with the Puja stick. This may be because wall is 5 mm thick to accommodate the dynamic range of data variations, which makes it too rigid to resonate, whereas the wall of the Tibetan singing bowl is only 2-mm thick and vibrates more freely.

Limiting the thickness so it will resonate required rethinking the mapping of the data onto the shape. Mapping the time series around the circumference rather than down the shape profile was tried. The pairs of systolic/diastolic data values were

Figure 12.3 (a) Tibetan Singing Bowl cast in Bronze (Barrass 2021); (b) Blood Pressure Singing Bowl with profile mapping (Barrass 2021); (c) Hypertension Singing Bowl (Barrass 2021); (d) Chemo Singing Bowl with Bezier spokes (Barrass 2021).

assigned to radial spokes that connect the rim to the base. The systolic pressure modulates the radial displacement of the upper half of the spoke, and the diastolic pressure modulates the lower half. The idea is that the modulation of the upper and lower parts of each spoke inward and outward should produce an individual acoustic effect at each spoke. Rubbing the rim should activate the spokes to additively synthesize an acoustic sonification of the entire dataset as each of the spokes vibrates in a slightly different way. The Hypertension Singing bowl, shown in Figure 12.3c, is 100 mm in diameter, with volume 18.7 cm^3 and weighs 162 g.

The Hypertension Singing Bowl sings at a dominant frequency of 609 Hz, with four or five partials that vary over time and a 2-Hz tremolo. Striking it produces an interesting 'whispering' effect for about 2 seconds that may be due to acoustic interference between vibrating spokes (Barrass 2014, 2016).

When I showed the Hypertension Singing Bowl to a friend she mentioned that she had a blood pressure dataset recorded during a year of chemotherapy for cancer. This dataset provided the means to further explore the effect of data on the sound of the singing bowl. In order to increase the effects of the data values the data pairs were mapped to control points on S-shaped Bezier splines that extended the spokes further inwards and outwards from the bowl, as seen in the Chemo Singing Bowl shown in Figure 12.3d.

The Chemo Singing Bowl sings with a dominant frequency of 598 Hz, but it is faint and does not resonate for long. When struck it clanks like a crumpled tin can, with inharmonic partials that interfere for 10 seconds or so. I was disappointed because the bowl was intended to be a present for my friend who had so generously provided the data. However my feelings about the sound changed when she heard it:

it sounds exactly as I imagine to have sounded while having chemo! It's painful to experience it, but quite accurate – the sound is dry and heavy, without much resonance, just like I felt!

This insight made me realize that although we often think of datasets as objective measurements, a healthcare dataset can have traumatic experiences associated with it. Why should the sonification of data from an unpleasant experience sound pleasant? The dissonant sound of the Chemo Singing Bowl is true to the data and to the experience it was measured from.

Conclusion

These experiments with acoustic sonification and data physicalizations open the door to many new and exciting possibilities. The parametric tuning fork demonstrates that computer-based Auditory Icon mappings can be realized in a physical form. Adding more variation to the shape parameters of the tuning fork allows more data values and multidimensional data points to be physicalized in this form. However these early prototypes have also raised the issue that many variations do not vibrate well enough to produce an acoustic sonification. These experiments highlight the tight coupling between shape, material and acoustics and the need for further investigation of the acoustic properties of 3D printed sounding objects. They also point to the opportunities that CAD/CAM provides to explore innovative acoustic shapes.

The 3D printed bells demonstrate the effect that different materials such as steel, brass and bronze have on timbre and resonance due to their effects on the speed of sound. The Binaural Data Bells demonstrate the mapping of the data onto the shape profile of the bell so that the entire dataset can be heard all at once when it is struck. The pair of bells allows an appreciation of the effectiveness of the sound to allow the immediate perception of small differences between these two large datasets that are difficult to distinguish visually or through touch.

The data to shape profile mapping strategy from the bells was employed to map a year of personal blood pressure measurements onto the shape of a singing bowl. The musical metaphor of the singing bowl was chosen because of its association with health and well-being. This design choice changes how the acoustic sonification will sound, and introduces an additional mode of interaction by rubbing the rim with a puja stick to make it sing, as well as striking it to make it ring. However the Blood Pressure Singing Bowl did not sing very well because the walls were too thick and rigid to resonate. A different mapping strategy where the data values effected the displacement of a set of radial spokes designed to vibrate in an additive manner like a set of tuning forks was more successful. The Hypertension singing bowl sings and makes an interesting whispering sound when it is struck that may be due to acoustic interference between the spokes. If this mapping is effective as an acoustic sonification then a Healthy Blood Pressure Singing Bowl made from a dataset measured after medical treatment should sound different. The effect of the dataset on the sound harks back to pre-industrial times when hand-made singing bowls each had a distinctive sound. The Chemo Singing Bowl demonstrates another mapping of data onto the shape that is intended to accentuate the effect of the data on the acoustics. In this case the blood pressure measurements were recorded during chemotherapy treatment and have wild swings and chaotic variations. The Chemo Singing Bowl does not sing very beautifully and sounds dissonant when struck. This raised the issue of the aesthetics of the acoustic sonification. Must sonifications always sound pleasant? The unpleasant clank of the Chemo Singing Bowl points to the possibility that acoustic sonifications could also add emotional effects to data physicalizations. The production of singing bowls shaped by health data could be a case study for the Industry 5.0 revolution based on mass personalization in mass production (Østergaard 2018).

References

Alexander, J, Isenberg, P, Jansen, Y, Rogowitz, BE & Vande Moere, A 2019, 'Data physicalisation (Dagstuhl Seminar 18441)', *Dagstuhl Reports*, vol 8, no. 10, pp. 127–47, DOI:10.4230/DagRep.8.10.127.

Barrass, S 2012, 'Digital fabrication of acoustic sonifications', *Journal of the Audio Engineering Society*, vol. 60, no. 9, pp. 709–15.

Barrass, S 2014, 'Acoustic sonification of blood pressure in the form of a singing bowl', in *Proceedings of the Conference on Sonification in Health and Environmental Data*, York University, UK.

Barrass, S 2016, 'Diagnosing blood pressure with acoustic sonification singing bowls', *International Journal of Human-Computer Studies*, vol. 85, pp. 68–71, https://doi.org/10.1016/j.ijhcs.2015.08.007.

CCRMA 2013, *3D printing for acoustics workshop*, CCRMA, https://ccrma.stanford.edu/workshops/pa3d2012/2013/.

Dakota Ultrasonics 2020, *References: Appendix A velocity table*, Dakota Ultrasonics, https://dakotaultrasonics.com/reference/.

Fletcher, NH & Rossing, TD 1998, *The physics of musical instruments*, Springer, New York.

Gaver, WW 1993, 'Synthesizing auditory icons', in *Proceedings of the INTERACT '93 and CHI '93 Conference on Human Factors in Computing Systems*, pp. 228–35, https://doi.org/10.1145/169059.169184.

Ghassaei, A 2012, *3D printed record*, Amanda Ghassaei, http://www.amandaghassaei.com/3D_printed_record.html.

Hermann, T, Hunt, A & Neuhoff, JG (eds) 2011, *The sonification handbook*, Logos Publishing House, Berlin.

Jense, A 2012, 'Possibilities for 3D printing musical instruments', Masters Dissertation, University of Twente, http://3dprintedinstruments.wikidot.com/.

Kramer, G (ed.) 1994, *Auditory display, sonification, audification and auditory interfaces*, SFI Studies in the Sciences of Complexity, Proceedings Volume XVIII, Addison-Wesley Publishing Company Reading, MA, USA.

Left Field Labs 2013, *Music drop*, Left Fields Labs, https://www.leftfieldlabs.com/work/music-drop/.

Lipson, H 2013, *Fully functional loudspeaker is 3D printed*, Cornell University, http://www.cornell.edu/video/fully-functional-loudspeaker-is-3-d-printed.

Miller, J 2013, *Vacuum pump muffler*, Design & Make, http://jmillerid.com/wordpress/2013/03/vacuum-pump-muffler/.

Østergaard, EH 2018, *The 'human touch' revolution is now under way*, International Society of Automation, https://www.isa.org/intech-home/2018/march-april/features/welcome-to-industry-5-0.

Rocchesso, D & Fontana, F (eds) 2003, *The sounding object*, Ass. Culturale Mondo Estremo.

Shapeways 2013, '3D printing enters the Bronze Age', blog post, *Shapeways*, https://www.shapeways.com/blog/archives/2296-3d-printing-enters-the-bronze-age-at-shapeways.html.

Wersényi, GY 2010, 'Representations of HRTFs using MATLAB: 2D and 3D plots of accurate dummy-head measurements', in *Proceedings of the 20th International Congress on Acoustics (ICA)*, Sydney, Australia, 23–27 August 2010, https://www.acoustics.asn.au/conference_proceedings/ICA2010/cdrom-ICA2010/papers/p45.pdf.

Wolter, J 2013, *Gramohorn 3D printed acoustic speaker*, Gramohorn, http://www.gramohorn.com/.

Zaggo 2009, *Whistle*, Thingiverse, https://www.thingiverse.com/thing:1046.

13
MAKING WITH CLIMATE DATA: MATERIALITY, METAPHOR AND ENGAGEMENT

Mitchell Whitelaw and Geoff Hinchcliffe

Introduction

This chapter reports on a practice-led research project investigating the tangible visualization (or physicalization) of climate data. Working with the Australian National University's (ANU) Climate Change Institute (CCI), the authors designed and produced an open-ended edition of data-objects: small, laser-cut climate coasters. Each represents one year's temperature data for a single location, in relation to the long-term average. This data translation concept was further developed through the design of a web application, which allowed for an expanded range of data and locations. It also broadened the reach of the project, and enabled users to customize and produce coasters of their own. Reflecting on this work and the contexts of data physicalization and climate communication three key points emerged. Firstly, that data physicalization – making data-objects – can make a useful contribution to the challenge of engaging audiences with climate change data, in the context of an increasingly polarized debate. Second, the affordances of materiality and metaphor are significant here. The material form engages senses of smell and touch, reframing prosaic communication of data as a more immediate encounter; while the metaphor or functional form of the coaster invokes an everyday context of conviviality and conversation. Third, a distinctive hybrid approach to data physicalization, where computational workflows for digital fabrication are adapted for the web is of significant value. We show how this combined approach worked to increase the audience and relevance of the project, as well as to validate the design of the tangible object. The makerly approach adopted here, based on software- and data-driven sketching and experimentation, alongside material prototyping, enabled movement between physical and screen-based visualization. As an instance of 'making data', this project operates within a broader networked context of cultural and technical data practices.

Making climate data physical

As mentioned above, this project originated from a conversation in late 2017 with researchers from the ANU CCI. Discussions of potential data visualization collaborations focused on the need to expand the climate-related discourse, to draw more people into the climate conversation and engage with them more effectively. As Bolson and Shapiro (2018) show, simply gaining the public's attention is a significant challenge; moreover, climate change discourse in the United States is increasingly polarized and partisan. Tranter (2013) shows the same dynamic at work in Australia. Conversations also touched on a growing weariness amongst our communities resulting from a continuous stream of confronting climate news – what Kerr (2009) called 'climate fatigue'.

In response to these overarching challenges and aims, we advocated for the potential of novel forms of data visualization, and physicalization in particular, as well as the value of localized, current data in contrast to the global and national overviews common to much climate-related reporting. Climate data visualizations ought to be attention-getting, inclusive rather than divisive, spark interest rather than fatigue, and motivate curiosity, interest and even action. CCI colleagues were supportive, and proposed a rapid, experimental visualization project: the design and production of a tangible visualization based on data detailing the City of Canberra's temperature in 2017. These data-objects would be small, robust and cheap to produce, and would be distributed at the CCI's 2018 Climate Update forum; a public event providing a snapshot of Australian climate change data, science and policy.

This response builds on previous projects by the authors, such as *Weather Bracelet* (Whitelaw 2009) and *Measuring Cup* (Whitelaw 2010), which demonstrate practical approaches to weather and climate data physicalization. Based on location-specific datasets, these objects encoded detailed time-series data in 3D printed geometry, investigating the affordances of tangibility in representing environmental data; but they were produced in tiny quantities as self-initiated experiments. This project introduced two important new factors: the need for fast and affordable production at scale; and collaboration with domain experts strongly committed to both accurate representation and public engagement.

Given the need to develop a novel physical representation of Canberra climate data, in an edition of over a hundred, with a limited budget and timeframe, development focused on laser cutting as a mode of fabrication. Laser cutting was accessible, fast and flexible, and could involve affordable, sustainable materials such as plywood or cardboard. Based on previous experience with digital fabrication, work began with the sketching of potential designs. These sketches were not hypothetical concepts, but more like working prototypes. By using data sourced readily from the Australian Bureau of Meteorology and the coding framework p5.js[1] (McCarthy 2020), we were able to generate visual concepts through a process of code-based experimentation and iteration based on actual (rather than imagined) data. The visualization coalesced around a disc-like shape, where time-series data is shown as a set of radial line graphs encoding daily and monthly average maximum temperatures, as well as their relation to local long-term averages. The use of a radial layout for an annual time-series resonates with the annual seasonal cycle (and in turn the earth's orbital cycle), echoing the approach used in *Weather Bracelet* and *Measuring Cup*, where the radial layout of an annual cycle creates the outer edge of both forms.

As illustrated in Figure 13.1, the visualization design was developed through an iterative process of sketching, testing, prototyping, consultation and annotation. Fundamental questions addressed through this process included how much data to show, and how and where to show it. The design quickly settled on a layout where monthly values and averages are shown on the outer edge; this privileged the simpler and more legible monthly values, while the unlabelled daily data on the inner graph visually supports and validates these monthly averages. For consistency both daily and monthly time-series are shown as anomalies, that is, as difference from long-term monthly average. Values above the long-term monthly average are plotted outside the reference line, and below average values inside it. The above-average area of both graphs is etched, drawing attention to these signals of a warming trend.

Full scale paper prototypes were produced (Figure 13.1c and d) which proved invaluable in discussing design decisions with collaborators in the CCI. Based on these discussions the inclusion of daily minimum temperatures in the inner graph (Figure 13.1c) seemed to be an unnecessary complication that impaired legibility. Hand-annotation in the form of drawn notes on the laser cut prototypes proved useful, enabling quick modifications and visual notations of discussions around tick marks, labelling, and the alignment of inner and outer time series. The radial lines in the final design that mark out the months and their anomaly values are evident in Figure 13.1c. Similarly, the etching of the above average portion of the daily graph is shown here as an annotation.

Early fabrication tests (Figure 13.1e) played multiple roles, helping to resolve physical scale, as well as refining the graphical encoding of data and its translation into laser fabrication. A key discovery was the effect of combining raster (area) etching with vector etching (essentially a low-powered cut that scores the surface of the material). The vector etch provides a crisp edge that improves the legibility and detail of the daily graph (see Figure 13.1g). This process culminated in a design, generated through a combination of dynamic code-driven visualization (for the graph elements) and static typography and layout design to resolve type for labels, legends, data attribution and credits.

The idea of a coaster arose fairly organically through the visualization process. Early software sketches used the more generic term 'disc', with some variants

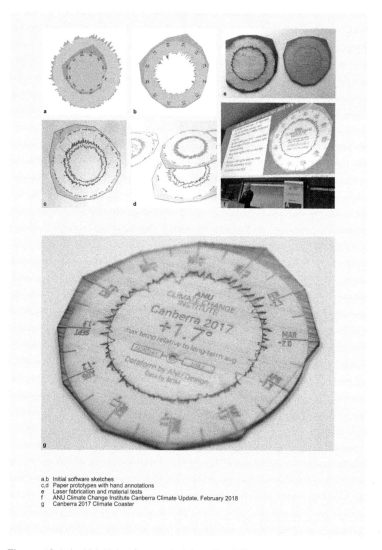

a,b Initial software sketches
c,d Paper prototypes with hand annotations
e   Laser fabrication and material tests
f   ANU Climate Change Institute Canberra Climate Update, February 2018
g   Canberra 2017 Climate Coaster

Figure 13.1 (a, b) Initial software sketches; (c, d) Paper prototypes with hand annotations; (e) Laser fabrication and material tests; (f) ANU Climate Change Institute Canberra Climate Update, February 2018; (g) Canberra 2017 Climate Coaster. All works and images by Mitchell Whitelaw (a–d) and Geoff Hinchcliffe (e–g).

including a quite un-coaster-like central hole. As the design developed around a radial data layout, laser cut from thin plywood, 'coaster' emerged as a more appropriate term. In doing so it clarified design aims that resonated with earlier investigations, of dataforms as small wearable or handle-able objects intended for an everyday context (Whitelaw 2012). Unlike *Weather Bracelet* (technically wearable but in practice uncomfortable) or *Measuring Cup* (a small and only semi-functional vessel) the coaster offered a simple form that could be functional while also unobtrusively occupying a commonplace desk- or table-top environment.

The first edition of coasters was cut from recycled bamboo plywood and given to attendees of the CCI's Climate Update event in Canberra 2018. The coasters were greeted with great enthusiasm and observing them in the wild provided us with rich insights and affirmed the proposition that physical dataforms could be a catalyst for activating the climate conversation. The novelty of the coaster form, the texture of the bamboo and especially the smell of the wood served as easy access points for convivial discussion and reflection. People were animated by the physicality of the coasters and intrigued by their smell, but were also interested in their production and whether more could be made, whether they could be made for other locations and whether people could make their own. These questions were used to drive the next phase of the project.

Networked making

In order to make more coasters, for more locations, and ideally allow anyone to make their own, the code written to generate the coaster was converted into a freestanding web application.[2] Technically, this process was made easier by the fact that this code used Javascript libraries that run natively in a web browser. To address more locations, Bureau of Meteorology (BOM) data for 111 Australian sites was accessed, and the code adjusted to accommodate the dramatic range of temperature variations evident in these geographically diverse sites. An added benefit of using the BOM's ACORN-SAT data is that it features historical data for much of the twentieth century, which allowed for the visualization of multiple years for each location (Australian Bureau of Meteorology 2020a).

Web visualizations were developed through a further process of data-driven sketching, focused on adapting the physical coaster design, to be tailored for the dataset and to handle the wide variation in data across multiple sites and years (Figure 13.2a and b). The final site took the form of a single page web app that allows visitors to generate coasters based on 111 locations over a thirty-year period, or to prepare and upload data from other locations (Figure 13.2c). The app offers visitors the option of downloading SVG files which can be used for laser cutting, as well as image files for printing or social media sharing (Figure 13.2d, and e). As a simple Javascript application, it uses no database or server-side scripts, and instead runs in the user's web browser, loading data from CSV text files. All of the calculation and visual rendering are computed in the browser rather than on a web server, and as such, the app is lightweight, fast to load and responsive to the user's input.

In developing the app we looked beyond immediate functional aims (more coasters, more locations, more makers) and took the opportunity to leverage the affordances of the web browser to create an interface that is concerned with data visualization as much as user input. For example the map interface, which allows for the selection of a specific location, also uses coloured dots to visualize the annual temperature anomaly for each site, providing a unique national overview for the selected year. Similarly, a timeline graphs the annual anomaly for the selected location over a thirty-year period, while clicking the graph selects the year to be displayed (Figure 13.2c2). In addition to selecting an individual year, the app allows the thirty-year period to be played as an animated sequence in which the coaster visualization and interface elements transform and transition between states. The additional interface visualizations are based on the same daily maximum temperature recordings that underpin the coaster, with each visualization representing a different scale; the coaster shows daily, monthly and annual anomaly for a single year in a single location, while the map and timeline zoom out even further. This means that the map can represent an overview of 100+ locations (Figure 13.2c1), with the timeline showing daily maximum temperatures over thirty years.

A final notable quality of the web app is that it pursues a different visual aesthetic to the distinctive bamboo texture of the physical coaster. The visual design of the app-based coaster seeks to respond to its browser context and uses colour and tone to accentuate the coaster form and the climate data it represents. The coaster visualization seen in the browser is an SVG image embedded within the HTML webpage. The SVG file format was used in the initial sketch because of its compatibility with a laser cutting workflow; but as a browser compatible image format, it could also be embedded in the app interface. A distinct advantage of SVG proved to be its portability; code-generated SVG graphics could be opened and edited using the desktop graphics application Affinity Designer (AD). AD was useful for tuning the visual aesthetics and allowed for the grouping and labelling of the different elements to be exported as an SVG image. These changes could then be returned to the web application and merged with data-driven graphics.

While the process of converting the coaster code into a public web app was made easier by the underlying Javascript code, the decision to use these libraries was not motivated by the intention of creating a website, which had not been included in the initial brief. The browser is not only a vehicle for websites but a highly accessible development platform and ecosystem. Modern browsers are powerful and as a platform, the web and its related technologies (HTML, SVG, CSS, Javascript, WebGL) are highly accessible. The browser as a development

MAKING WITH CLIMATE DATA

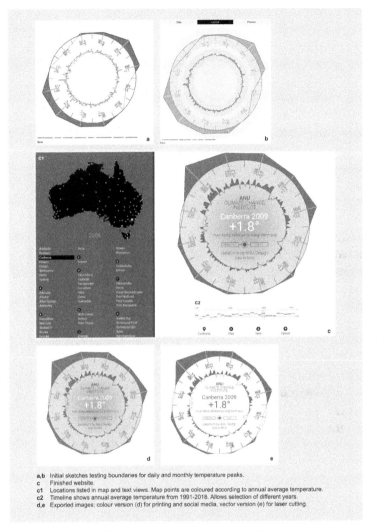

Figure 13.2 (a, b) Initial sketches testing boundaries for daily and monthly temperature peaks; (c) Finished website; (c1) Locations listed in map and text views. Map points are coloured according to annual average temperature; (c2) Timeline shows annual average temperature from 1991 to 2018. Allows selection of different years; (d, e) Exported images; colour version (d) for printing and social media, vector version (e) for laser cutting. All works and images by Geoff Hinchcliffe.

platform is home to innumerable code libraries and generous communities of practice. This context makes it a compelling choice for a creative producer.

Rather than being simply a by-product of the physical data-objects, the web app is an integral component of the whole coaster project. Making software production tools public is a unique attribute of the digital fabrication workflow that should be embraced and explored in other projects. The rationale and benefit of a public-facing website goes beyond facilitating DIY production and has the potential to expand a project in other significant ways. Through the development of the coaster website it was possible to extend the reach of the work. For example the ability to transform a coaster based on location, year or user supplied data is integral to localized representation of climate data, but can also be considered a form of user customization; another compelling opportunity afforded by a digital production workflow. User customization has been exemplified in web applications which permit parametric manipulation of jewellery and clothing designs through sophisticated browser-based interfaces (see for example Nervous System, 2014). But where these apps focus on customization for personal expression, the modest levels of customization in the Climate Coaster app supported localization, exploration and validation, offering personally relevant insights into the data. The app allows users to generate a coaster for their town or city, and as importantly, provides opportunity to explore and compare different locations, to gain an appreciation of the variation between different regions, and ultimately to better understand the workings of the visualization and the data being represented.

Making conversation

In both tangible visualization and web app forms, the Coaster was successful in sparking interest and engagement across a wide set of different contexts, from community groups to government departments and environmental organizations, as well as other areas in the university. In considering these engagements as well as the media coverage attracted, the project showed how the combination of tangible data-object and customizable web platform helped create conversations around climate change and climate data.

In the months following the February 2018 Canberra Climate update, further collaborations with the CCI took place to develop a coaster for a Brisbane-based event. In another iteration artwork was provided to a local activist group Canberra Climate Action, to print paper coasters for distribution at the Canberra Multicultural Festival. The ACT Government's Environment Planning and Sustainable Development Directorate also commissioned additional Canberra coasters to distribute at public events. Following the launch of the web application in May 2018, the Sydney-based Investor Group on Climate Change commissioned 100 coasters for a workshop on climate risk and investment, co-hosted by a major Australian bank. In these cases the modest form of the coaster and its propositional combination of climate data – as shared concern – and low-stakes everyday object, helped carry it into different contexts and to different audiences.

The web application also brought the project mainstream media attention and combined with the novel appeal of climate data in coaster form provided the headlines for media both locally and nationally (ANU Reporter 2018; Green 2018; Sydney Morning Herald 2018). Also notable was the engagement from regional Australian media, who were interested to discuss local concerns, trends and patterns that the web app made apparent – such as the extreme warming anomalies observed in outback Queensland (Bhole & Varley 2018). These instances indicate that fine-grained localization can provide an effective channel for engaging with climate data, especially in often marginalized rural and regional areas.

Discussion

Tangible engagement

The ongoing public life of the Climate Coaster provides some evidence of public engagement in a cultural context marked by polarization and fatigue (Althor, Watson & Fuller 2016; Colvin et al. 2020; Kerr 2009; Smith & Mayer 2019). However the question of how data visualization can support engagement with climate change is complex; in a 2019 paper Windhager, Schreder and Mayr consider the design space of climate change visualizations focused on public engagement, and include the Climate Coaster web application in a sample of thirty-seven visualizations. The authors note that the conventional (objectivist) approach of information visualization – to 'abstain from everything but the chart' and 'just *show the data*' – is untenable in our troubled and polarized social context, where the 'inconvenient' message of climate change encounters many forms of resistance, from fatigue to psychological defence mechanisms and active disinformation (Windhager, Schreder & Mayr 2019, p. 4). In response they advance a multi-level model of cognitive, affective and behavioural engagement that spans attention, observation, exploration, reflection, opinion formation and action. The authors identify a brace of visualization techniques that address these forms of engagement. The Climate Coaster adopts many of these: aesthetic appeal to engage visual attention; animation (in the web application) to guide viewing. Windhager, Schreder and Mayr (2019) recognize the value of personalization or localization to engage users in analysis and reflection. This tallies with the experience in this project, and echoes work in climate communication such as Scannell and Gifford's study showing that a local framing of climate change messaging created greater engagement, particularly among those 'more attached to their local areas' (2013, p. 26). The Coaster design also adopts some of the visualization rhetoric that Windhager, Schreder and Mayr (2019) link with opinion formation. In the Climate Coaster project data is shown in a way that emphasizes the anomaly (difference from 1960 to 1990 average), and visually highlights the warm (positive) anomalies through etching or colour. The data provenance, from the Australian Bureau of Meteorology, is cited to rhetorically emphasize the credibility of both the source data and its visual representation.

While Windhager, Schreder and Mayr (2019) do not address tangible or physical visualization, the nascent literature in that field supports both the functionality and engagement values of data-objects. Jansen, Dragicevic and Fekete (2013) provide evidence that physical visualizations can be more efficient than on-screen equivalents, attributing this to the role of touch and physical manipulation. Tangible visualizations have also been shown to be more memorable than screen-based displays (Stusak, Schwarz & Butz 2015). In a major review, Jansen et al. (2015) summarize the benefits of data physicalization, such as its exploitation of active perception and engagement of non-visual senses. This echoes observations from this project: the coasters sit around on tables and bookshelves, at times they are handled and regarded absent-mindedly, they insert themselves into other conversations, they even prevent hot drinks from damaging precious table surfaces. This persistent presence is a key feature of physical dataforms as Jansen et al. note, 'since physicalisations can be anywhere and are always "on," they can be used as ambient data displays and support casual visualization.' We agree that 'data physicalisations pique interest, and this interest could in turn be leveraged to have people spend more time and effort exploring and understanding important and complex data' (Jansen et al. 2015, p. 3230). Similarly Sosa et al. argue that '[data-objects] are particularly suited for design activism' through enabling access and supporting sense-making, providing 'a verifiable backdrop where conversations and dialogue led by the public can be grounded and articulated' (2018, p. 1693). This usefully summarizes the aims of the Climate Coaster: to provide access to relevant data, in a verifiable and engaging form, in order to prompt and support a public conversation. While the Climate Coasters cannot hope to *solve* climate communication, such devices can be used to reconvene the conversation in an effort to diminish the polarization that has come to characterize the climate discourse.

Metaphor and materiality

The novelty of tangible data is one driver for engagement – in this case the Coaster's functional form worked to bring detailed data (in an unfamiliar form) to a wide audience. In analysing how tangible visualizations map data to physical forms, Zhao and Moere (2008) use the concept of metaphor, drawn from the field of tangible computing, to describe the way recognizable physical forms can provide a bundle of pre-existing concepts. Such forms should be distinct and identifiable (provide a 'single mental image'), provide physical and cultural affordances or cues for interaction, and be widely known or familiar (termed 'intuitiveness') (Zhao & Moere 2008, p. 345). In applying this lens to the mapping of data to form, Zhao and Moere focus on metaphorical distance, and classify physicalizations according to the 'closeness' of their data representation, and familiarity of their physical forms.

By this formulation the coaster form is a metaphor; certainly it provides a single, familiar mental image, as well as a set of affordances for interaction. Moreover, it brings with it certain cultural affordances, connotations and contexts. Zhao and Moere (2008) inherit metaphor from the domain of human computer interaction, where it serves a functional role focused on familiarity, tapping users' pre-existing knowledge to make interaction 'intuitive'. In this case metaphor is equally a discursive or poetic strategy. It exploits familiarity, but also makes a proposition about how and where the object belongs. Found on tables in a pub, a cafe or living room, the coaster is an artefact of a convivial social setting. This object signals its intention, to prompt conversation about local climate in these settings – at the same time putting the proposition that climate data can, in fact, be represented in coaster form. In fact it is a functional coaster, so metaphor begins to lose its meaning here; rather the form is a functional type strategically appropriated.

The material affordances of the form are also significant. In observing people interacting with the coasters, we can see how they are physically *encountered* before they are *read*. The process of touching, feeling and smelling, establishes an affective setting within which the more prosaic, and often confronting, climate data is regarded. As a contrast, consider the context of the climate chart embedded within a news article reporting on the latest dire Intergovernmental Panel on Climate Change (IPCC) warnings. In that context, the graph must be concise and economical in its delivery of key findings. The climate coaster is unambiguous in its representation of temperature trends, but when encapsulated within a typically benign domestic object it invites a slower and more reflexive consideration of the data. Rather than only reading the data, people use touch to *feel* the peaks in monthly temperatures. Smell also proved to be a significant characteristic: daily temperatures are burnt into the surface of the bamboo and above average temperatures burn more material and produce a stronger smell. People could smell the cumulative effect of days exceeding the long-term average as well as feel the peaks of the monthly anomalies. In Australia this data is stark: the average maximum temperature for 2017 was a full degree above the long-term average; 2019 was the hottest year yet recorded, at over 1.5 degrees above average (Australian Bureau of Meteorology 2020b).

Making data: Workflows and networks

The Climate Coaster project shows how data physicalization and everyday data-objects can contribute effectively to the engagement challenges that Windhager and co-authors identify. It also provides a useful case study in makerly physicalization as a technical and creative process. Jansen et al. (2015) identify the technical complexity of physicalization workflows as a key challenge in the field. Workflows here are the sequences of technical processes (such as data preparation, visualization design and fabrication) that making with data demands. In response Swaminathan et al. (2014, p. 3845) and collaborators have presented a tool with an 'integrated workflow', intended to 'lower the barriers to producing physical visualizations'.

Recognizing the value of this work, the Climate Coaster offers a contrasting model of process. Swaminathan et al. (2014) seek to design a 'pipeline', a seamless chain of technical processes delivering a predictable outcome. By contrast this project was developed through formative cycles of sketching, prototyping and conversation. Experimentation with materials and processes played an important role. Finally the technical opportunities of a Javascript toolset were exploited, with public data sources used to rework the project as a web application. This was a crucial move, significantly amplifying the project's impact and utility, but also representing a kind of diversion of the physicalization pipeline: appropriating a technical process and translating and adapting it for a new context. We characterize this approach as *makerly*. While the maker movement has linked this term firmly to physical fabrication, it can be applied equally to software based practices founded on practical experimentation, bricolage and sketching. This project shows how a makerly approach can situate physicalization within a broader, networked context.

This networked context includes technical protocols and infrastructures – the standards and languages of the web, for example – but also entails an expanded social context for the circulation, representation and interpretation of data. In an immediate sense the coaster web application depends on public data sources, available online. It also participates in a networked context where data visualization is an active form of cultural practice and consumption. As Eric Roddenbeck of visualization studio Stamen argues, visualization is a cultural medium in its own right (Rodenbeck 2018). As a public form, the emerging culture of web-based visualization is most potent when it deals with data as a matter of shared concern. The proliferation of visualization and data journalism in online news media in recent years shows this clearly; a nascent, multidisciplinary 'data practice' is arising focused on the cultural, political and creative potential of data in an increasingly digitized culture (Whitelaw 2017). The question of access and agency in this domain is crucial: we recognize the privileged position that enables our own work – including technical knowledge and experience, and ready access to expensive equipment. There are promising signs of broad participation in making with data; community craft projects such as Tempestry, creating knitted visualizations of temperature data, lead the way (Tempestry

Project 2020). In this spirit makers are invited to upload custom datasets as well as download and produce their own coasters. Rather than simplified technical workflows, the future of making with data as a matter of community and culture in a distributed, networked context.

Conclusion

The climate change discourse has demonstrated that scientific facts alone will not necessarily change understanding, and in some cases, may even entrench contrary beliefs. Clearly there is a need to recalibrate the climate conversation, and as Windhager, Schreder and Mayr (2019, p. 7) argue, to 'go beyond the study of cerebral visualization design' and consider 'elements and strategies of cognitive, affective, and behavioural engagement'. The Climate Coaster project demonstrates that physicalization can be used to respond to the same challenges and offers unique opportunities for eliciting affective and reflective engagement. It shows how physicalization can be used to achieve a balance between prosaic and poetic modes of representation and engagement; from an object that is read to one that is encountered. The coaster metaphor, along with the object's physical properties, seeks to prompt reflective consideration. Most critically, the coaster seeks to move the conversation from an insurmountable global scale to something more approachable, local and familiar. The coaster brings climate data to a personal scale; it lives in domestic space on tables in kitchens, living rooms and offices, and it makes climate data something that people can touch, feel and even smell.

Built from the same browser-based workflow as the tangible visualization, the Climate Coaster web app has proven to be a crucial component of the whole project. The web allowed the project to reach a vastly increased audience and to connect with national media organizations. Situating the coaster alongside the software that generates it allowed an audience to appreciate the provenance of the coaster objects and to gain much deeper insight into the data being represented. Being able to explore and interrogate the data, to see how it changes between locations and time periods, adds significantly to the veracity of the physical coaster.

Finally, this project offers a case study in making data: partly in making data tangible, and the creative agency this entails; but also in the cultural and technical contexts that surround and support this makerly practice. The Climate Coaster relies on a model of networked making that is open and inclusive. If as Roddenbeck argues, visualization is a cultural medium for our time, it's crucial that making with data be as broad, diverse and accessible as possible.

Notes

1. p5.js is an open-source Javascript library for creative coding, created by Lauren Lee McCarthy. See http://p5js.org
2. http://gravitron.com.au/climatecoaster

References

Althor, G, Watson, JEM & Fuller, RA 2016, 'Global mismatch between greenhouse gas emissions and the burden of climate change', *Scientific Reports*, vol. 6, no. 1, p. 20281, DOI:10.1038/srep20281.

ANU Reporter 2018, 'Drink coasters worth talking about', *ANU Reporter*, The Australian National University, accessed 17 April 2020, https://reporter.anu.edu.au/drink-coasters-worth-talking-about.

Australian Bureau of Meteorology 2020a, *Long-term temperature record: Australian climate observations reference network – surface air temperature*, accessed 17 April 2020, http://www.bom.gov.au/climate/data/acorn-sat/.

Australian Bureau of Meteorology 2020b, *Annual rainfall, temperature and sea surface temperature anomalies and ranks*, accessed 14 May 2020, http://www.bom.gov.au/climate/current/annual/aus/2019/annual-summary-table.shtml.

Bhole, A & Varley, R 2018, 'Beer coasters show outback towns have the highest rising temperatures', *ABC News*, accessed 17 April 2020, https://www.abc.net.au/news/2018-05-31/beer-coasters-highlight-hottest-locations/9817564.

Bolsen, T & Shapiro, MA 2018, 'The US news media, polarization on climate change, and pathways to effective communication', *Environmental Communication*, vol. 12, no. 2, pp. 149–63, DOI:10.1080/17524032.2017.1397039.

Brace, C & Geoghegan, H 2011, 'Human geographies of climate change: Landscape, temporality, and lay knowledges', *Progress in Human Geography*, vol. 35, no. 3, pp. 284–302, DOI:10.1177/0309132510376259.

Colvin, RM, Kemp, L, Talberg, A, De Castella, C, Downie, C, Friel, S, Grant, WJ, Howden, M, Jotzo, F, Markham, F & Platow, MJ 2020, 'Learning from the climate change debate to avoid polarisation on negative emissions', *Environmental Communication*, vol. 14, no. 1, pp. 23–35, DOI:10.1080/17524032.2019.1630463.

Gifford, R 2011, 'The dragons of inaction: Psychological barriers that limit climate change mitigation and adaptation', *American Psychologist*, vol. 66, no. 4, pp. 290–302, DOI:10.1037/a0023566.

Green, J 2018, 'Climate change beer coasters', *ABC Radio National*, Australian Broadcasting Corporation, accessed 17 April 2020, https://www.abc.net.au/radionational/programs/drive/climate-change-coasters/9800852.

Jansen, Y, Dragicevic, P & Fekete, J-D 2013, 'Evaluating the efficiency of physical visualizations', in *Proceedings of the SIGCHI Conference on Human Factors in Computing Systems*, pp. 2593–602, https://doi.org/10.1145/2470654.2481359.

Jansen, Y, Dragicevic, P, Isenberg, P, Alexander, J, Karnik, A, Kildal, J, Subramanian, S & Hornbæk, K 2015, 'Opportunities and challenges for data physicalization', in *CHI '15: Proceedings of the 33rd Annual ACM Conference on Human Factors in Computing Systems*, Association for Computing Machinery, New York pp. 3227–36.

Kerr, RA 2009, 'Amid worrisome signs of warming, "climate fatigue" sets in', *Science*, vol. 326, no. 5955, pp. 926–8, DOI:10.1126/science.326.5955.926.

McCarthy, L 2020, *p5.js*, accessed 14 May 2020, https://p5js.org/.

Nervous System 2014, *Cell cycle: 3d-printable jewelry design app inspired by microscopic cellular structures*, accessed 17 April 2020, https://n-e-r-v-o-u-s.com/cellCycle/.

Pousman, Z, Stasko, J & Mateas, M 2007, 'Casual information visualization: Depictions of data in everyday life', *IEEE Transactions on Visualization and Computer Graphics*, vol. 13, no. 6, pp. 1145–52.

Rodenbeck, E 2018, *What is data visualization for?*, accessed 17 April 2020, https://hi.stamen.com/what-is-data-visualization-for-83c3a736d568.

Scannell, L & Gifford, R 2013, 'Personally relevant climate change: The role of place attachment and local versus global message framing in engagement', *Environment and Behavior*, vol. 45, no. 1, pp. 60–85.

Schmitt, MT, Neufeld, SD, MacKay, CML & Dys-Steenbergen, O 2019, 'The perils of explaining climate inaction in terms of psychological barriers', *Journal of Social Issues*, vol. 76, no. 1, pp. 123–35, DOI:10.1111/josi.12360.

Shaw, A, Sheppard, S, Burch, S, Flanders, D, Wiek, A, Carmichael, J, Robinson, J & Cohen, S 2009, 'Making local futures tangible – synthesizing, downscaling, and visualizing climate change scenarios for participatory capacity building', *Global Environmental Change*, vol. 19, no. 4, pp. 447–63.

Sheppard, SRJ 2005, 'Landscape visualisation and climate change: The potential for influencing perceptions and behaviour', *Environmental Science & Policy: Mitigation and Adaptation Strategies for Climate Change*, vol. 8, no. 6, pp. 637–54, DOI:10.1016/j.envsci.2005.08.002.

Smith, EK & Mayer, A 2019, 'Anomalous anglophones? Contours of free market ideology, political polarization, and climate change attitudes in English-speaking countries, Western European and post-Communist states', *Climatic Change*, vol. 152, no. 1, pp. 17–34, DOI:10.1007/s10584-018-2332-x.

Sosa, R, Gerrard, V, Esparza, A, Torres, R & Napper, R 2018, 'Data objects: Design principles for data physicalisation', in *DS 92: Proceedings of the DESIGN 2018 15th International Design Conference*, pp. 1685–96, https://doi.org/10.21278/idc.2018.0125.

Stusak, S, Schwarz, J & Butz, A 2015, 'Evaluating the memorability of physical visualizations', in *Proceedings of the 33rd Annual ACM Conference on Human Factors in Computing Systems*, pp. 3247–50.

Swaminathan, S, Shi, C, Jansen, Y, Dragicevic, P, Oehlberg, LA & Fekete, J-D 2014, 'Supporting the design and fabrication of physical visualizations', in *Proceedings of the SIGCHI Conference on Human Factors in Computing Systems*, pp. 3845–54.

Sydney Morning Herald 2018, 'ANU presents climate change in beer coaster and bracelet form', *Sydney Morning Herald*, 24 May, accessed 17 April 2020, https://www.smh.com.au/environment/climate-change/anu-presents-climate-change-in-beer-coaster-and-bracelet-form-20180524-p4zhb3.html.

Tempestry Project 2020, *Tempestry Project*, accessed 17 April 2020, https://www.tempestryproject.com/.

Tranter, B 2013, 'The great divide: Political candidate and voter polarisation over global warming in Australia', *Australian Journal of Politics & History*, vol. 59, no. 3, pp. 397–413, DOI:10.1111/ajph.12023.

Whitelaw, M 2009, *Weather Bracelet*, accessed 17 April 2020, http://mtchl.net/weather-bracelet/.

Whitelaw, M 2010, *Measuring Cup – Mitchell Whitelaw*, accessed 17 April 2020, http://mtchl.net/measuring-cup/.

Whitelaw, M 2012, 'Weather bracelet and measuring cup: Case studies in data sculpture – Mitchell Whitelaw', accessed 17 April 2020, http://mtchl.net/weather-bracelet-measuring-cup-data-sculpture/.

Whitelaw, M 2017, 'Australasian data practices: Mining, scraping, mapping, hacking', *Artlink*, vol. 37, no. 1, accessed October 2021, https://www.artlink.com.au/articles/4574/australasian-data-practices-mining-scraping-mappin/.

Windhager, F, Schreder, G & Mayr, E 2019, 'On inconvenient images: Exploring the design space of engaging climate change visualizations for public audiences', in R Bujack, K Feige, K Rink & D Zeckzer (eds), *Workshop on visualisation in environmental sciences (EnvirVis)*, The Eurographics Association, DOI:10.2312/envirvis.20191098.

Zhao, J & Moere, AV 2008, 'Embodiment in data sculpture: A model of the physical visualization of information', in *Proceedings of the 3rd International Conference on Digital Interactive Media in Entertainment and Arts*, pp. 343–50.

14
WATERFALLS AS A FORM OF AI-BASED FEEDBACK FOR CREATIVITY SUPPORT

Georgi V. Georgiev and Yazan Barhoush

Introduction

In our daily lives, we face an extensive range of practical problems that can be solved by employing novel and creative solutions. The ability to construct such solutions can empower us, enable us to transform our environment and even extend our human attributes to the unknown. However, the creativity and success (or lack thereof) of our solutions is often attributed to simple chance, hard work or innate talent.

This chapter explores whether an AI-based system aimed at creativity support can provide real-time, implicit feedback for conversations involving design thinking. The cornerstone of the developed approach is that the system itself is able to determine the success of a design solution as it is generated. Furthermore, the two main issues explored in this research are the complexity and comprehension of the feedback offered and a conversation around intrusiveness of the system in the creative process. To address these issues, a prototype system that analyses creative design thinking conversations in real time and provides implicit feedback in the form of an 'anti-gravity' illusory mini waterfall system has been developed and explored. The guiding principle behind this approach is that the system will be able to determine the success of the solutions as they are generated, even before we subconsciously feel, know or consciously determine their fate (Georgiev & Georgiev 2018). According to the approach, such solutions can be considered as successful if they are novel, useful and adopted in practice.

We might imagine that a consultative AI-based creativity support system could be deployed as part of a distributed home assistant technology, such as

Google Assistant or Amazon Alexa, to aid in our everyday problem solving. Such a system could help with addressing complex problems, and sensemaking (Weick 1995), with the goal being to help people select ideas that are novel, creative and ultimately, successful. In creative problem solving, sometimes we must make a mistake to learn from it. A consultative AI-based creativity support system can help us identify mistakes while we are in the process of making them. This might prevent us from investing effort in ideas that are less creative and unsuccessful in addition to facilitating reflection, learning and skill acquisition. Failing fast is pre-planned and instrumental for innovation (Leifer & Steinert 2011).

In a data-saturated world, it can be difficult to make decisions or imagine solutions that are novel or creative (Weinstein et al. 2014). Furthermore, complex feedback that requires much cognitive resources or time can hamper creativity or creative problem solving (Norman & Stappers 2015). A consultative AI-based creativity support system could perhaps help navigate this complexity by providing feedback in a simple manner.

To address the aforementioned issues, a prototype system was developed that can analyse design problem-solving conversations in real time and provide implicit feedback though a dynamic data physicalization – which in this case takes the form of an 'anti-gravity' mini waterfall. The metaphor of the waterfall was used as it resonates with both the nature of problem-solving conversations and the concept of flow in creativity. The playful anti-gravity concept relates to human emotions, such as surprise (Becattini et al. 2017) and inspiration. AI-generated recommendations were presented in a physical form to make them feel more tangible and related to the physical/natural world we live in, the water-based media was well-suited to this purpose.

AI-based creativity support

An explicit list of rules is required for the construction of an AI-based creativity support system to allow machines to compute the creativity or future success of a design solution. Current AI-based support systems do not provide unattended feedback or require the interaction of the user with the system. For example, Han and colleagues (2018) developed a computational tool for assisting designers in generating creative ideas during the early stages of design. The tool is based on analogical reasoning and can improve the fluency and flexibility of idea generation and the usefulness of ideas (Han et al. 2018).

In the project explored in this chapter, semantic networks were employed to provide a structural representation of knowledge in the form of graphs (mathematical structures used to model relations between pairs of words) (Miller & Fellbaum 1991). After exteriorizing and representing knowledge in the form of a semantic network, a number of graph-theory measures were employed for quantitative analysis (Steyvers & Tenenbaum 2005).

A recent study by Georgiev and Georgiev (2018) analysed a dataset of design problem-solving conversations in real-world settings by using a sizable number of semantic measures. The study utilized four different semantic variables to quantify design thinking conversations: polysemy, abstraction level, information content and semantic similarity.

More information on these variables is as follows:

- **Polysemy** is the number of direct links between a word node X and its meaning nodes, accounting for the number of meanings of the word node. For example, the 'car' node has five meaning nodes: 'auto', 'railcar', 'gondola', 'elevator car' and 'cable car'. While these nodes are not generated in a specific conversation or context, they represent a model of human thinking. Certainly, in actual problem-solving conversations, there can be numerous other nodes. For example, polysemy appears during designers' verbalizations, and it shows the multiplicity of significations that an object can have (Dabbeeru & Mukerjee 2011). Polysemy has been identified as an essential manifestation of the richness, flexibility and adaptability in meaning potential in thinking (Fauconnier & Turner 2011).

- **Abstraction** in this context is the normalized fraction of the length of the shortest path from the root word node to a word node X and the length of the maximal shortest path from the root to any node in the network. Abstraction indicates the extent to which the word node is generalized, compared to the most specific instance. For example, the word 'vehicle' is more abstract than the word 'boat'. It is known that the abstraction of specific ways of thinking can lead to novel ideas (Ward, Patterson & Sifonis 2004). Moreover, abstraction is a key requirement for the successful use of external sources in design creativity (Goldschmidt 2011).

- **Information content** (IC) is the bits (amount) of information carried by a word node inside the graph. This is measured inside the graph structure of all words represented in WordNet, which is a tree-like hierarchical and interconnected database. IC is measured as the normalized fraction of the number of 'leaves' (terminal nodes) of the word node in the tree and the maximal number of leaves in the network (whole tree). IC is a measure of the informativeness of a unit. For example, IC was found to be an effective method of quantifying design fixation (when consciously or unconsciously adhere to prior ideas, unable to generate new ones) (Gero 2011).

- **Semantic similarity** of two word nodes (Fellbaum 2012; Miller & Fellbaum 1991), X and Y, is measured by the IC of the least common subsumer of the two words (the most specific concept that is an ancestor of both words in a semantic network), essentially quantifying the similarity of the two word nodes. The least common subsumer (LCS) of X and Y is the most specific word node ancestor of both X and Y in the 'is-a' hierarchy (e.g. the LCS of 'car' and 'boat' is 'vehicle'). As an example, semantic similarity has been used to assess the novelty potential of the resulting combination of two concepts (Nomaguchi et al. 2019).

Georgiev and Georgiev (2018) found that three semantic factors can predict the success of generated ideas that have implications for creativity: divergence of semantic similarity, increased information content and decreased polysemy. The following examples illustrate this premise:

- Divergence of semantic similarity: This occurs when, during the design thinking process, a pair of concepts A and B is substituted by another pair of concepts C and D, which are more dissimilar compared to the A and B pair.
- Increased information content: This refers to when concept E is substituted by concept F, which carries more information than E.
- Decreased polysemy: This occurs when a concept G is substituted by another concept H that is less polysemous.

The temporal dynamics of these semantic factors identifies real-world processes in human problem solving that are relevant to the success of produced solutions. However, more importantly, these factors are easily computable, and hence straightforwardly implementable in AI-based creativity support systems. Thus, there is potential for the real-time monitoring of design thinking using AI, which may improve our training, learning and skill acquisition.

Two main issues can be envisioned regarding such feedback:

1. the complexity and comprehension of the feedback might influence the flow of the design thinking process, and
2. the intrusiveness of the system 'telling' the users engaged in design thinking conversations could influence the trend towards success.

The types of data we used are the four semantic variables outlined above. Each of these has a single direction; hence, the overall data have four dimensions. The density of the data depends on the intensity of the conversation analysed. A typical problem-solving conversation has high density.

Analysis of design-thinking conversations

A real-time analysis system that calculates and visualizes the semantic variables of a design thinking conversation was developed. Analysing a natural real-time conversation, although data intensive and not entirely clean (owing to the possible use of jargon and unfinished sentences), can provide rich information regarding the fundamental processes that underlie design thinking (Becattini et al. 2020; Casakin & Georgiev 2021; Georgiev & Georgiev 2018).

In this experiment, the system recognizes the speech of two participants and measures and visualizes four semantic parameters (e.g. convergence and divergence) of the participants' speech in real time. In the initial testing, the time

WATERFALLS AS A FORM OF AI-BASED FEEDBACK

from recording speech and calculating semantic variables to a visual response (plot of the consequent calculation of variables as shown in Figure 14.1b) on screen took approximately 3 to 5 seconds.

The developed conversation analysis system performed three main tasks:

1. Transcribing the conversation into text with a Speech-to-Text (StT) subsystem.
2. Part-of-Speech (PoS) tagging, where nouns in texts are tagged, and the measurement of semantic variables.
3. Calculation and output of the semantic variables through screen-based visualization or other means.

In this research design, the thinking was quantified by using four different semantic variables: polysemy, abstraction level, information content and semantic similarity.

The first experiments with the system were performed to explore the functionality of the system and the possibility of feedback mechanisms. We tested the system with two conversations, each with a different pair of people. The test participants were university students, and all of them spoke English proficiently as a second language. The participants were tasked with 'Designing a solution for the dark and cold winters in Oulu', a town in Northern Finland where

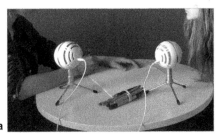

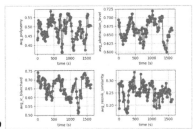

Figure 14.1 Design thinking conversation during the initial testing of the real-time analysis and evaluation system (a) Design thinking conversation feedback with separate; (b) and compound; (c) plots of real-time conversation data. In example (c), four semantic measures are plotted on the y axis, taking values on the axis z over time on the axis x. Images: Yazan Barhoush.

the experiments took place. They were asked to do this using pen and paper, as shown in Figure 14.1a. The participants were asked to work and converse about this task for at least 20 minutes until they felt that they were done. After providing solution(s) for the task, the prototype screen-based visualization output of the system was shared with the pairs of participants. The AI-interpreted data generated during the conversation was shown in the format of Figure 14.1b immediately after the conversation. The meanings of the four semantic variables visualized were also explained to the participants in simple terms. The participants were then interviewed and asked to answer a set of questions related to the data visualization. The explorative example visualization of the same data, as shown in Figure 14.1c, was developed later.

These initial experiments demonstrated that the AI data interpretation system performed in a satisfactory manner. However, the participants identified problems with understanding and interpreting the different variables.

Feedback

As demonstrated by the results of the preliminary study, the explicit feedback in the form of plots (Figure 14.1b and c) was not adequately clear when presented to the participants after the end of their conversations. The participants experienced problems with both understanding and interpreting the feedback owing to the complexity of the graphs. The visualized data was presented at the end of each conversation as it was thought that the feedback, if presented in this form during the conversation, would be distracting, especially because of the complexity of the visualized data and the comprehension required to make sense of it. Feedback in this form during the conversation could negatively influence the flow of the design thinking process.

All participants had some difficulty in making sense of the visualizations or relating them to what was discussed in the conversation. Initially, the participants had some problems with understanding the different variables. One participant suspected that the abstraction level fluctuated because when coming up with ideas, they tended to start with a general idea, which was then focused into a more concrete idea. The participants noted that the system seemed interesting and helpful. When asked about what they thought about the usage of the system, one participant noted that it could help them with critically thinking about the way they speak and cause them to use a more information-rich vocabulary. The system also made the participants ponder on the nature of language and the relationship between language and thinking.

Based on these qualitative observations a more simplified and implicit feedback form that would fit better in the overall design thinking process was proposed as previous research had suggested that conveying implicit feedback is potentially useful in the context of creativity (Georgiev & Nagai 2011).

A Prototype of an 'anti-gravity' illusory feedback system

Based on the results of the conversation analysis experiment, a prototype system that focused on more implicit feedback was developed. The premise for this experimental prototype was to have a binary representation in the form of yes/no (successful/unsuccessful or creative/less creative) trajectory in the trend of the conversation, based on a single semantic variable. We used the divergence/convergence of semantic similarity as the variable with highest potential in terms of the prediction of successfulness or creativity (Georgiev & Georgiev 2018). A waterfall metaphor was used to physicalize this data in real time.

Water and falling water curtains have been used to visualize data and information for several decades. For example, Moere (2008) proposed ambient displays using water, turning everyday spaces into interfaces by changing the states of liquids and those of other media contained in such liquids with data-driven values and representing information using water as a communication medium.

In this experiment, the visual effect of the waterfall as it visualized the data was either the normal effect of water flowing downwards, or that of 'anti-gravity' (creating what is known as the levitating-water effect), where the water freezes in the air or flows upwards (Barhoush et al. 2018). We connected the unsuccessful or less creative trend to the normal effect and the successful or creative trend to the anti-gravity effect (Figure 14.2). Although water flow is a continuous series of close, flowing water droplets, the 'binary representation' is not based on a series of water droplets but on changes in the frequency of the light of the waterfall. At particular frequencies, light creates the perception of water going upwards or freezing in mid-air, but at other frequencies it the water appears to fall as normal. Thus, in this setup a binary visualization of up (anti-gravity) and down (normal) was viewable.

The visualized data can be observed in real time during the conversation instead of during playback after the conversation as in the earlier experiments. The use of water and the waterfall metaphor played with the way in which we think and make creative decisions – creative moments are disruptive and may be surprising, like the idea of water following upwards.

The AI-based system consisted of microphones, a laptop computer with an AI-based conversation analysis system and a mini waterfall system in a closed-box container. The implemented system used two microphones, one for each of the participants. A natural language processing (NLP) pipeline software module was responsible for the calculation of the four semantic variables. In the implemented system, the NLP pipeline module transformed the input text data through a series of steps to a calculation value for each of the four semantic variables.

The NLP module starts with a StT subsystem using Google speech recognition and performs PoS tagging, where nouns in texts are tagged. Then, the module loads corresponding graphs and takes the text from StT processing and the created list of nouns. In the following step, values of each of the four semantic measures are calculated (see Becattini et al. (2020) for example implementations of four variables). In the last step, the output of the semantic variables is created through visualization with the waterfall. In the case of this prototype, only the semantic similarity variable was utilized as it is proven to be the most influential in terms of the successfulness of ideas generated in creative problem-solving conversations (Georgiev & Georgiev 2018). Selection of this variable also allowed for more straightforward feedback – the identified trend of semantic similarity based on a moving window of five nouns either downwards or upwards. In previous research, the downward trendline of semantic similarity has been

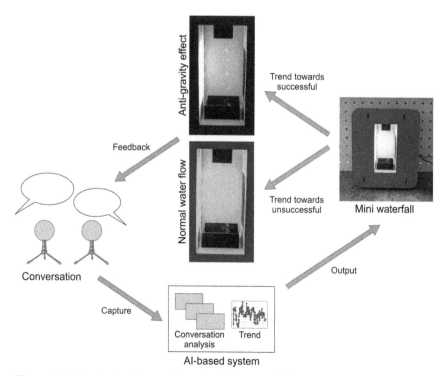

Figure 14.2 Feedback with an anti-gravity illusion waterfall. Image: Yazan Barhoush and Georgi Georgiev.

identified as a feature of successful and possibly creative ideas, whereas the upward one (more similar) is a feature of unsuccessful ideas that are possibly less creative (Georgiev & Georgiev 2018).

The physically prototyped container includes water tanks, a pump and a large strobe light (LED light that was switched on/off at certain frequencies to create the anti-gravity effect) controlled by an Arduino microcontroller and powered by an external power supply (Barhoush et al. 2018). All of the parts of the waterfall system were designed and fabricated in a Fab Lab, including the 3D printing, laser cutting and electronic board production processes.

Discussion and conclusion

Implicit feedback from the anti-gravity illusion waterfall was observed to have the potential to address some of the earlier perceived issues with regard to AI-based feedback on design thinking conversations. Preliminary testing of the system with existing pre-recorded conversations demonstrated that the system can provide simple feedback via the normal and anti-gravity effect. Further work will include larger-scale testing of the proposed system.

In particular, the waterfall can help unravel the complexity of the data and facilitate better comprehension of the trends of the participants' conversations. In addition, the intrusiveness of the AI system and visualized data was mitigated by the implementation of the mini waterfall, which could become a part of an interior space where the participants are engaged in design thinking conversations.

The implementation of this type of data in a physical, interactive object opens further possible directions for interaction, tangibility and experimentation. The tangibility of data has been identified as a powerful way to create memorable user engagement (Petrelli et al. 2017). The customization of solutions via data visualization in different forms is deemed to be critical from a human-centredness perspective (Prendiville, Gwilt & Mitchell 2017). A possible further exploration of the feedback could be focused on other interactions. An example of such interactions is the comprehension and emotions that a participant would experience if they could put their hand in the water and feel the changes of the stream of 'AI data' in real-time.

In this study, we explored a prototype AI-based system aimed at implicitly supporting creativity by providing real-time feedback for design thinking conversations via an illusory waterfall. The developed prototype AI system addressed two main issues with regard to such feedback: the complexity and comprehension of the feedback and the intrusiveness of the system. By analysis of data generated during creative problem-solving conversations with an AI programme, content feedback in the form of an anti-gravity mini waterfall was shared in an implicit, human centred manner. To create a hybrid 'data-object', an AI-based system is proposed that capitalizes on the potential of digital AI technologies to be combined with real-world affordability in a novel and informative way. This project provides only a glimpse of the manner in which these types of systems can be created, and further research regarding successfully developing and deploying such hybrid systems is certainly needed.

Acknowledgements

Great thanks are due the students of the course Applied Computing Project 2, Eemeli Ristimella, Mikko Lehto, Timo Mattila and Dung 'Daniel' Nguyen who implemented the system with the authors of the study. The feedback of the editor of this book, Prof. Ian Gwilt, on different stages of this study is greatly appreciated. This research has been partially financially supported by Academy of Finland 6Genesis Flagship (grant 318927).

References

Barhoush, Y, Mustonen, M, Ferreira, D, Georgiev, GV, Nguyen, D & Pouke, M 2018, 'The gravity of thought: Exploring positively surprising interactions', in *Proceedings of the 20th International Conference on Human-Computer Interaction with Mobile Devices and Services Adjunct, MobileHCI '18*, Association for Computing Machinery, New York, NY, USA, pp. 333–8, https://doi.org/10.1145/3236112.3236160.

Becattini, N, Borgianni, Y, Cascini, G & Rotini, F 2017, 'Surprise and design creativity: Investigating the drivers of unexpectedness', *International Journal of Design Creativity and Innovation*, vol. 5, no. 1-2, pp. 29–47, https://doi.org/10.1080/21650349.2015.1090913.

Becattini, N, Georgiev, GV, Barhoush, Y & Cascini, G 2020, 'Exploring the applicability of semantic metrics for the analysis of design protocol data in collaborative design sessions', in *Proceedings of the Design Society: DESIGN Conference* 1, pp. 1205–14, https://doi.org/10.1017/dsd.2020.141

Casakin, H & Georgiev, GV 2021, 'Design creativity and the semantic analysis of conversations in the design studio', *International Journal of Design Creativity and Innovation*, vol. 9, no. 1, pp. 61–77, https://doi.org/10.1080/21650349.2020.1838331.

Dabbeeru, MM & Mukerjee, A 2011, 'Learning concepts and language for a baby designer', in JS Gero (ed.), *Design computing and cognition '10*, Springer Netherlands, Dordrecht, pp. 445–63, https://doi.org/10.1007/978-94-007-0510-4_24.

Fauconnier, G & Turner, M 2011, 'Polysemy and conceptual blending', in B Nerlich, Z Todd, V Herman & DD Clarke (eds), *Polysemy: Flexible patterns of meaning in mind and language*, De Gruyter Mouton, Berlin and New York, pp. 79–94.

Fellbaum, C 2012, 'WordNet', in *The Encyclopedia of Applied Linguistics*, American Cancer Society, https://doi.org/10.1002/9781405198431.wbeal1285.

Georgiev, GV & Georgiev, DD 2018, 'Enhancing user creativity: Semantic measures for idea generation', *Knowledge-Based Systems*, vol. 151, pp. 1–15, https://doi.org/10.1016/j.knosys.2018.03.016.

Georgiev, GV & Nagai, Y 2011, 'The taste of criticism: Enhancing feedback for creativity', in *Proceedings of the 8th ACM Conference on Creativity and Cognition, C&C '11*, Association for Computing Machinery, New York, NY, USA, pp. 337–8, https://doi.org/10.1145/2069618.2069685.

Gero, JS 2011, 'Fixation and commitment while designing and its measurement', *The Journal of Creative Behavior*, vol. 45, no. 2, pp. 108–115, https://doi.org/10.1002/j.2162-6057.2011.tb01090.x.

Goldschmidt, G 2011, 'Avoiding design fixation: Transformation and abstraction in mapping from source to target', *The Journal of Creative Behavior*, vol. 45, no. 2, pp. 92–100, https://doi.org/10.1002/j.2162-6057.2011.tb01088.x.

Han, J, Shi, F, Chen, L & Childs, PRN 2018, 'A computational tool for creative idea generation based on analogical reasoning and ontology', *AI EDAM*, vol. 32, no. 4, pp. 462–77, https://doi.org/10.1017/S0890060418000082.

Leifer, LJ & Steinert, M 2011, 'Dancing with ambiguity: Causality behavior, design thinking, and triple-loop-learning', *Information Knowledge Systems Management*, vol. 10, no. 1–4, pp. 151–73, https://doi.org/10.3233/IKS-2012-0191.

Miller, GA & Fellbaum, C 1991, 'Semantic networks of English', *Cognition*, vol. 41, no. 1–3, pp. 197–229, https://doi.org/10.1016/0010-0277(91)90036-4.

Moere, AV 2008, 'Beyond the tyranny of the pixel: Exploring the physicality of information visualization', in *2008 12th International Conference Information Visualisation*, pp. 469–74, https://doi.org/10.1109/IV.2008.84.

Nomaguchi, Y, Kawahara, T, Shoda, K & Fujita, K 2019, 'Assessing concept novelty potential with lexical and distributional word similarity for innovative design', in *Proceedings of the Design Society: International Conference on Engineering Design*, vol. 1, no. 1, pp. 1413–22, https://doi.org/10.1017/dsi.2019.147.

Norman, DA & Stappers, PJ 2015, 'DesignX: Complex sociotechnical systems'. *She Ji: The Journal of Design, Economics, and Innovation*, vol. 1, no. 2, pp. 83–106, https://doi.org/10.1016/j.sheji.2016.01.002.

Petrelli, D, Marshall, MT, O'Brien, S, McEntaggart, P & Gwilt, I 2017, 'Tangible data souvenirs as a bridge between a physical museum visit and online digital experience', *Personal and Ubiquitous Computing*, vol. 21, no. 2, pp. 281–95, https://doi.org/10.1007/s00779-016-0993-x.

Prendiville, A, Gwilt, I & Mitchell, V 2017, 'Making sense of data through service design–opportunities and reflections', in D Sangiorgi & A Prendiville (eds), *Designing for service: Key issues and new directions*, Bloomsbury Academic, London, pp. 227–36.

Steyvers, M & Tenenbaum, JB 2005, 'The large-scale structure of semantic networks: Statistical analyses and a model of semantic growth', *Cognitive Science*, vol. 29, no. 1, pp. 41–78, https://doi.org/10.1207/s15516709cog2901_3.

Ward, TB, Patterson, MJ & Sifonis, CM 2004, 'The role of specificity and abstraction in creative idea generation', *Creativity Research Journal*, vol. 16, no. 1, pp. 1–9, https://doi.org/10.1207/s15326934crj1601_1.

Weick, KE 1995, *Sensemaking in organizations*, Sage, Thousand Oaks, California.

Weinstein, EC, Clark, Z, DiBartolomeo, DJ & Davis, K 2014, 'A decline in creativity? It depends on the domain', *Creativity Research Journal*, vol. 26, no. 2, pp. 174–84, https://doi.org/10.1080/10400419.2014.901082.

15
DATA AS ACTION: CONSTRUCTING DYNAMIC DATA PHYSICALIZATIONS

Jason Alexander

Introduction

A Data Physicalization is defined as a 'physical artefact whose geometry or material properties encode data' (Jansen et al. 2015). Such representations can be traced back thousands of years to the Sumerians using clay tokens to represent quantitative data (Schmandt-Besserat 2010) and have evolved over time to become teaching and research tools (Vande Moere & Patel 2010), and art forms (Zhao & Moere 2008). It is only recently that Data Physicalization as a research field was formalized (Jansen et al. 2015) as the physical world analogy to Data Visualization.

There are many demonstrated benefits of Data Physicalizations. These include their ability to leverage our perceptual skills (including active perception, depth perception, non-visual senses and intermodal perception), by making data more widely accessible, enhancing cognition and learning, and by engaging large audiences with data (Jansen et al. 2015). These benefits though must be weighed by the caution that significant further scientific study is still required to fully understand our perceptions and ability to read data from these representations (Sauvé et al. 2020).

The majority of current Data Physicalizations are static representations of a dataset. They are fundamentally limited compared to their digital counterparts as they are non-interactive: they cannot update their data or datasets, they cannot conduct computations and they cannot employ standard data visualization tools (e.g. sorting, annotating (Heer & Shneiderman 2012)). To bring all of these elements into the physical world, physicalizations must include computation and be physically dynamic, allowing the user to interact and manipulate the dataset, and for data points to change and update based on those interactions.

Constructing such dynamic physicalizations is challenging; this chapter seeks to better understand these challenges by examining the motivations and benefits dynamic physicalizations bring over their static counterparts, compiling a range of current approaches to their construction, describing progress in creating and evaluating dynamic data physicalizations, and ending with a discussion of the challenges that remain for dynamic physicalizations to become a mainstream visualization tool.

The motivation for dynamic data physicalizations

Dynamic data physicalizations have a number of key advantages over their static counterparts:

- **Reusability:** when the underlying dataset of a dynamic data physicalization changes, be it due to an update or a completely newly dataset, it adjusts its physical state to reflect this change. In static physicalizations, no such change is possible and so a new physicalization must be constructed. Given their physical nature, this is resource inefficient and unsustainable in the long-term. The reusability of dynamic data physicalizations is a key argument for their adoption.

- **Interactivity:** physically dynamic representations can respond to human interaction – be it direct touch and manipulation or indirect commands – allowing the user to manipulate the dataset to better serve their purpose (e.g. filtering, sorting, annotating), in a similar manner to visualization tools. This ensures the user's data view can be configured for the greatest efficiency and suitability for the data-task at hand.

- **Animations and demonstrations:** dynamic physicalizations support animations of time-series data (including live updates) and can be used to demonstrate a data process. The style of animations can also be used to convey meaning between two data points (e.g. to show variance in a dataset) providing an additional communication channel.

- **Multi-form:** complex dynamic physicalizations can also manipulate their geometric shape and properties to show the same data in different forms (imagine for example, a physical bar chart morphing into physical pie chart). By using self-assembly and reconfiguration dynamic physicalizations can be multi-form, significantly increasing the opportunities for reuse.

While a range of prototypes and construction approaches for the first three of these motivations have already been shown, we are yet to see demonstrations of multi-form physicalizations.

Approaches to dynamic data physicalization

All dynamic data physicalizations require actuation to generate physical movement. There are many actuation approaches including electro-mechanical, pneumatic, hydraulic, organic or human-driven. Choosing a particular actuation technique can be difficult and is usually based on a number of functional and non-functional requirements. Taher, Vidler and Alexander (2017) characterize vertical actuation approaches for shape-changing interfaces (Alexander et al. 2018; Sturdee & Alexander 2018). Their taxonomy highlighted the following features: speed of actuation, granularity (number of stable states), actuation force, actuator size (or footprint), complexity of control and feedback method. Physicalization designers must also consider the accuracy of representation and the desired interaction from the end-users. In this section we briefly review current approaches, with examples, that demonstrate the range of actuation already possible for data physicalizations.

Electro-mechanical actuation

Electro-mechanical actuators rely on fundamental physical principles to generate motion through an interaction between magnets and coils of wire (Taher, Vidler & Alexander 2017). Commonly this occurs through off-the-shelf DC, stepper or servo motors. Electro-mechanical approaches are typically cheap, easy-to-control and provide high-resolution positioning.

Electro-mechanical actuation is a common approach for creating dynamic physicalizations. Examples of its use include EMERGE (detailed below), a dynamic physical bar chart (Taher et al. 2015, 2017), CairnForm that uses shape-changing ring chart to display ordinal data (Daniel, Rivière & Couture 2019), and Sweeny's dynamic physical pie and bar charts for community data engagement (Lindley et al. 2017). Electro-mechanical actuation can also be used to physically reshape an object through extrusion and milling (Weichel et al. 2015), through robotics to move or re-arrange data-objects, or by using multiple drones to self-assemble into data representations (Gomes et al. 2016).

Pneumatic and hydraulic approaches

Pneumatic actuation uses compressed air to achieve actuation, while hydraulics manipulate fluid for the same effect. Pneumatic approaches use compressed air acting on a piston in a cylinder to create actuation along a linear path. One of their key advantages over hydraulics is that the operating fluid is air, so leakage is not of concern (and does not contaminate surrounding areas). A hydraulic actuator consists of a hollow cylindrical tube along which a piston can slide. Fluid is pumped into this tube to create actuation. As hydraulic fluids are nearly impossible to compress, hydraulic actuators can exert large forces.

The use of pneumatic and hydraulic approaches for explicit data physicalization is limited, however the Aegis Hyposurface (Goulthorpe, Burry & Dunlop 2001) provides room-scale surface actuation using 576 pneumatic pistons; Gemotion (Kawaguchi 2006) also demonstrates physical surface rendering using pneumatics, at a smaller scale.

Levitating data

Several approaches exist for levitating objects, including acoustic and magnetic levitation. Acoustic levitation uses acoustic transducers that produce sound waves with a certain amplitude and phase (Omirou et al. 2015). By placing two of these transducers vertically opposite each other, with both emitting waves with the same amplitude and phase, objects are trapped, and levitated, in the space between the low pressure nodes of the generated standing wave (Omirou et al. 2015). To move objects, the phase difference between the transducers is changed (Courtney et al. 2010); two-dimensional manipulation of the object requires multiple transducers and is achieved by controlling the phase (Seah et al. 2014) or the amplitude of the waves generated by the transducers (Foresti et al. 2013).

Floating charts utilizes acoustic levitation to position free-floating objects (such as the point markers in a scatter plot) in mid-air (Omirou et al. 2016). Thread woven between floating beads can also be used to show relationships. LeviPath (Omirou et al. 2015) levitates objects in free-air and includes the ability to move them in 3D paths to illustrate functions or trajectories.

Responsive materials

Responsive (or 'Smart') materials have one or more properties that can be changed in a controlled fashion by an external stimulus. Examples of these stimuli include moisture, electric or magnetic fields, light or temperature. Perhaps the most common are Shape Memory Alloys (SMA) that can be deformed when cold but return to their pre-deformed state when heated.

Responsive materials are yet to be widely deployed in data physicalizations, but have seen use in decorative artefacts (Nabil et al. 2018), shape-changing interfaces (Nojima, Ooide & Kawaguchi 2013), and to produce smooth and silent movement in haptic systems (Poupyrev et al. 2004).

Organic growth

By controlling the environmental parameters of a living organism, their growth can be altered to reflect an underlying dataset. Examples include Cercós et al. (Cercós et al. 2016) who altered the amount of water and light provided to a plant in relation to human physical activity, and Thorsten Kiesl, Harald Moser and Timm-Oliver Wilks who created the 'Garden of Eden' where lettuces were cultivated in sealed plexiglass domes, each feed with the same real-time pollution levels as the capitals of the G7 countries. In these examples, the organic (living) medium creates a powerful and relatable representation of the underlying dataset. Unlike many of the other approaches in this section, organic growth is not always reversible (e.g. a plant cannot 'ungrow' to reduce its height) making its use only suitable in some contexts.

Human-centric actuation and construction: Constructive visualization

Movement in a data physicalization can also be 'human powered', where the end-user physically manipulates the data in the physicalization to either construct, destruct, rearrange or add data points. Constructive visualization is 'the act of constructing a visualization by assembling blocks, that have previously been assigned a data unit through a mapping' (Huron et al. 2014). It is simple (minimal skills are required), expressive (construction takes place within the constraints of the given environment) and dynamic (physicalizations and be rebuilt and adjusted) (Huron et al. 2014). Constructive visualizations are often token-based (Huron, Jansen & Carpendale 2014): participants either arrange tokens into groups or are provided with a token to place into a representative 'bucket' (often to show political or social preference). A more formal example is Cairn, a data collection, visualization and analysis tool for FabLab spaces (Gourlet & Dassé 2017).

Examples of dynamic data physicalizations

In this section, we examine three examples of dynamic data physicalizations that are electro-mechanically actuated: EMERGE, a physical 3D bar chart, ShapeClip, a toolkit for prototyping dynamic physicalizations and PolySurface an approach for fabricating semi-solid surface physicalizations.

EMERGE: A dynamic physical 3D bar chart

EMERGE is a fully interactive physically dynamic bar-chart (Figure 15.1), where a 10 × 10 grid of actuated, touch-sensitive, back-drivable columns dynamically display datasets. EMERGE is designed to support interactions required for the fundamental visualization tasks of annotation, navigation, filtering, comparison, organization and sorting. Interaction with the dataset is additionally mediated by a series of touchscreen panels that display axis information and provide input for controls. The overall design was inspired by Jansen, Dragicevic and Fekete's swappable bar charts (2013).

The hardware consists of 10 × 10 array of square, actuated plastic rods that are individually linked to 100 motorized potentiometer sliders that provide 100 mm of travel. A series of linkages allows the sliders to be stacked appropriately below the interaction surface (Figure 15.1, right). Each rod is illuminated by an RGB LED and each of the four sides of the data-display is augmented by a tablet to display axis labels and provide additional control.

Each bar is individually interactive and updatable; this allows EMERGE to support a range of typical visualization tasks including annotation (pulling a bar), filtering (hiding rows, columns or individual data points), organization (e.g. swapping rows on touchscreens) and navigation (scrolling in both axes on touchscreens). Together these operations mean that EMERGE can not only provide an updatable data-display, but that it supports and range of actions and tasks. For example, we have conducted a range of studies that include tasks where users explored, discussed and presented data using the EMERGE

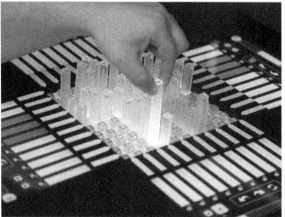

Figure 15.1 EMERGE, a physically dynamic bar-chart; (left) a user directly interacts with a bar by pulling it; (right) linkages connect linear actuators to bars. Image credits: Faisal Taher (Lancaster University) and Jason Alexander (University of Bath). Reproduced with permission.

platform (Taher et al. 2015, 2017). Examples of the data used in these studies included the UK rainfall dataset.[1] The average rainfall was encoded as the bar height, by regions across the UK (y-axis) for 103 years (x-axis), and in another experiment the European Values Survey (European Values Study Group 2011) that consisted of ratings (bar height) from inhabitants of forty-six European countries (y-axis) on thirty-one topics (x-axis) was visualized.

The investigations with EMERGE focused on translating a familiar representation to the physical world together with familiar visualization operations. There is still significant research required to understand whether this is the correct approach, what other representations would provide an equally or more effective data communication platform, and in understanding the role dynamic interaction plays in data interpretation and understanding.

ShapeClip: A toolkit for prototyping dynamic physicalizations

One of the key challenges exposed in the creation of EMERGE was the diverse technical skillset required to engage in creating dynamic physicalizations. The required skills include electrical and mechanical engineering, computer science, human interface design and information visualization expertise. Such a high bar for entry will prevent large audiences from creating dynamic physicalizations, in an attempt to address this problem a toolkit that would lower the requirements to engage with such physical representations was designed.

For this, ShapeClip (Figure 15.2, left) (Hardy et al. 2015), a modular hardware tool capable of transforming any computer screen into a vertically actuating shape-changing display was developed (Alexander et al. 2018). ShapeClips have two light sensors on the bottom that capture the brightness of the light being emitted from a display and convert that into an actuation height (black for fully retracted, white for fully extended). This simplicity of use means that physicalization designers do not require any knowledge of electronics or programming in order

 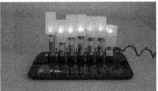 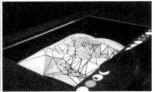

Figure 15.2 Two ShapeClip modules (left); A row of ShapeClip modules (centre); A PolySurface physicalization of a volcano (right). Image credits: (left, centre) John Hardy (H&E Inventions), Faisal Taher (Lancaster University) and Jason Alexander (University of Bath); (right) Aluna Everitt (University of Oxford) and Jason Alexander (University of Bath).

to produce dynamic data physicalizations, simply the ability to change the colour on a display (which can be as simple as a painting or slideshow application). Their design means they are portable (can be battery powered), scalable (you can use as many as you fit onto a screen), fault-tolerant and support runtime re-arrangement.

An example of their use in physicalizations is shown in Figure 15.2, centre – again a bar-chart representation, in this case of audio data. Sturdee et al. describe many more use-cases (Sturdee et al. 2015), demonstrating the viability of down-scaling physicalizations that utilize vertical actuation. ShapeClips have also facilitated several other physicalization projects, including PolySurface (Everitt & Alexander 2017) (see below) and TableHop (Sahoo, Hornbæk & Subramanian 2016).

To improve their scalability a version of ShapeClips that use serial communication to trigger height movement, rather than placement on the screen was developed. While this increases the technical skill required, it does produce more reliable installations, especially when the number of ShapeClips in an artefact is greater than ten.

PolySurface: Semi-solid data physicalizations

While EMERGE and ShapeClip provide robust solutions to producing vertically actuating surfaces (which are perfect for e.g. physical bar charts), their resolution means they are limited in their ability to dynamically represent more complex surface geometries (for example landscape topographies). To address this challenge, we created the PolySurface (Everitt & Alexander 2017), a rapid prototyping approach for building semi-solid surfaces – those that combine thin solid Perspex components and a stretchable continuous surface. A key driver for PolySurface was again the desire for a process that allowed non-technical users to engage in the development of dynamic data physicalizations. PolySurface seeks to segment input data such that it produces templates that maximize continuous surfaces (to reduce the number of required actuators) and provides sufficient flexibility to allow height control for dynamic surface changes.

PolySurfaces are best suited to three-dimensional (x,y,z) data. Fabricating a PolySurface is a six-step method. First, the (x,y) data is segmented to produce polygonal meshes to produce cutting patterns for step 2. Second, the generated polygonal mesh is laser cut on lightweight polypropylene. Third, this mesh is then glued onto a stretchable spandex material to provide a flexible sub-surface. Fourth, visual displays are designed, based on the input data. Fifth, ShapeClips (Hardy et al. 2015) are placed under the material surface at keys points to provide vertical actuation. Sixth, when desirable, toolkits such as UbiDisplays (Hardy & Alexander 2012) can be used to provide interaction (e.g. layer selection or configuration). An example of a volcano physicalization designed and built using the PolySurface approach is shown in Figure 15.2, right.

Challenges for dynamic data physicalizations

Dynamic data physicalizations are even more immature than their static counterparts. There are significant challenges to overcome before data physicalizations, let alone dynamic data physicalizations become a trusted and mainstream data visualization tool. Here is a summary of those challenges:

- **Technical:** the community has seen several approaches to prototyping dynamic physicalizations – each technical approach comes with its own advantages and disadvantages. In all cases, there are trade-offs – often between complexity of implementation and resolution of output (e.g. electromechanical actuators are easy to control, but do not scale-down easily). The key technical challenges are both developing new (or improving current) approaches to meet the requirements of dynamic physicalizations, and then providing access to these approaches to those who are visualization, but not technical, experts.

- **Designing data mappings:** there is a very large design space for mapping values onto physical dimensions that becomes more complex when that physical dimensions can change shape or size. In the physical world, these shape changes must obey the laws of physics (something that is not required digitally). It is therefore unclear whether dynamic physicalization mappings can and should follow the understanding we have from the information visualization community or whether a new set of guidelines and approaches to data mapping is required. For physicalization standardization to occur (see below) data mapping and dynamic data mapping must be well understood.

- **Perception of movement:** the speed and style of 'change' in dynamic physicalizations impacts on the user's perception and understanding of the underlying dataset. Whereas extremely fast movement may not allow the observer to understand the change that has occurred, extremely slow movement may become frustrating or require frequent revisitation to understand the full dataset. The community must understand the implications of our perception of movement on our interpretation of any underlying dataset in order for dynamic physicalizations to be a reliable and consistent community medium.

- **Interaction and control:** the tangibility of physicalizations means that datapoints can be directly manipulated by the user, even unintentionally. There is a need to build an understanding of the correct approaches to interaction with physicalizations (e.g. the expected outcome of manipulating a data point) so that a common understanding can be built across physicalizations, facilitating transfer of learning. Exposing interaction and control mechanisms will also require significant study.

- **Sustainability:** although most dynamic physicalizations allow data and dataset updates to support reuse, some implementation approaches do not. For example, many organic approaches are 'one shot' – once growth has occurred it cannot be reversed. Dynamic physicalizations also require more components (making recycling harder) and greater energy than their static counterparts. Building sustainable (in all meanings of the word) physicalizations will play an important role in their future as mainstream data representations.

- **Standardization:** over time, and based on strong empirical evidence, visualizations have become standardized, with clear guidelines on how to map values to different representations and how to apply different visual guidelines. For dynamic physicalizations to become intuitive to understand and reach the mainstream in the same manner, a similar level of standardization and guidelines will be required. This requires significant scientific study to understand the correct way to convey physical data and the implications of movement on conveying that data.

Conclusion

Dynamic data physicalizations represent the future of physical data representations. Their dynamicity supports data updates and user interaction – making them reusable, significantly reducing concerns around the resources and sustainability of one-shot physicalizations. There are a diverse set of engineering approaches to building such physicalizations, ranging from traditional electromechanical actuation to responsive materials and organic growth. Our work has demonstrated prototype physicalization systems and uncovered some of the key challenges in this space. These challenges include the technical construction of these artefacts, mapping data from digital values onto dynamic physical spaces, the end-user's perception of movement, interaction and control of physicalization, their sustainability, and the future standardization of physicalizations so the data they convey becomes as intuitive as their purely digital counterparts. Dynamic physicalizations provide a powerful, exciting and compelling advance on static physicalizations that we will see evolve and mature in the coming years.

Acknowledgements

This chapter is the cumulation of several years of research into dynamic data physicalizations together with PhD students, post-doctoral researchers and colleagues. Particular thanks goes to the co-authors of the three case studies featured: Faisal Taher, John Hardy, Abhijit Karnik, Christian Weichel, Yvonne

Jansen, Kasper Hornbæk, Jonathan Woodruff, John Vidler and Aluna Everitt. Various elements of this work were funded by GHOST, a European Commission 7th Framework Programme FET-open project (grant #309191) and MORPHED, an EPSRC project (grant #EP/M016528/1).

Note

1. UK rainfall data is available for download from the MetOffice: https://www.metoffice.gov.uk/research/climate/maps-and-data/uk-and-regional-series

References

Alexander, J, Roudaut, A, Steimle, J, Hornbæk, K, Alonso, MB, Follmer, S & Merritt, T 2018, 'Grand challenges in shape-changing interface research', in *Proceedings of the 2018 CHI Conference on Human Factors in Computing Systems*, Montreal QC, Canada, pp. 1–14.

Cercós, R, Goddard, W, Nash, A & Yuille, J 2016, 'Coupling quantified bodies. Affective possibilities of self-quantification beyond the self', *Digital Culture & Society*, vol. 2, no. 1, pp. 177–82.

Courtney, CRP, Ong, C-K, Drinkwater, BW, Wilcox, PD, Demore, C, Cochran, S, Glynne-Jones, P & Hill, M 2010, 'Manipulation of microparticles using phase-controllable ultrasonic standing waves', *The Journal of the Acoustical Society of America*, vol. 128, no. 4, EL195-EL199, DOI:10.1121/1.3479976.

Daniel, M, Rivière, G & Couture, N 2019, 'CairnFORM: A shape-changing ring chart notifying renewable energy availability in peripheral locations', in *Proceedings of the Thirteenth International Conference on Tangible, Embedded, and Embodied Interaction*, Tempe, Arizona, USA.

European Values Study Group 2011, 'European values study 2008: Integrated dataset (EVS 2008).' Cologne, Germany: GESIS Data Archive.

Everitt, A & Alexander, J 2017, 'PolySurface: A design approach for rapid prototyping of shape-changing displays using semi-solid surfaces', in *Proceedings of the 2017 Conference on Designing Interactive Systems*, Edinburgh, United Kingdom.

Foresti, D, Nabavi, M, Klingauf, M, Ferrari, A & Poulikakos, D 2013, 'Acoustophoretic contactless transport and handling of matter in air', in *Proceedings of the National Academy of Sciences*, vol. 110, no. 31, pp. 12549–54, DOI:10.1073/pnas.1301860110.

Gomes, A, Rubens, C, Braley, S & Vertegaal, R 2016, 'BitDrones: Towards using 3D nanocopter displays as interactive self-levitating programmable matter', in *Proceedings of the 2016 CHI Conference on Human Factors in Computing Systems*, San Jose, California, USA.

Goulthorpe, M, Burry, M & Dunlop, G 2001, 'Aegis Hyposurface©: The bordering of university and practice', in *Reinventing the discourse – how digital tools help bridge and transform research, education and practice in architecture* (Proceedings of the Twenty First Annual Conference of the Association for Computer-Aided Design in Architecture), pp. 344–9.

Gourlet, P & Dassé, T 2017, 'Cairn: A tangible apparatus for situated data collection, visualization and analysis', in *Proceedings of the 2017 Conference on Designing Interactive Systems*, Edinburgh, United Kingdom.

Hardy, J & Alexander, J 2012, 'Toolkit support for interactive projected displays', in *Proceedings of the 11th International Conference on Mobile and Ubiquitous Multimedia*, Ulm, Germany, pp. 1–10.

Hardy, J, Weichel, C, Taher, F, Vidler, J & Alexander, J 2015, 'ShapeClip: Towards rapid prototyping with shape-changing displays for designers', in *Proceedings of the 33rd Annual ACM Conference on Human Factors in Computing Systems*, Seoul, Republic of Korea.

Heer, J & Shneiderman, B 2012, 'Interactive dynamics for visual analysis', *Queue*, vol. 10, no. 2, pp. 30–55, DOI:10.1145/2133416.2146416.

Huron, S, Jansen, Y & Carpendale, S 2014, 'Constructing visual representations: Investigating the use of tangible tokens', *IEEE Transactions on Visualization and Computer Graphics*, vol. 20, no. 12, pp. 2102–11, DOI:10.1109/TVCG.2014.2346292.

Huron, S, Carpendale, S, Thudt, A, Tang, A & Mauerer, M 2014, 'Constructive visualization', in *Proceedings of the 2014 conference on Designing interactive systems*, Vancouver, BC, Canada, pp. 433–42, https://doi.org/10.1145/2598510.2598566.

Jansen, Y, Dragicevic, P & Fekete, J-D 2013, 'Evaluating the efficiency of physical visualizations', in *Proceedings of the SIGCHI Conference on Human Factors in Computing Systems*, Paris, France, pp. 2593–602, https://doi.org/10.1145/2470654.2481359.

Jansen, Y, Dragicevic, P, Isenberg, P, Alexander, J, Karnik, A, Kildal, J, Subramanian, S & Hornbæk, K 2015, 'Opportunities and challenges for data physicalization', in *Proceedings of the 33rd Annual ACM Conference on Human Factors in Computing Systems*, Seoul, Republic of Korea, pp. 3227–36, https://doi.org/10.1145/2702123.2702180.

Kawaguchi, Y 2006, 'The art of gemotion in space', in *Tenth International Conference on Information Visualisation (IV'06)*, pp. 658–63, DOI:10.1109/IV.2006.105.

Lindley, SE, Thieme, A, Taylor, AS, Vlachokyriakos, V, Regan, T & Sweeney, D 2017, 'Surfacing small worlds through data-in-place', *Computer Supported Cooperative Work (CSCW)*, vol. 26, no. 1, pp. 135–63, DOI:10.1007/s10606-017-9263-3.

Nabil, S, Everitt, A, Sturdee, M, Alexander, J, Bowen, S, Wright, P & Kirk, D 2018, 'ActuEating: Designing, studying and exploring actuating decorative artefacts', in *Proceedings of the 2018 Designing Interactive Systems Conference*, Hong Kong, China, pp. 327–39, https://doi.org/10.1145/3196709.3196761.

Nojima, T, Ooide, Y & Kawaguchi, H 2013, 'Hairlytop interface: An interactive surface display comprised of hair-like soft actuators', in *2013 World Haptics Conference (WHC)*, 14–17 April 2013, pp. 431–5, DOI:10.1109/WHC.2013.6548447.

Omirou, T, Perez, AM, Subramanian, S & Roudaut, A 2016, 'Floating charts: Data plotting using free-floating acoustically levitated representations', *2016 IEEE Symposium on 3D User Interfaces (3DUI)*, 19–20 March 2016, pp. 187–90, DOI:10.1109/3DUI.2016.7460051.

Omirou, T, Marzo, A, Seah, SA & Subramanian, S 2015, 'LeviPath: Modular acoustic levitation for 3D path visualisations', in *Proceedings of the 33rd Annual ACM Conference on Human Factors in Computing Systems*, Seoul, Republic of Korea, pp. 309–12, https://doi.org/10.1145/2702123.2702333.

Poupyrev, I, Nashida, T, Maruyama, S, Rekimoto, J & Yamaji, Y 2004, 'Lumen: Interactive visual and shape display for calm computing', *ACM SIGGRAPH 2004 Emerging Technologies*, Los Angeles, California, https://doi.org/10.1145/1186155.1186173.

Sahoo, DR, Hornbæk, K & Subramanian, S 2016, 'TableHop: An actuated fabric display using transparent electrodes', in *Proceedings of the 2016 CHI Conference on Human Factors in Computing Systems*, San Jose, California, USA, pp. 3767–80, https://doi.org/10.1145/2858036.2858544.

Sauvé, K, Potts, D, Alexander, J & Houben, S 2020, 'A change of perspective: How user orientation influences the perception of physicalizations', in *ACM SIGCHI Conference on Human Factors in Computing Systems (CHI '20)*, Honolulu, HI, USA, pp. 1–12, https://doi.org/10.1145/3313831.3376312.

Schmandt-Besserat, D 2010, *How writing came about*, University of Texas Press, Austin.

Seah, SA, Drinkwater, BW, Carter, T, Malkin, R & Subramanian, S 2014, 'Correspondence: Dexterous ultrasonic levitation of millimeter-sized objects in air', *IEEE Transactions on Ultrasonics, Ferroelectrics, and Frequency Control*, vol. 61, no. 7, pp. 1233–6, DOI:10.1109/TUFFC.2014.3022.

Sturdee, M & Alexander, J 2018, 'Analysis and classification of shape-changing interfaces for design and application-based research', *ACM Computing Surveys*, vol. 51, no. 1, Article 2, DOI:10.1145/3143559.

Sturdee, M, Hardy, J, Dunn, N & Alexander, J 2015, 'A public ideation of shape-changing applications', in *Proceedings of the 2015 International Conference on Interactive Tabletops & Surfaces*, Madeira, Portugal, pp. 219–28, https://doi.org/10.1145/2817721.2817734.

Taher, F, Hardy, J, Karnik, A, Weichel, C, Jansen, Y, Hornbæk, K & Alexander, J 2015, 'Exploring interactions with physically dynamic bar charts', in *Proceedings of the 33rd Annual ACM Conference on Human Factors in Computing Systems*, Seoul, Republic of Korea, pp. 3237–46, https://doi.org/10.1145/2702123.2702604.

Taher, F, Jansen, Y, Woodruff, J, Hardy, J, Hornbæk, K & Alexander, J 2017, 'Investigating the use of a dynamic physical bar chart for data exploration and presentation', *IEEE Transactions on Visualization and Computer Graphics*, vol. 23, no. 1, pp. 451–60, DOI:10.1109/TVCG.2016.2598498.

Taher, F, Vidler, J & Alexander, J 2017, 'A characterization of actuation techniques for generating movement in shape-changing interfaces', *International Journal of Human–Computer Interaction*, vol. 33, no. 5, pp. 385–98, DOI:10.1080/10447318.2016.1250372.

Vande Moere, A & Patel, S 2010, 'The physical visualization of information: Designing data sculptures in an educational context', in M Huang, Q Nguyen, K Zhang (eds), *Visual information communication*, Springer, Boston, MA. https://doi.org/10.1007/978-1-4419-0312-9_1.

Weichel, C, Hardy, J, Alexander, J & Gellersen, H 2015, 'ReForm: Integrating physical and digital design through bidirectional fabrication', in *Proceedings of the 28th Annual ACM Symposium on User Interface Software & Technology*, Charlotte, NC, USA, pp. 93–102, https://doi.org/10.1145/2807442.2807451.

Zhao, J & Vande Moere, A 2008, 'Embodiment in data sculpture: A model of the physical visualization of information', in *Proceedings of the 3rd International Conference on Digital Interactive Media in Entertainment and Arts*, Athens, Greece, pp. 343–50, https://doi.org/10.1145/1413634.1413696.

SECTION FOUR

MAKING DATA: TRAJECTORIES

In this concluding chapter we reflect on some of the learnings from this book and consider what might be the next steps for data physcialization. How will the ongoing rapid technological change impact on the capacity to make data-objects and inform the next generation of the data-object, and consider, what needs to happen for individuals and communities to more readily read and accept these new and immerging forms of communication.

16
MAKING DATA: THE NEXT GENERATION

Ian Gwilt and Aaron Davis

Introduction

In the Foreword, Karel van der Waarde astutely divided the intention of creating data-objects into two broad categories: on one hand looking for patterns and trying to figure out what data might mean, and on the other, as a means of communicating and bringing insight into complex information. Thinking about the physicalization of data in this way allows us to grasp the abstract, and to capture and interact with scales that are beyond our immediate perceptive capacities, including both the very large and the very small. As designers of these artefacts, our work in this space has the opportunity to facilitate the bringing forth of data into public space, and into a discourse that extends beyond the traditional silos of academic knowledge. The physical nature of the object also allows us to experience this data both emotionally and cognitively (Kennedy 2015), and exposes contestations within our own interpretations of the data-object, as well as in those of others. In what contexts we should consider creating these kinds of data informed objects, whether they can become a two-way dialogic experience of story-building, and how the understandings we build through data physicalization can extend us beyond binary certainty into a new more complex and pluralistic knowledge making system emerge as future areas of interest.

Through the course of this book we have seen how the act of making data can touch on all walks of life and influence the way we make sense of the world. From aiding in better understandings of personal and public healthcare or unpacking the complexities, economics and politics of Big Data, to cultural and creative applications of data and the facilitation of a better knowing of ourselves and our relationship with the natural world, the making of physical representations of data offers an opportunity to have an embodied experience of data in a way that comes naturally to us. The data-object offers a different form of information visualization or information translation from conventional representation techniques, quite literally adding texture and tone to data. This relationship between digital and material paradigms, and our expectation and understanding of material objects and digital content is played out through the data-object. In these new hybrid forms, the visual languages and typologies which we might have traditionally ascribed to one or the other, digital or physical, become increasing blurred.

The human need to make data

Proprioception is part of the human sensory toolkit, so it is little wonder that there has always been an instinctive interest in physicalizing numeric data. Physical objects that are informed by data present us with an alternative way to interact with data beyond screen- and paper-based statistical lists or graphical representation. Throughout history, this making and representation of data has been achieved by using the common materials and tools of the time; we make piles of things, we represent one thing with another and we measure and craft numbers into physical forms. The tools we use to amplify our data making and representing abilities have taken various forms over millennia, with the abacus, the slide rule, mechanical calculating machines, and eventually digital calculators and computers taking an innate calculative ability, and abstracting it to the point where the data being represented takes on an ephemeral and theoretical, rather than physical quality.

The rise of data and the sum of human knowledge is inexorably connected to the rise of digital computing and the start of the information age from the mid twentieth century. Negroponte's book *Being Digital* (1995) brought the potential in this shift towards digital information to public consciousness. Since then, we have seen the capacity to generate and store data grow exponentially, roughly in line with Moore's Law (1965). Our abilities to interpret this ever-expanding pool of data have also grown, though perhaps not at the same rate. In many fields, we rely on black boxed processes (Latour 1999) that exclude the agency of human interpretation and establish binary fact, despite hidden interpretive bias or data inaccuracies.

In a post-digital era, there is a concerted effort to make large amounts of public and 'open data' available to the community, but there is still much work to do in interpreting these data sets in a way that is comprehensible and of use to everyday citizens. Data visualization techniques, information graphics and 'dashboard' designs have begun to make the translation and comprehension of data more accessible on computer screens. However, if these data sets are to live outside of the computer screen – conflated with the metaphors, values and affordances of the 'real/material word' object forms – the crafting of such representations becomes important. As Sennett describes, the affordances of physical artefacts are influenced by the tools and materials we use to create them (2009). These material affordances and choices will also influence the way we read and value the underlying data (Gwilt 2013).

Moreover, we should not forget the transcontextuality of objects, given objects accrue value by an individuals' interaction with them (Benjamin 1969). Objects, and by extension objects that are described by data, are able to hold multiple contexts, exist across multiple contexts, and be understood in multiple ways. Data is one thing, but how it is visualized, used and valued is open and contestable. This places us in a unique moment where we might consider how the physicalization processes we are collectively developing might be used to rebalance our systems of knowledge, and challenge the de facto privileging of access to knowledge through the complexity and abstract codification of data interpretation systems. For example, as we have read in earlier chapters, the physicalization of difficult to comprehend ecological systems data has a particular power in building ecological literacy in the Anthropocene. Physical representations of data seem to allow for a more comprehensible interpretation of phenomena that change in a time and space that is outside of our daily lived experience. In the context of climate change, the immediacy of the digital, and the complexity of the data that is collected, prevents us from dwelling on the fundamental macro-scale changes that are occurring in our physical world.

Our understanding of the relationship between our personal lived-experience and planetary phenomena occurring at the scale of millennia could perhaps be compared to a shift from anecdotal evidence ('bad') to 'hard' science ('good'). But this privileging of the universal over the particular belies our own interpretive abilities, and the social power that comes from a deep collectively constructed understanding of problems. The ability of the individual and the community to relate to and interact with a physicalization of a large and somewhat uninterpreted data set may foster an understanding of the relationship between the particular and the universal without dismissing the former. This is in many ways similar to the affordance created by the Campbell-Stokes Sunlight Recorder that was described in the introduction to this book.

As we have seen through the book, who produces these physical data interpretations, where these data driven objects are encountered and by which people, can be as many and varied as are the potential readings and reactions to the objects themselves. Understanding does not automatically lead to behaviour change but the potential to generate an empathetic experience through the use of physical data interpretations is something to be valued.

The democratization of access (through scale) has been a consistent theme in innovation in Western human history – from the 1440 Gutenberg printing press, to the use of casting techniques in the industrial revolution, and the eventual development of mass-produced consumer goods. The history of access to data, and tools for capturing, understanding and representing data, has had an analogous history. Technologies allowing the storage, transmission and manipulation of data have shifted (sometimes bumpily) from access based on privilege to more democratized forms of access, and in more recent years the open data movement has gained significant pace. However, while data is increasingly available to us, comparatively less innovation has occurred in the democratization of interpretation, representation and general engagement with data. A common idea which Fry picked up on in his chapter is that even if I could see my data, it is in a form that is unintelligible to me, but in that very same form, it is incredibly useful to Mark Zuckerberg (CEO, Facebook).

Microsoft Office and Microsoft Excel (as well as Google sheets and other free and open-source platforms) could be argued to be the last big development in the accessibility of the ability to manipulate, interpret and represent data, yet these technologies require a complex set of technological, educational and cognitive resources – not to mention the assumption that people are interested in generating and discussing graphs. The static and in many ways definitive representation of the graphing techniques enabled by these technologies also restricts the ability to build a culture of discursion around data, forcing more binary conclusions of 'interesting or not', or 'useful or not'.

The explicit nature of numerical lists, and graphs may on the face of it be more understandable than a physical object (as a way of representing data), however we should not leap to the conclusion that everyone can read graphs and tables, and even if they can, that they understand their meaning. This is perhaps a similar principle to the ability for an English speaker to 'read' but not necessarily understand other Latin-based languages. The understanding of the physicality of objects is something that is innately human, and although interpretation is still necessary, we see potential for the data-object to more easily cut across cultural, educational and language barriers than a list, table or graph.

In recent decades, the world's governments, researchers, citizens and industries have been capturing data at an ever-increasing rate. The open science, and open government movements have generated open data sets that appear to be sitting ripe for the picking, but outside of state-sponsored hackathon events, often appear to have little ability to enter into public discourse. This presents an interesting and quite fundamental opportunity for data physicalization practitioners, to determine the ways in which people can translate and represent data. While it is daunting to consider that the field is on the precipice of developing the next set of default representations (pie chart, bar graph, line graph, scatter plot etc.), the opportunities to do this in a way that is based on facilitating meaningful engagement with data, like climate change or other environmental impact data, are profound.

Returning for a moment to the question of who the authorship of these data-objects is something that we must consider carefully. These may indeed become 'everyday objects' that are shaped by the practices of their application as described by Shove et al. (2007), but if this is the case, shaped by whom, for which practices, and for who's benefit are interesting questions to consider. The opportunities for these objects to be deliberately designed to support new forms of discourse should not be under-estimated. Research has shown that data-objects can be discursive and contested, because their meaning and form is often contestable and may take some work to decode and understand (Gwilt, Yoxall & Sano 2012). The contemporary trend towards the discounting of knowledge if it doesn't fit within one's own belief system suggests the tools and techniques used to represent and physicalize data should carefully consider how these representations are fostering shared discourse rather than representing singular truth. Whether or not we trust those who are making data-objects is also likely to have a large impact on their impact in the world. Opaque artificial intelligence and machine learning systems often make the origins (and reliability) of data difficult to decipher, but recent advancements in digital transparency through blockchain-based technologies offer the potential for integrating concepts of data-provenance and traceability. How these enter into or are reflected by the physical artefacts is not well understood, but perhaps offer an opportunity to rebuild trust in the data that is being physicalized.

Technological advancements

In this period of rapid technological advancement the practice of physicalizing data in ways that take advantage of digital technologies is still in its infancy. Industry 4.0 introduced the work to cloud computing, robotics, Big Data and AI, and this has been swiftly followed up by the concept of Industry 5.0/6.0 which recognizes the importance of the human experience within these technological constructs. As such, you could say the data-object is perfectly positioned to take advantage of this industry 5.0/6.0 thinking. 3D printing technologies will become quotidian; in the way that many households now own a 2D ink on paper printer, the capacity to print three dimensional objects will soon become common place, making it easy for more people to create physical representations of data using 3D printing technologies. However, in a word suffering from the effects of overproduction we should be cautious of this capacity. Some careful thinking needs to be applied to the wholesale production of physical data-objects and the resources that go into their creation, use and disposal. When the creation of 3D printed data-objects does become mainstream then the adoption of a carefully considered service system based on a circular economy model is critical.

We could learn from the graphic design and print media industries that have engaged with the whole of lifecycle impact of their products. While it may have been economic factors and supply issues that forced the printing industry from animal skin parchments to timber-based paper-stock, the shift from old growth forest to recycled and sustainably managed plantation timbers, as well as the gradual shift to soy and vegetable based inks is based on an understanding of the bigger picture, and more externalized impacts the industry has. For the production of physical data-objects, we may well use the same ethical principles to determine that 3D printed plastics are not an appropriate form for producing data-objects.

The capabilities of adaptive and integrated digital technologies offer the potential for proximate and distributed, synchronous and asynchronous interaction and responsiveness. This is something that appears to be incongruous with the concertized data-object, which is fixed in time, space and form. How we might think about successfully combining the material properties of data-objects with digital attributes is something written about before (Gwilt 2013, 2015). Without doubt, careful consideration around this combination is required if we are to create data-objects that capitalize on the potential of both of these paradigms to enhance our understanding and experience of data. Remembering that what you gain by physicalizing data such as tangibility, uniqueness, physical presence and the patina of use might entail a trade-off in digital potentials such as networkability, replicability, ephemerality, and visa-versa. The end game would appear to be to arrive at a data-object (or set of data-objects) which is enhanced through the physical-digital partnership. The consideration of how digital and material properties and attributes are integrated into a digital or physical object, and to what ends, is important because if handled poorly, this combination risks the diminishment of both paradigms.

As we have seen in Jason Alexander's chapter on constructing dynamic data physicalizations the move towards developing morphogenic physical surfaces and objects that can change in real-time is already underway. Georgiev and Barhoush's experimental perceptual waterfall that tracks creative collaboration in real-time also shows us that data physicalization is not restricted to the creation of static objects. Predictive AI tools, machine learning algorithms, computer imaging technologies will soon be used to automatically generate data-objects on demand and there may indeed be a new hierarchy of data to uncover that guides us to determine which sets of data are best understood through static means, and which require dynamism and four-dimensional representation. We might also explore which data sets should be interrogated and understood by individuals and which require a community of exploration to unpack the pluralistic meanings that are embodied in the data.

Next steps – cultural awareness

To say there is an agreed or universal next step in the development of data physicalization technologies and approaches would be antithetical to the concepts presented in this book. There are indeed many next steps in many different directions that will guide the development of this field.

One of the key areas that strikes us in reviewing the contribution of this book and the context within which it will sit, is the need to develop a more nuanced cultural awareness of how data might be realized in material and digitally enabled hybrid forms – in effect, the onto-epistemological qualities of the data-object. Treating the data-object as a category of representation rather than a defined form of representation might allow us to explore their potential as dynamic, culturally informed and communally developed (bottom-up) objects rather than prescribed (top-down) representations of data.

The celebration of the inexactness of the data-object that is discussed explicitly in Bettina Nissen's chapter, and is evident across almost all other chapters, begins to suggest opportunities for us to shift away from an obsession with the precise, and to frame conversations around meanings and interpretations. This could be described as an obfuscation of the prescriptive or 'correct' interpretation that is present in the codified knowledge system of traditional data presentation. The ability to question the authority of data that is implicit in this approach may allow us to support the community to engage in a more postmodern understanding of the world where a universal interpretation is not necessarily taken as truth.

By allowing communities to contest interpretation, and enter into dialogic argument about these representations of the world around them, the data-object may succeed where computer-based collaboration and representation techniques have failed (see the example of Google Wave in Sennett 2012), engaging in pluralistic interpretation and respectful but meaningful debate. This contestation could also emerge from the building of discourse around what data means, rather than what it says. This shift from unequivocal indexical representation to metaphor is a common technique used in design processes, shifting discourse from the question of 'what?', to the more fundamental question of 'why?'.

However, there is still the need to establish in broad terms a recognizable set of agreed conventions and typologies for data-driven objects before we can move onto the second generation of examples.

At the risk of perpetuating a dubiously attributed quote, we are still very much in the Henry Ford trap of asking people what they want rather than what they want to achieve. Rather than focusing on what people want ('a faster horse'/a data-object), we might do well to consider what people are trying to achieve ('getting from one place to another more quickly'/stimulating engagement with data). With this understanding, we could then work toward the development of a 'visual' syntax for three-dimensional data physicalizations that can allow us to move forward from indexical representation to more symbolic and metaphorical data translations.

We hope that in the future, digitally inflected data-objects will become more culturally accepted and expected, that they are active and responsive, both physically and digitally, documenting our interaction with them, helping us to better connect with ecology of systems within which we exist. More specifically, we see a critical role for data-objects in supporting education based on multiple readings of data, and the democratization of sense-making, and communal empowerment.

References

Benjamin, W 1969, 'The work of art in the age of mechanical reproduction', in H Arendt (ed.), *Illuminations*, Schocken Books, New York, pp. 217–51.

Gwilt, I, Yoxall, A & Sano K 2012, 'Enhancing the understanding of statistical data through the creation of physical objects', in A Duffy, Y Nagai & T Taura (eds), *The 2nd international conference on design creativity* (Proceedings), UK, Design Society, pp. 117–24.

Gwilt, I 2013, 'Data-objects: Sharing the attributes and properties of digital and material culture to creatively interpret complex information', in D Harrision (ed.), *Digital media and technologies for virtual artistic spaces*, IGI Global, Pennsylvania, USA, pp. 14–26.

Gwilt, I 2015, 'Big data – small world: Materializing digital information for discourse and cognition', in D Harrison (ed.), *Handbook of research on digital media and creative technologies*, IGI Global, Pennsylvania, USA, pp. 288–301.

Kennedy, H 2015, 'Seeing data: Visualisation design should consider how we respond to statistics emotionally as well as rationally', blog post, *London School of Economics and Political Science*, 22 July, accessed April 2021, https://blogs.lse.ac.uk/impactofsocialsciences/2015/07/22/seeing-data-how-people-engage-with-data-visualisations/.

Latour, B 1999, *Pandora's hope: Essays on the reality of science studies*, Harvard University Press, Cambridge, Massachusetts.

Moore, GE 1965, 'Cramming more components onto integrated circuits,' *Electronics*, vol. 38, no. 8, pp. 114–117.

Negroponte, N 1995, *Being digital*, Knopf, New York.

Sennett, R 2009, *The craftsman*, Penguin Books, London.

Sennett, R 2012, *Together: The rituals, pleasures and politics of cooperation*, Yale University Press, New Haven, CT.

Shove, E, Watson, M, Hand, M & Ingram, J 2007, *The design of everyday life*. https://doi.org/10.5040/9781474293679

INDEX

AI-based system
    conversation analysis experiment 214–19
    creativity support deployment 211–12
    design thinking conversation 214–16
    explicit and implicit feedback 216–19
    list of rules 212–13
    natural language processing (NLP) module 218
    prototype screen-based visualization output 211–12, 216–19
    semantic measures 213–14
    water and falling water curtains, example 217
Air Quality Balloons (Kuznetsov's project) 50
Amazon 59, 99–100
    Alexa 212
A Meter of Jungle (Dion, Mark) 99
Amphibious Architecture (Benjamin and Jeremijenko) 100–1
analogue technologies 2, 10
'A New Paradigm for Personal Data, Five Shifts to Drive Trust and Growth'(Facebook) 65
Animal Tracker 75
Anti-mass (sculpture) 16
Apple 60
Arctic Sea Ice/Albedo (art work) 14
Art & Language collective 28
art forms
    art vocabulary 27
    complex concepts 26
    conceptual and material and practice 27–30
    digitality and hybridity 26–7
    industrial objects 28
art object 4, 19, 25, 27–31, 37, 121
Azure (Microsoft) 60

Being Digital (Negropont, N) 240
Bergson, Henri 73
    on illusion of motion 80
    theory of duration 78–9
Bezos, Jeff 59
Big Data 2, 30, 32, 37, 75, 92, 102, 126, 243
    influence 239
biomedical data
    common practice 169–70
    digital visualizations 171–2
    4D data 172, 180
    future trends 178–9
    hybrid methods 176–8
    immersive digital visualization 173–4
    physical construction 169–71
blockchain-based technologies 5, 64, 243
    socio-material translations 127–30, 136
Blood Swept Lands and Seas of Red 30

Calibra 64
Cambridge Analytica system 60, 62
    barriers to transparency 62–3, 65
Campbell-Stokes Sunlight Recorder 2, 241
Cartesian coordinate system 12, 41, 176
choreographic approaches 73–4, 82
    example 77
cinema's movement. See also choreographic approaches
    frames per second (fps) 78
    moving images in 74
    pull, audio-visual exploration 77–9, 81–2
    time/events duration 79–80
    wave breaking moments 79–80, 82
Clever Country (documentary) 41, 43, 50, 94

climate change 3–5, 36. *See also* climate data; ecological data
  indigenous knowledge 94
climate data
  Bureau of Meteorology (BOM) date 199
  Canberra Climate Action 202
  Climate Coaster project 195, 202–7
  engagement challenges 205–7
  Javascript application 199–200
  network context 205–7
  networked making 199–202
  physicalization 195–9
  by-product 201–2
  SVG image 200
  tangibility 203–5
  web app related technologies 200–3
cloud computing 3, 243
cognition 44–5, 110, 132, 142, 223
  traditional concept 11
Collateralized Debt Obligations (CDOs) 63
computer aided design (CAD) modelling programme 19
computer numeric controlled (CNC) machines 18
computer science 58–9, 169, 229
  data forms 1–2
Cosmos (Jarman and Gerhardt) 30, 96–8
Counting the Costs (Marsh, D) 98
Covid-19 pandemic 65
craft-thinking 25, 29
Crisis of Credit Visualized (Jarvis, J) 67
Cuoghi, Roberto 17

data. *See also* next generation
  analogous history 241–2
  as asset and as system 59–62
  definition and functions 9–10
  as interaction/transaction 61
  physical forms and materials 11
  sonification 185
  as-strategic insight 61
data dividend 59
data driven platforms, privacy abuses 60
DataMarket.com 60
data-objects
  authorship 242–3
  Burning Acres (Stever) 160–4
  climate change 153–4, 156, 162, 164
  Climate Clock (Kong) 154–7

climate data 195–6, 201, 204–5
Disruption: The Materiality of Global Temperature (Pereira-Vega) 157–60
forms and constructions 9
future generation 242–4, 246
importance 3, 242–3
inexactness of 245
manifestation theory 153–4
next generation 3
philosophical significance 7
pre-digital 2
data ownership models 3, 7, 59–60
data physicalization
  actuation approaches 225–6
  advantages 224
  AI-based creativity support 212, 217, 219
  art object 25–8, 30, 32, 34, 37
  biomedical application 169–79
  challenges 231–2
  climate change 153, 159–60, 162–4
  climate data 195–9
  constructive visualization 227
  definition 223
  demonstration of benefits 223
  ecological data 97, 101
  electro-mechanical actuation 225
  environmental data 41–52
  floating charts, use of 226
  human-centric actuation 227
  hybrid digital material 107–10, 112, 117, 119–21
  hydraulic approaches 225–6
  magnetic levitation 226
  organic growth 227
  personal data 142–4, 146, 148, 150
  pneumatic actuation 225–6
  PolySurface 230–1
  responsive materials 226
  ShapeClip 229–30
  socio-technical systems 57, 66
  sonic data 183–5, 191
  tangible translations 125–6, 128–9, 132–3, 135–6
  technological advancements 243–4
  visualization of movement 82
data sculpture 14–15, 48, 50–1
  global temperature 157–60, 163–4

INDEX

data visualization 10
  AI-based system 216, 219
  art objects 27
  in biomedical applications 170–4, 177–9
  choreographic approaches 73–4
  climate change 203–9
  climate data 196, 200, 203, 206
  contemporary computation 80
  conversation analysis experiment 217–19
  data physicalization and 223, 231, 240
  design thinking 58
  ecological data 91–4
  environmental themes 45–9
  graphic forms of diagrams and maps 12
  human and non-human movement 73–5, 79–80, 83
  hybrid approaches 2–3, 5
  movement interrelations 74, 79, 83
  movement of data 73–5, 79–80, 83
  over-use and cultural saturation 2
  physicalization 10, 18, 49, 52
  public projections and murals 47
  Sankey visual conventions 75
  six visual variables 12
  social system 58
  tangible poetics 143–4, 146
  visual effect of the waterfall 217
design
  AI-based system 214–16
  biomedical data 171–8
  climate change visualizations 203–7
  hybrid digital material 119–20
  socio-material interactions (currency and value) 131–3
Design Methods movement 66
Design Research Unit 66
digital information
  common conception 10
  emergent practice of data making 3
distributed cognition 11
Dourish, Paul 57
Duchamp, Marcel 25–8, 31–3, 37
  Bride 26, 31–3
  Creative Act, The 27
  infrathin, definition 33
  Large Glass 26–7, 31–2, 37

  l'inframince 26, 32, 34, 37
  Readymades 25–32, 37

ecological data
  affective power of the non-human 93–101
  production and communication 91–3
  projects, examples 93–101
  science communication 89–91
  'songlines' concept 94–5, 101
  Zakpage 93–4, 101
ecosystem 34–5, 41, 50–1, 61, 67, 100, 200
  virtual and real 36
Eden, Michael 29
EMERGE 225, 227, 230
  3D bar chart 228–9
environmental data
  climate change 41, 43, 50
  common themes and formats 45–9
  contextual and embedded displays 44–5
  display modality 43, 51–2
  novel digital interfaces 41–2
  physical visualization techniques 42–3
  role of data enactment 49–52
  visualization strategies 45, 47–52

'Facebook and an Examination of its Impact on the Financial Services and Housing Sectors' 64
Feral Robotic Dogs (Jeremijenko's project) 50
For Forest 51
Forsythe, William 73–4, 79, 82–4
  One Flat Thing Reproduced 83
  Synchronous Objects 74, 79, 82–3
For What It's Worth (Marsh) 97
Fourier theory 185
fourth-dimensional space (cyberspace) 26
Fused Deposition Modelling (FDM) printer 19

General Data Protection Regulation of 2016–18 (EU) 58
Gerhardt, Joe 30, 96–8, 101
Google Assistant 212
Greenpeace 43
Grewingk Glacier (sculpture) 14

health. *See also* biomedical data;
    personal user data, *Lifestreams*
    (digital healthcare domain)
    biosensor monitoring 143–4
    climate change, impact on 156
    Facebook's business interests 65–6
    hypertension or high blood pressure
        189
    Parkinson's Disease 146–7
    sonification of data 191–2
    wealth *versus* 115
Heer, Jeffrey 58, 223
Helmholz, Hermann von 184–5, 187
Humby, Clive 59
hybrid digital-material
    Chesters Roman Fort and the Clyton
        Museum (case study) 114–16
    EU project meSch–Material
        Encounters with Digital Cultural
        Heritage (MeSch) 108
    'Fort Pozzacchio: Voices from the
        Past' (case study) 111–14
    'The Hague and the Atlantic Wall: War
        in the City of Peace', exhibition at
        MUSEON (case study) 116–19
    museum asset, cultural experiences
        119–20
    museum context, challenges
        107–11
    usability issues 108

Ice Watch (Eliasson, Olafur) 99
IDEO 66
Industry 4.0 3
Inheritance (Berger and Keto) 95–6
installation *Lines (57° 59' N, 7° 16'W,*
    Niittyvirta and Aho's) 100
Interactive Data Lab (University of
    Washington) 58
Internet of Things 2–3, 108

James, William 76
Jarman, Ruth 30, 96–8, 101
Jerwood Open Forest 96

Kelley, David 66

Lachajczak, Nik 93–4
Libra 64

Lippard, Lucy 27–9
    Conceptual Art 29
    *Six Years: The Dematerialization of the
        Art Object* 27

machine learning algorithms 62, 243–4
MacKenzie, D 58
Mass (Colder Darker Matter, sculpture) 16
materials 26, 29, 31, 37, 41–2, 48, 51,
    95–6, 126, 136, 144, 150, 157,
    159–60, 164, 183–5, 191, 197,
    232, 240–1. *See also* hybrid
    digital-material; 3D printing
    technologies
    aesthetic forms 15
    physical characteristics 13–14
    responsive or smart 226
    subtle qualities 15–16
    symbolic significance 16
Max Planck Institute, *Movebank* project
    75
McCune, Doug 30
Meadows, Donella 66
Microsoft Office and Excel 242
Minard, Joseph 75
Mind in Motion (Tversky, Barbara) 11
mining 59–60
moving data 73, 82, 100
    artistic approaches 73–4, 82, 84
    dance/dancer positions 79, 82–5
    data analytic approach 76
    high speed cameras 80
    imagistic techniques 74
    non-linear multiplicity 77
    patterns 74
    process-based approaches 76–7
    relational approach 74, 77, 83–4
    timestamp values 75–6, 78, 81, 83
    visual analytics approach 75
Moving Stories (Schiphorst, Thecla) 84

new media art 58
next generation
    cultural awareness 244–6
    data-object 239–40
    data visualization techniques 240–3
    material objects 239–40
    technological advancements 243–4
Noë, Alva 44, 142

INDEX

Orlikowski, WJ 58

Page, Alison 93–5
Parker, Cornelia 16
personal user data
    data manifestation *theory* 149–50
    exploitations 57
    guiding principle 141–6
    Lifecharm 145–6
    Lifestreams (digital healthcare domain) 143–8
    Presidential Trump-Pence campaign 60
Pesce, Gaetano 17
physical objects 2–3, 9, 19, 110, 121, 185, 240
PolySurface 230–1
public data sculptures 48

radical choreographic theory 73
RFID codes 29
Rittel, Horst 66

Samsung 60
Scott, SV 58
Semiologie Graphique (Bertin, Jacques) 12
ShapeClip 229–30
Shift-Life, The 34–6
Simon, Herbert 66
smart environments 3
sociomateriality, definition 58
Socio-Technical Systems (STSs)
    current deficits 63
    data-based interactions 57–9, 61–7, 69
    design thinking 58, 66–9
    digital infrastructures 57–8
    financial products 63–4
    human-scale reasoning 63–5, 69
    interactions with digital data 66
    interpretation style 62, 64–5, 69
    long wall extraction 62
    technical language 64
sonic data
    additive synthesis 185
    Auditory Icons 185–7
    bell shape acoustics 187
    CAD/CAM model 186
    Chemo Singing Bowl 190–2

Head Related Transfer Function (HRTF) 187–8
information mapping 185
physicalizations 183
singing bowl, acoustic effect 189–91
3D printed musical instruments 183–4
tuning forks 185–7
Special Interest Group on Computer–Human Interaction (SIGCHI) 58
Spiral Jetty (Smithson, Robert) 99
Sunflower Seeds (Weiwei, Ai) 29–30

tangible translations
    accessibility, audience *versus* accuracy 134–5
    Alternative Rates of Exchange 133
    blockchain 127–8
    Block Exchange workshop 128–9, 134, 136
    concepts of technologies 125–7
    cryptocurrency 127–8
    Crypto-Knitting Circles (project) 127
    Currency After Money (project) 127, 131–2
    data representation 135–6
    distributed ledger technologies 127–8
    GeoCoin 131–2
    interaction design 131–3
    material engagement 128–31
    Strings of Distributed Value workshop 129–30
    Swap Market context 128
    transparency issues 136–7
    Weaving Crypto-Ledgers workshop 129
Tavistock scholars 57–8, 61, 65–6, 69
3D printing technologies
    AI-based system 219
    biomedical applications 171–8, 180
    climate data 196
    concept of representation 12–13
    data physicalization 227–9
    graphic forms of diagrams and maps 12
    musical instruments 183–4, 186–9, 191
    next generation 243–4
    print processes 19, 25
    technological advancement 243
Trends in Water Use (sculpture) 14
2008–9 financial crisis 67

typology
- AI-based creativity support systems 211–12, 214, 216
- artistic practice 149
- biomedical application 171–2, 175–7, 179
- computer aided design (CAD) model 19
- data manifestation 154
- digital representation 170
- electro-mechanical actuation 225
- hybrid digital material 108, 110, 112
- inframince 32
- interaction affordance 205
- *makerly* 206
- material artefacts 17
- sonification 185, 191
- 3D printout 175–7
- visual analytics 75–6, 141

visualization techniques. *See also* data visualization
- aggregated movement pathways 75
- contemporary computation 80
- human and non-human 73
- practice-based thinking 73

Visualizing Finance Lab 66

visual thinking 66–7

Waarde, Karel van der 239

Western educational systems 10

Whitehead, Alfred North 76–7, 82, 144

Words and Objects after Conceptualism (Beech, D.) 28

Zeno's arrow of time 80

Zuckerberg, Mark 61, 64–5, 242